The Right to Know

The Right to Know

Your Guide to Using and Defending
Freedom of Information Law
in the United States

Jacqueline Klosek

PRAEGER

An Imprint of ABC-CLIO, LLC

Santa Barbara, California • Denver, Colorado • Oxford, England

Library of Congress Cataloging-in-Publication Data

Klosek, Jacqueline, 1972–
    The right to know : your guide to using and defending freedom of information law in the
    United States / Jacqueline Klosek.
      p. cm.
    Includes bibliographical references and index.
    ISBN 978–0–313–35927–9 (hard copy : alk. paper) — ISBN 978–0–313–35928–6 (ebook)
1. Freedom of information—United States. 2. Government information—United States. 3.
United States. Freedom of Information Act. I. Title.
KF5753.K58 2009
342.7308′53—dc22   2009011656

13 12 11 10 09 1 2 3 4 5

This book is also available on the World Wide Web as an eBook.
Visit www.abc-clio.com for details.

ABC-CLIO, LLC
130 Cremona Drive, P.O. Box 1911
Santa Barbara, California 93116-1911

This book is printed on acid-free paper (∞)

Manufactured in the United States of America

This book is dedicated to Thomas Lozinski and Jason Klosek.

Contents

Preface

The importance of freedom of information to democracy cannot be over-stated. As James Madison once wrote:

> [A] popular Government, without popular information, or the means of acquir-ing it, is but a Prologue to a Farce or a Tragedy; or, perhaps, both. Knowledge will forever govern ignorance: And a people who mean to be their own Gover-nors, must arm themselves with the power which knowledge gives.[1]

Although written so many years ago, the words of Madison continue to hold truth, and perhaps even a new sense of urgency in the modern era. It has been nearly two centuries since Madison wrote of the importance of the freedom of information, and in that time the size of our country and our government has grown tremendously. The activities of government and the complexities of those activities have also multiplied. At the same time, con-temporary situations and political factors have been prompting some con-stituencies to push for greater secrecy in government. All of these factors call upon us to focus anew on information freedom.

The federal Freedom of Information Act (FOIA), in effect since 1967, has helped to ensure that the public has the means for acquiring the knowledge of which Madison spoke with such great eloquence so many years ago. Over the years, courts and commentators alike have reaffirmed the important role that the FOIA plays in our democracy. The Supreme Court reiterated the important principles underlying the FOIA just a few years ago, and the obser-vations of the Court in this regard are well worth repeating:

> FOIA is often explained as a means for citizens to know 'what the Government is up to.' This phrase should not be dismissed as a convenient formalism. It defines a structural necessity in a real democracy. The statement confirms that, as a

general rule, when documents are within FOIA's disclosure provisions, citizens should not be required to explain why they seek the information. A person requesting the information needs no preconceived idea of the uses the data might serve. The information belongs to citizens to do with as they choose. [2]

Despite the fundamental importance of information freedom to our democracy, recently there has been a palpable trend away from openness and towards increased secrecy. This movement had already commenced during the earliest phases of the Bush administration, but it took on new urgency after 9/11. Following the 2001 terrorist attacks, public access to information concerning government affairs, private industry, environmental risks, and health and safety issues became the subject of much controversy. Of particular concern was the release of information about chemical factories, nuclear facilities, and other sensitive facilities. However, we witnessed a clamping down on access to information in many other areas.

Since 2001, public information needed by individuals to protect themselves, their families, and their communities has been disappearing from the Internet and other publicly available sources at a startling pace. While it is not clear that the removal of such information has had a positive impact on our security, there is evidence to suggest that the absence of such information has hindered our ability to obtain information about important issues, such as environmental protection[3] and women's rights.[4]

Even when the information removed from the Internet might bear some relation to national security, such as the case of certain types of environmental data, recent analysis has shown that the redacted information is generally not detailed enough to aid terrorists in planning a successful attack.[5] Given this fact, removing it has a disproportionately high impact on citizens who need information to better understand what their government is up to and to be better prepared to protect themselves from certain risks, such as the harm that may result from residing in close proximity to a contaminated facility.

Individuals who were vociferous about the suppression of such information contended that the United States was potentially putting itself at risk by making it available to the public. After all, they argued, terrorists could use that information to advance their dangerous plots. While it is very likely that many people who argued for increased secrecy truly believed that the public availability of such information could put the country at risk, it is equally possible that some had other motivations. For example, an alternative might be that representatives of certain private industries desire suppression because more limitations on the right to freedom of information might help to reduce the legal, regulatory, and public relations-related consequences of full disclosure? Likewise, isn't it possible that various governmental actors may desire to keep certain information private for reasons other than a fear of terrorism?

This issue also raises another, even more important, question, namely: Isn't it possible that suppressing information could be more dangerous than disclosing it? Are the risks of terrorists accessing and exploiting this information outweighed by the dangers of government actors and/or private industry harming the public by carrying out certain dangerous activities in secrecy, with little or no accountability? It is the theory of this author that historically, the risks of allowing governments to operate in secrecy and of permitting private industry to operate free of citizen oversight far outweigh the risks that potential terrorists will access information through freedom of information laws and use it to commit a terrorist attack.

Despite public conception, in the modern world threats to national security may come not only from large, foreign countries but may also result from smaller, multinational, and even domestic groups. The reality is that persons and groups that threaten national security may not be easy to identify and eliminate. Accordingly, it is incumbent that the government and industry place the most emphasis on taking steps to reduce vulnerabilities to a terrorist attack. A policy of simply trying to hide the vulnerabilities by taking a broad cloth to suppress government information is not necessary, nor is it sufficient, to address terrorist threats.

Further, while the threat of terrorism is quite real, it is this author's contention that from a long-term, more fundamental perspective, the threats that governmental secrecy and suppression pose to our safety, security, and liberty are far more grave. With this premise in mind, this book seeks to explore the importance of freedom of information, examine the attacks it has been under, and emphasize the need for its protection.

It is an opportune time for such reflection. Data from recent years suggest that freedom of information has been under considerable attack. While an increase in secrecy may have been expected post 9/11, it is more concerning that secrecy had been continuing to increase many years after the attacks of 2001.[6]

With the recent election of Barack Obama as president, there is hope for improved openness and better administration of the FOIA. Early evidence suggests this will prove to be the case. This is very fortunate, as the stakes are simply too high for any other option.

The FOIA is far more than an instrument for liberal-leaning activists. It is a tool that is fundamental to the accurate and complete portrayal of history.[7] Using notable examples from several key areas, this book will highlight a number of significant revelations that have been made through the FOIA. Examples discussed herein will include revelations uncovered through the FOIA and other similar laws that expose government corruption, identify perpetrators of environmental harm, uncover harm and abuse to animals, including endangered species, demonstrate the risks of various drugs and medical procedures, and identify the hazards of various products, among others. Many of the revelations that were uncovered through the FOIA have helped lead to significant changes in matters of great importance to our society and our world. Accordingly, there is a clear need to protect, defend, and promote the FOIA and associated legislation.

Notes

1. Letter from James Madison to W. T. Barry (August 4, 1822) in *The Writing of James Madison* 103 (Gailard Hunt ed. 1910).

2. *NARA v. Favish*, 541 U.S. 157, 171-72 (2004) (citation omitted).

3. Christopher H. Schmitt & Edward T. Pound, Keeping Secrets: *The Bush Administration Is Doing the Public's Business Out of the Public Eye. Here's How—and Why*, U.S. *News and World Report*, December 22, 2003, available at: http://www.usnews.com/usnews/news/articles/031222/22secrecy.htm.

4. Mary Thorn, National Council For Research On Women, Missing: Information About Women's Lives (2004), available at: http://www.ncrw.org/misinfo/report.pdf. The report details, for example, the removal of the *Handbook on Women Workers* and fact sheets on women workers from the U.S. Department of Labor site.

5. John C. Baker et al., *Rand National Defense Research Institute, Mapping the Risks: Assessing the Homeland Security Implications of Publicly Available Geospatial Information* 71 (2004), available at http://www.rand.org/pubs/monographs/2004/RAND_MG142.pdf.

6. OpenTheGovernment.org, Secrecy Report Card 2008: Indicators of Secrecy in the Federal Government, a Report by OpenTheGovernment.org, available at http://www.openthegovernment.org/otg/SecrecyReportCard08.pdf (last visited September 20, 2008).

7. For a general discussion of the importance of the FOIA to historians, see Mathew Silverman, *National Security and the First Amendment: A Judicial Role in Maximizing Public Access to Information*, 78 Ind. L. J. 1101 (2003).

Acknowledgments

This book would never have come to life without the help, support, and contributions of many. I wish to thank Jon Whiten for his superb research skill, tremendous attention to detail, and enthusiasm. His passion for the issue covered in this book was evident and helped to motivate me whenever I thought of giving up on this work. I also am very thankful for the research assistance of Chris Grubic, Nick Liptak, and Lisa Ugelow.

On a personal level, gratitude is owed to many individuals who have been by my side throughout this process. First, I wish to thank my brother Jason for being an inspiration to me. I am awestruck by his perseverance and dedication and find great inspiration in him. I also owe thanks to my parents, my aunt Mare, Michael, Michelle, Mathew, and Meredith, who are my best cheerleaders and who believe in and support every crazy thing I try to do. I am also very grateful to Thomas Lozinski, who served as a constant source of support, encouragement, and humor throughout this process. In addition to this invaluable personal support, he proved to be a superb research assistant. He has kept me grounded and has helped me to get out and play when the work got to be too much. This book would never have been finished without him. Finally, I thank my best friend Brian for showing me what really matters, helping me to achieve balance and filling my every day with pure joy.

The information contained in this book reflects my own views and opinions and is not an official opinion of my employer, Goodwin Procter LLP.

Introduction

A government by secrecy benefits no one. It injures the people it seeks to serve; it damages its own integrity and operation. It breeds distrust, dampens the fervor of its citizens and mocks their loyalty.

—Senator Edward V. Long[1]

Freedom of information is the bedrock of democracy. While it is clear that one needs access to information in order to participate fully in government processes and to have a healthy democracy, the widespread movement to legislate the right to information is of relatively recent origins. The pace of this movement has been become more rapid in recent years, however, and over the course of the past decade numerous countries have enacted formal statutes guaranteeing their citizens' right of access to government information. In the United States, freedom of information has a longer history than it does in those countries that are taking part in this relatively recent trend. Although the main federal legislation, the Freedom of Information Act (FOIA), was not enacted until the later half of the twentieth century, the concept of information freedom has been embraced by many of our country's leaders throughout history. Back in 1861, Abraham Lincoln observed, "Let the people know the facts, and the country will be safe." More recently, in 1962, President John F. Kennedy contended: "We seek a free flow of information . . . we are not afraid to entrust the American people with unpleasant facts, foreign ideas, alien philosophies, and competitive values." Still even more recently, when vetoing the Intelligence Re-authorization Bill in 2000, President Bill Clinton contended: "We must never forget that the free flow of information is essential to a democratic society." In addition, as will be discussed further in Chapter Two, principles of information freedom existed in the U.S. legal system even prior to the enactment of the FOIA.

Across the globe, other countries have been recognizing the importance of ensuring access to information held by the government, and to date more than 60 countries have enacted freedom of information laws. Elsewhere, even in the absence of specific legislation, citizens are asserting their right to know and are enjoying success on a number of fronts. While it is true that these laws vary tremendously from country to country and can often face serious implementation problems, it cannot be denied that the overall trend is producing much more government accountability, and often dramatic results.

In the United States, journalists, advocates, and ordinary citizens have used freedom of information laws to reveal a wide range of information. Notable examples include the following:

- Using documents obtained through the Freedom of Information Act, the U.S. Public Interest Research Group (PIRG) found that nearly one-third of major industrial facilities and government-operated sewage treatment plants had significantly violated pollution discharge regulations in 2000 and 2001, but relatively few of those plants were prosecuted for the violations.

- At least a dozen women died in 2004 from blood clots apparently caused by their use of a new birth control patch, Ortho Evra, according to federal drug safety reports released to the Associated Press under the FOIA. Dozens more women, most in their late teens and early twenties, suffered strokes and other clot-related problems after using the patch. Despite claims by the FDA and manufacturer Ortho McNeil that the patch was as safe as using birth control pills, the reports appear to indicate that the risk of dying or suffering a blood clot was about three times higher than with birth control pills.

- In 2003, the *New York Times* used the FOIA to obtain from the Food Safety and Inspection Service meat inspectors' reports that suggested the agency was lax in enforcing safety procedures at slaughterhouses. The *Times* found that contaminants were often present in food as it was processed at meat-packing plants even *after* it had gone through the plant's safety processes. The *Times* also concluded that inspectors' reports and recommendations to take action often went unheeded.

- Utah's *The Desert News* published FOIA documents in 1995 showing that U.S. Army scientists had exposed hundreds of sailors to germ and chemical warfare tests in the 1960s. In 2002, the Pentagon officially acknowledged using chemical and biological warfare agents in the tests, which finally allowed hundreds of affected veterans to receive disability and health benefits previously denied them.

- In an ongoing series of reports, the *Sun-Sentinel* of Florida used the FOIA to examine wasteful patterns of post-disaster spending by the Federal Emergency Management Agency (FEMA), including $31 million in fraudulent claims related to 2004's Hurricane Frances and the enormous scope of fraud from Hurricane Katrina. The paper's reporting led to a number of federal investigations, U.S. Senate and congressional hearings, changes in FEMA policies nationally, and the indictments of more than two dozen people on fraud charges.

- In 2005, *USA Today* revealed, via a FOIA request, that the Bush administration paid well-known media figure Armstrong Williams to promote the No

Child Left Behind Act. On that report's heels, the *Washington Post* learned through FOIA that the U.S. Department of Agriculture paid a writer to pen favorable stories about federal conservation programs.

- Documents obtained by the American Civil Liberties Union in 2004 through FOIA show that the Federal Bureau of Investigation (FBI) attempted to seek court permission to secretly review confidential materials—such as business, doctor, university, or library records—without the knowledge of the target of the investigation, as outlined in the controversial section 215 of the Patriot Act. Previously, Attorney General John Ashcroft had denied any usage of section 215.

- Department of Justice documents obtained under the FOIA by the *Des Moines Register* in 2005 showed that the Justice Department has greatly broadened the definition of terrorism since 2001 to seek congressional funding and authorization for greater police power. Justice Department memoranda showed that officials broadened record-keeping practices so that they could increase the reported number of "terrorism-related cases."

These are only some of the numerous examples of cases where individuals, journalists, and/or associations have used freedom of information laws to obtain very important information about significant issues impacting our society. Freedom of information laws and activism under such laws have led to many significant changes in a wide range of areas, including human rights, environmental preservation, health care, and consumer protection, many examples of which will be discussed in this book.

This book would be remiss if it did not also examine the ironic fact that during the past few years as other countries have begun strengthening their information access laws, the United States has been backtracking and limiting access to information. Even prior to the horrendous attacks of 9/11, Congress had ordered a re-review of the hundreds of millions of pages declassified under President Clinton. Since 9/11, the Bush administration has clamped down on openness and information access in major ways. Matters are expected to change dramatically under the Obama administration and, in fact, have already begun to do so. This is fortunate given the extremely important role that information access has to play in the health and strength of a democracy.

Chapter One will focus intensively on the origins and philosophical underpinnings of information freedom.

Chapter Two will explore freedom of information law in the United States. In doing so, it will examine the components and history of the federal FOIA and key state statutes. This chapter will also introduce the main problems that plague the effective administration of existing freedom of information laws, including access fees, administrative delays, the culture of secrecy, and the overuse of secrecy classifications.

The next five chapters will examine how individuals and organizations have been able to utilize freedom of information laws to make tremendous revelations and effect extraordinary change.

Chapter Three will focus specifically on the tremendous role that freedom of information laws play in helping journalists and activists uncover and reveal details about various environmental hazards. The actual and potential scope of freedom of information activism in the area of the environment is truly profound. From acid rain to zoos, individuals have obtained accurate information about the true status of questionable situations existing in the environment, detected perpetrators of environmental harm, and provided support for greater environmental protection. This chapter will also offer concrete advice for acquiring information regarding environmental issues through existing freedom of information laws and open government initiatives.

Chapter Four will examine the role that freedom of information and open government can play in protecting human health. It will explore significant cases in which journalists and other individuals were able to gather information about various health risks and issues via freedom of information laws. Finally, it will provide strategies for obtaining information about health issues from the government.

Chapter Five will examine how freedom of information laws can contribute to the protection of safety in a number of different ways. By exploring case studies, this chapter will show how freedom of information laws have been used to expose significant safety risks in a number of different domains.

In Chapter Six, attention will shift to government waste and corruption. This chapter will show how open government initiatives help to limit governmental corruption and crime. Using actual case studies, it will also show how researchers have used freedom of information laws to obtain significant details about governmental impropriety.

In Chapter Seven, attention will be directed at human rights and civil liberties. This chapter will show the successes and failures that individuals have experienced in gathering data and other information regarding human rights and civil liberties using freedom of information laws. It will also make suggestions as to how freedom of information efforts can better advance human rights, freedoms, and individual liberties.

Chapter Eight will show, in startling detail, how the terrorist attacks of September 11, 2001, and the resulting war on terror have impacted open government and information freedom initiatives. This chapter will analyze recent trends in information access in the United States and show why a departure away from free access to information is dangerous to our freedom and safety as well as to the integrity of our democracy.

Drawing upon the case examples presented in previous chapters, Chapter Nine will present important lessons that can be learned from the current administration of existing freedom of information laws. It will also present best practices for those attempting to secure information via such laws for the purpose of bringing about social change.

Notes

1. 110 Cong. Rec. 17,087 (1964) (Statement of Senator Long).

Chapter One

The Genesis of Freedom of Information Law

Let the people know the facts, and the country will be safe.
—President Abraham Lincoln, 1861

1. Overview

Although the United States is regarded as having well-developed freedom of information laws, it was not the first country to pass legislation to recognize and protect this freedom. This honor goes to Sweden, which enacted the Freedom of Information Act in 1766.[1] Despite Sweden's long history with freedom of information, however, it is only within the last quarter of a century that information freedom has gained widespread recognition in both the United States and internationally. Today, nearly 70 countries[2] have enacted laws intended to shed light on government operations.

A new trend towards information freedom is rapidly emerging in the international community, and laws recently enacted across the globe are breathing new life into the concept of information access. The U.S. Freedom of Information Act (FOIA) is now more than 40 years old, but many of the laws enacted in other countries have been passed within the last decade or so. Many of these new laws take a fresh and modern approach to information freedom. For example, while the FOIA covers only the executive branch of government, the newer laws of some countries include even private companies.

This chapter presents a brief overview of the history and development of this important right.

2. Rationale for Information Freedom Legislation

Freedom of information has been recognized not only as crucial to participatory democracy, accountability and good governance, but also as a fundamental human right. Authoritative statements and interpretations by a number of international bodies as well as national developments in countries around the world all agree that information freedom is an important part of modern democracy.

The right to freedom of information refers primarily to the right to access information held by a wide range of governmental agencies. It reflects the principle that public bodies do not hold information on their own behalf, but rather for the benefit of all members of the public. Accordingly, individuals should be able to access this information unless there is an overriding public interest reason for denying access. However, the right to freedom of information goes beyond the passive right to access documents upon request and includes a second element, a positive obligation by governments to publish and widely disseminate key categories of information of public interest.

In the contemporary era, another important aspect of the right to freedom of information is starting to emerge, namely the right to truth. This facet of information freedom refers to the obligation of governments to ensure that people know the truth about serious incidents of human rights abuse and other traumatic social events, such as major rail disasters, illnesses, and/or threats to safety. In such cases, it is not enough for public authorities simply to provide access to their files, or even to actively publish key documents they hold. Rather, it is incumbent on the government to ensure that the matter is fully investigated and that the results of that investigation are made public.

The primary human right and constitutional source of the right to freedom of information is the fundamental right to freedom of expression, which includes the right to seek, receive, and impart information and ideas, although some constitutions also provide separate, specific protection for it. In a more general sense, the right to information can also be derived from the recognition that democracy, and indeed the whole system for protection of human rights, cannot function properly without freedom of information. In that sense, it is a foundational human right upon which other rights depend.

The right to freedom of information can only be effective if it is guaranteed by law and if the means by which it is to be exercised are set out clearly in legislation or, for international governing bodies, in binding policy statements. Over time, authoritative statements, court decisions, and national practices have elaborated certain minimum standards that such laws and policies must meet. Generally, these include, among other things:

1. a strong presumption in favor of disclosure (the principle of maximum disclosure);
2. broad definitions of information and public bodies;
3. positive obligations to publish key categories of information;
4. clear and narrowly drawn exceptions, subject to a harm test and a public interest override;
5. effective oversight of the right by an independent administrative body.

3. Information Freedom on the Global Scale

Around the world, freedom of information is increasingly recognized as a fundamental human right, most commonly as an aspect of the right to freedom of expression. No democratic government can now seriously seek to deny members of the public the right to freedom of information. Indeed, the rapid proliferation of freedom of information laws in countries in all regions of the world is a dramatic global trend and one of the most important democratic developments of recent times.

While the United States is well regarded as being a leader in democracy and for having a well-developed system of information freedom, freedom of information did not originate in the United States, as noted above. This section examines the evolution of information freedom on the world stage and, in doing so, will show how the historical origins of information freedom are impacting the evolution and growth of this right in the modern age.

3.1 International Organizations

3.1.1 The United Nations

The United Nations has a long history of recognizing and advocating for freedom of information. The United Nations acknowledged this right even before the United States had adopted the FOIA. In 1946, during its first session, the UN General Assembly adopted Resolution 59(1), which states, in part: "Freedom of information is a fundamental human right and is the touchstone of all the freedoms to which the United Nations is consecrated. Freedom of information implies the right to gather, transmit and publish news anywhere and everywhere without fetters. As such it is an essential factor in any serious effort to promote the peace and progress of the world."[3]

In the ensuing years, the United Nations continued to recognize the right to information. In international human rights instruments that were to follow, however, freedom of information was not set out separately but was addressed as part of the fundamental right of freedom of expression, which includes the right to seek, receive, and impart information. The Universal

Declaration of Human Rights (UDHR), adopted by the UN General Assembly in 1948,[4] is generally considered to be the flagship statement of international human rights. Article 19 of the UDHR guarantees the right to freedom of expression and information in the following terms: "Everyone has the right to freedom of opinion and expression; this right includes freedom to hold opinions without interference and to seek, receive and impart information and ideas through any media and regardless of frontiers."

The International Convention on Civil and Political Rights (ICCPR), a legally binding treaty, was adopted by the UN General Assembly in 1966.[5] The corresponding provision in this treaty, also Article 19, guarantees the right to freedom of opinion and expression in very similar terms to the UDHR, stating:

1. 1. Everyone shall have the right to hold opinions without interference.

2. 2. Everyone shall have the right to freedom of expression; this right shall include freedom to seek, receive and impart information and ideas of all kinds, regardless of frontiers, either orally, in writing or in print, in the form of art, or through any other media of his choice.

3. 3. The exercise of the rights provided for in paragraph 2 of this article carries with it special duties and responsibilities. It may therefore be subject to certain restrictions, but these shall only be such as are provided by law and are necessary:

   a. (a) For respect of the rights or reputations of others;

   b. (b) For the protection of national security or of public order (*ordre public*), or of public health or morals.

3.1.2 Organization of American States

Article 13 of the American Convention on Human Rights (ACHR),[6] a legally binding treaty, guarantees freedom of expression in terms similar to, and even stronger than, the U.N. instruments.[7] Furthermore, in a 1985 Advisory Opinion, the Inter-American Court of Human Rights, interpreting Article 13, recognized freedom of information as a fundamental human right, which is as important to a free society as freedom of expression. In doing so, the Court explained:

> Article 13 . . . establishes that those to whom the Convention applies not only have the right and freedom to express their own thoughts but also the right and freedom to seek, receive and impart information and ideas of all kinds. [Freedom of expression] requires, on the one hand, that no one be arbitrarily limited or impeded in expressing his own thoughts. In that sense, it is a right that belongs to each individual. Its second aspect, on the other hand, implies a collective right to receive any information whatsoever and to have access to the thoughts expressed by others.[8]

The Court also stated: "For the average citizen it is just as important to know the opinions of others or to have access to information generally as is the very right to impart his own opinion," concluding that "a society that is not well-informed is not a society that is truly free."[9] In so doing, the Court emphasized the critical role that freedom of information has in a democracy.

3.1.3 Council of Europe

Given that Sweden was the first country to enact a law recognizing freedom of information, it is not too surprising that Europe, generally, has a long history with information freedom. In addition to being recognized at the national level, European international and intergovernmental organizations have also respected the concept of a right to freedom of information for some years. The Council of Europe (COE) is an intergovernmental organization composed of 47 member states that is devoted to promoting human rights, education, and culture. One of its foundational documents is the European Convention on Human Rights (ECHR),[10] which guarantees freedom of expression and information as a fundamental human right in Article 10. Article 10 differs slightly from guarantees found in Articles 19 of the UDHR and ICCPR, and Article 13 of the ACHR, in that it protects the right to "receive and impart," but not the right to "seek," information.

3.2 National Protections for Freedom of Information

3.2.1 Constitutional Protection for Information Freedom

Given that freedom of information is so closely tied to freedom of expression, a right that is widely protected by national constitutions, it should not come as a great surprise that information freedom is constitutionally protected in many jurisdictions. The basis for such protection varies from country to country. In some, it comes in the form of judicial interpretation of general guarantees of freedom of expression, while in others it comes from specific constitutional provisions.

3.2.1.1 Judicial Interpretations

Let us consider first the issue of judicial protection for information access. A number of high courts in countries around the world have held that the right to access information is protected by the general constitutional guarantee of freedom of expression. As early as 1969, in the Hakata Station Film case, the Supreme Court of Japan established the principle that *shiru kenri* (the "right to know") is protected by the guarantee of freedom of expression in Article 21 of the Constitution.[11]

Years later, in 1982, the Supreme Court of India ruled that access to government information was an essential part of the fundamental right to freedom of speech and expression, protected by Article 19 of the Constitution of India. In doing so, the court maintained:

> The concept of an open Government is the direct emanation from the right to know which seems implicit in the right of free speech and expression guaranteed under Article 19(1)(a). Therefore, disclosures of information in regard to the functioning of Government must be the rule, and secrecy an exception justified only where the strictest requirement of public interest so demands. The approach of the Court must be to attenuate the area of secrecy as much as possible consistently with the requirement of public interest, bearing in mind all the time that disclosure also serves an important aspect of public interest.[12]

Courts in other jurisdictions have handed down similar rulings. For example, the Constitution of Pakistan does not expressly give a right of access to information. However, the Supreme Court ruled in 1993 that Article 19 includes a right of citizens to receive information.[13] In addition, in Israel the Supreme Court ruled in the 1990 Shalit case that citizens have a fundamental right to obtain information from the government.[14] Also, in France the Conseil d'Etat found in April 2002 that the right of administrative documents is a fundamental right under Article 34 of the Constitution. Furthermore, the Constitutional Court of South Korea ruled in 1989 that there is a constitutional right to information "as an aspect of the right of freedom of expression, and specific implementing legislation to define the contours of the right was not a prerequisite to its enforcement."[15]

While the United States has a well-developed system of freedom of information, its courts have not followed the lead of these other countries' courts and ruled that freedom of information is a constitutionally protected right. Rather, the U.S. Supreme Court has held that the First Amendment of the Constitution, which guarantees freedom of speech and of the press, does not "[mandate] a right to access government information or sources of information within government's control."[16]

3.2.1.2 Specific Constitutional Protections

While some jurisdictions have found constitutional protections for freedom of information through judicial interpretation, a number of countries specifically include the right to information among the constitutionally guaranteed human rights. Sweden is an interesting example, as the whole of its Freedom of the Press Act, adopted in 1766, has constitutional status. Sweden's Freedom of the Press Act includes comprehensive provisions on freedom of information. During the last decade, many countries that have recently adopted multiparty systems, or are otherwise in transition to democracy, have explicitly included the right to freedom of information in their constitutions. Examples include Bulgaria,[17] Estonia,[18] Hungary,[19] Lithuania,[20] Malawi,[21] Moldova,[22] the Philippines,[23] Poland,[24] Romania,[25] the Russian Federation,[26] South Africa,[27] and Thailand.[28]

In Latin America, constitutions have tended to focus on one important aspect of the right to information, namely the petition of habeas data, the right to access information about oneself, whether held by public or private bodies, and, where necessary, to update or correct it. For example, Section 43 of the Constitution of Argentina[29] states:

> Any person shall file this action to obtain information on the data about himself and their purpose, registered in public records or data bases, or in private ones intended to supply information; and in case of false data or discrimination, this action may be filed to request the suppression, rectification, confidentiality or updating of said data. The secret nature of the sources of journalistic information shall not be impaired.

In Mexico, the Constitution was amended in 1977 to include a right of freedom of information. Article 6 states, in part, "the right of information shall be guaranteed by the state." The Supreme Court made a number of decisions further enhancing that right. There are also statutory protections for freedom of information in Mexico. The Federal Law of Transparency and Access to Public Government Information was unanimously approved by Parliament in April 2002 and signed by President Vicente Fox in June 2002. It went into effect in June 2003. The law allows all persons to demand information in writing from federal government departments, autonomous constitutional bodies, and other government entities. Agencies must respond to requests in 20 working days.

In Panama, the Constitution was amended in 2004 to include a right of access to information. Article 43 gives all persons the right to access public information except in cases where it has been restricted by law. Article 42 allows individuals the right to access and control personal information held by public or private bodies. Article 44 gives the right of Habeas Data to enforce both of these rights of access in court. Again, there is also statutory protections for information freedom in Panama. The Law on Transparency in Public Administration was approved by the National Assembly in December 2001 and promulgated on January 22, 2002. The law gives the right for any person to ask for information in any form from government bodies. Individuals also have the right to access their own files and correct them. Government bodies must respond within 30 days. Fees can only be charged for reproduction.

Peru also recognizes a Constitutional right to information freedom. Article 2(5) of the country's Constitution states:

> All persons have the right: . . . To solicit information that one needs without disclosing the reason, and to receive that information from any public entity within the period specified by law, at a reasonable cost. Information that affects personal intimacy and that is expressly excluded by law or for reasons of national security is not subject to disclosure.

Access to information is constitutionally protected under the right of habeas data in Peru. Several cases have allowed the courts to establish their jurisdiction over, and support for, habeas data. The Law of Transparency and Access to Public Information was adopted in August 2002 and went into effect in January 2003. Under the law, every individual has the right to request information in any form from any government body or private entity that offers public services or executes administrative functions without having to explain why. Documentation funded by the public budget is considered public information. Public bodies must respond within seven working days, which can be extended in extraordinary cases for another five days.

The Parliament substantially amended the law in January 2003 following criticism of the excessive exemptions, especially relating to national security, and as a result of a lawsuit filed by the Ombudsman in the Constitutional Tribunal challenging the constitutionality of the Act.

Ecuador also recognizes a Constitutional right to information freedom. According to Article 81 of the Political Constitution:

> The state shall guarantee the right, in particular for journalists and social commentators, to obtain access to sources of information; and to seek, receive, examine, and disseminate objective, accurate, pluralistic, and timely information, without prior censorship, on matters of general interest, consistent with community values . . .
>
> Information held in public archives shall not be classified as secret, with the exception of documents requiring such classification for the purposes of national defense or other reasons specified by law.

The Organic Law on Transparency and Access to Public Information was adopted on May 18, 2004. The law gives citizens the right to demand public information in any format from public bodies and organizations that provide state services or are publicly owned. The request must be made in writing, and government bodies must respond within 10 days, but that deadline can be extended another five days.

3.2.2 Freedom of Information Legislation

Freedom of information laws have existed for more than 200 years, but very few are more than 20 years old. However, there is now a veritable wave of freedom of information legislation sweeping the globe, and in the last 10 years numerous such laws have been passed—or are being developed—in countries in every region of the world. As noted, the history of freedom of information laws can be traced back to Sweden, where information freedom has been protected since 1766. Another country with a long history of freedom of information legislation is Colombia, whose 1888 Code of Political and Municipal Organization allowed individuals to request documents held by government agencies or in government archives. The United States passed its freedom of information law in 1967, and several years later, in 1982, Australia,[30] Canada,[31] and New Zealand[32] followed suit.

A large number of countries have passed freedom of information laws since that time. In Asia, Hong Kong,[33] the Philippines,[34] South Korea,[35] Thailand,[36] and others have enacted such legislation. In Central and South America, a number of jurisdictions, including Peru,[37] the Autonomous Government of the City of Buenos Aires,[38] Belize,[39] and Trinidad and Tobago[40], have implemented information freedom laws. In Europe, the vast majority of countries have freedom of information laws, including Albania,[41] Bosnia and Herzegovina,[42] Bulgaria,[43] the Czech Republic,[44] Estonia,[45] Georgia,[46] Hungary,[47] Latvia,[48] Lithuania,[49] Moldova,[50] Slovakia,[51] Russia,[52] Ukraine,[53] and the United Kingdom.[54] Freedom of information laws are also present in the Middle East[55] region and in Africa.[56] Furthermore, a number of countries in all regions have prepared or are considering draft legislation. Therefore, when considered from a global perspective, the available data suggests that the trend is for freedom of information laws to develop and expand.

4. Conclusion

This chapter demonstrates the increasing importance that freedom of information is having on the international stage. While the United States has a history of information freedom that is longer than that of many other countries, jurisdictions around the world continue to recognize the important role that freedom of information has to play in democratic government. Recent information suggests that this trend is likely to continue on the international front in the coming years. The next chapter explores in detail the origins, scope, and limitations of U.S. information access laws.

Notes

1. The Freedom of Press Act, December 2, 1766 (Sweden). Following a *coup d'etat* in 1772, the Freedom of Press Act was repealed. A democratic government returned in 1809 and a new Freedom of the Press Act was adopted in 1810 and replaced by another in 1812, which remained in force until 1949.

2. David Banisar, *Freedom of Information Around the World 2006: A Global Survey of Access to Government Records Laws*, available at: http://www.freedominfo.org/documents/global_survey2006.doc (lasted visited August 5, 2008).

3. G. A. Res. 59(1) at 95 (December 14, 1946).

4. Universal Declaration of Human Rights, G. A. Res. 217A (III), at 71, U.N. Doc A/810 (December 10, 1948).

5. G. A. Res. 2300 A (XXI) at 55 (December 16, 1966).

6. Organization of American States, American Convention on Human Rights, adopted at San José, Costa Rica (November 22, 1969), entered into force July 18, 1978.

7. *Id.* at Article 13. Freedom of Thought and Expression, which provides:

- Everyone has the right to freedom of thought and expression. This right includes freedom to seek, receive, and impart information and ideas of all kinds, regardless of frontiers, either orally, in writing, in print, in the form of art, or through any other medium of one's choice.

- The exercise of the right provided for in the foregoing paragraph shall not be subject to prior censorship but shall be subject to subsequent imposition of liability, which shall be expressly established by law to the extent necessary to ensure:

  a. Respect for the rights or reputations of others; or

  b. The protection of national security, public order, or public health or morals.

- The right of expression may not be restricted by indirect methods or means, such as the abuse of government or private controls over newsprint, radio broadcasting frequencies, or equipment used in the dissemination of information, or by any other means tending to impede the communication and circulation of ideas and opinions.

- Notwithstanding the provisions of paragraph 2 above, public entertainments may be subject by law to prior censorship for the sole purpose of regulating access to them for the moral protection of childhood and adolescence.

- Any propaganda for war and any advocacy of national, racial, or religious hatred that constitute incitements to lawless violence or to any other similar action against any person or group of persons on any grounds including those of race, color, religion, language, or national origin shall be considered as offenses punishable by law.

8. *Inter-American Court of Human Rights, Compulsory Membership in an Association Prescribed by Law for the Practice of Journalism*, 30, Advisory Opinion OC-5/85 (November 13, 1985).

9. *Id.* at paragraphs 32, 70.

10. Council of Europe, Convention for the Protection of Human Rights and Fundamental Freedoms, E. T. S. No. 5, (November 4, 1950).

11. *Kaneko et. al v. Japan, Keishū* ll at 1490 (Sup. Ct. November 26, 1969).

12. *S. P. Gupta v. President of India* (1982) AIR (SC) 149, p. 234.

13. *Sharif v. Pakistan*, PLD 1993 S.C. 471.

14. H. C. 1601-4/90 Shalit et al. v. Peres el at., 44(3) P.D. 353.

15. Freedomofinfo.org resource page on South Korea, available at: http://www.freedominfo.org/countries/south_korea.htm (last visited October 1, 2008).

16. *Houchins v. KQED, Inc.*, 438 US 1, 1978, p. 15.

17. Constitution of the Republic of Bulgaria, art 41.

18. Constitution of the Republic of Estonia, art 44.

19. Constitution of the Republic of Hungary, art 61(1).

20. Constitution of the Republic of Lithuania, art 25(5).

21. Constitution of the Republic of Malawi, art 37.

22. Constitution of the Republic of Moldova, art 34.

23. Constitution of the Philippine Republic, art III(7).

24. Constitution of the Republic of Poland, art 61.

25. Constitution of Romania, art 31.

26. Constitution of the Russian Federation, art 24(2).

27. Constitution of the Republic of South Africa, art 32.

28. Constitution of the Kingdom of Thailand, art 58.

29. Constitution of the Argentine Nation, sect 43.

30. Freedom of Information Act, 1982 (Australia).

31. Access to Information Act, Chapter A-1 (Canada).

32. Official Information Act, 1982 (New Zealand).

33. Code on Access to Information, March 1995 (Hong Kong).

34. Code of Conduct and Ethical Standards for Public Officials and Employees, Republic Act 6713, 1987 (the Philippines).

35. Act on Disclosure of Information by Public Agencies, 1998 (South Korea).

36. Official Information Act, December 1997 (Thailand).

37. Law N 26301, 2 May 1994, implementing the constitutional right to habeas data (Peru).

38. Law No. 104, 1998 (the City of Buenos Aires).

39. Freedom of Information Act, 1994 (Belize).

40. Freedom of Information Act, 1999 (Trinidad and Tobago).

41. Law No. 8503 on the right to information about official documents, 1999 (Albania).

42. The Freedom of Access to Information Act, October 2000 (Bosnia and Herzegovina).

43. Access to Public Information Act, 2000 (Bulgaria).

44. Freedom of Information Law, 1999 (Czech Republic).

45. Public Information Act, 2000 (Estonia).

46. Law of Georgia on Freedom of Information, 1998 (Georgia).

47. Act No. LXIII of 1992 on the Protection of Personal Data and the Publicity of Data of Public Interest (Hungary).

48. Law on Freedom of Information, 1998 (Latvia).

49. Law on the Right to Receive Information from the State and Municipal Institutions, 2000 (Lithuania).

50. The Law on Access to Information, 2000 (Moldova).

51. Act on Free Access to Information and Amendments of Certain Acts (The Freedom of Information Act) (Slovakia).

52. Law on Information, Disclosure and Protection of Information, January 25, 1995, Act No. 24-FZ (Russia).

53. Law on Information, October 2, 1992, Law No. 2657-XII (Ukraine).

54. Freedom of Information Act, 2000, Chapter 36 (United Kingdom).

55. Freedom of Information Law, Law 5758-1998, May 1998 (Israel).

56. Promotion of Access to Information Act, Act No. 2, 2000 (South Africa).

Chapter Two

Freedom of Information Law in the United States

1. A Brief History of the Freedom of Information Act

1.1 Legislative History

The Freedom of Information Act (FOIA) was passed in the pre-Watergate 1960s, when a number of different constituencies were pushing for greater access to information held by the government.[1] Lead among these advocates of information freedom was the press. Citing a rash of random and largely unexplained denials of access to information held by the government, including denials for information about alleged cover-ups of mistakes made by the government, the press pushed vigorously for the enactment of legislation that would ensure greater information access.[2]

At the time, Congress was also a proponent for better access to information held by the executive branch of the government. It was not entirely surprising that the press had found an advocate in Congress given that legislators had been sparring with the executive branch over its Constitutional right to access executive materials for almost 200 years.[3] John Moss, a Democratic congressman from Sacramento, California, led that body's charge for information freedom. Supported by extensive press coverage and active lobbying by newspaper editors, Moss led hearings beginning in 1955 that documented and denounced excessive government secrecy and demonstrated why legislation to ensure information freedom was needed.[4]

Although the federal FOIA was not enacted until 1966, the United States actually has a fairly long history of providing access to certain public records. Some states have provided access to records for decades, even centuries: the first open records law was passed in Wisconsin shortly after it became a state in 1848.[5] In addition, court records and legislative materials have long been open to the public.

The first major federal legislative development occurred in 1946, when Congress enacted the Administrative Procedures Act[6] (APA). The APA required that government bodies publish information about their structures, powers, and procedures and make available "all final opinions or orders in the adjudication of cases (except those required for good cause to be held confidential and not cited as precedents) and all rules."[7]

The APA, however, was subject to broad exceptions. Specifically it allowed withholding of information relating to "any function . . . requiring secrecy in the public interest" and for internal management. It also authorized the disclosure of information to persons "properly and directly concerned except information held confidential for good cause found."[8] In practice, little information was actually released under this provision. Reform of the APA as a mechanism for achieving freedom of information was abandoned after it came to be seen as more of a withholding statute than a disclosure statute.[9] Beginning in the 1950s, media groups and Congress began advocating for a more comprehensive law that would ensure better access to documents and other information held by the government.

The enactment of the FOIA in 1966 was a momentous occasion, and it made the United States the third country in the world to enact freedom of information legislation. However, not everyone supported the idea of enacting legislation to protect information freedom. Even President Lyndon Johnson, who signed the law into force, reportedly had strong reservations about it.[10] While the President typically held formal bill signings for new legislation, he refused to hold a formal signing ceremony for the FOIA, instead signing the bill on July 4, 1966, while vacationing at his ranch in Texas. Nevertheless, upon signing the bill into law, Johnson made a statement that, on its surface, was supportive of the measure:

> This legislation springs from one of our most essential principles: a democracy works best when the people have all the information that the security of the nation permits. No one should be able to pull the curtains of secrecy around decisions which can be revealed without injury to the public interest.[11]

1.2 Philosophical Basis of the FOIA

While the FOIA was not enacted until the 1960s, and the concept of freedom of information is not a constitutionally protected right in the United States, the goals of the FOIA—namely an open government that remains accountable to its citizens—can be traced back clearly to the founding fathers of our country. The fact that these early leaders were aware of the risks and concerned by the prospects of a closed, inaccessible government operating in secrecy is particularly notable given that the government of their day was much smaller and far less bureaucratic than today's. James Madison clearly summed up this concern with his notable warning:

> Knowledge will forever govern ignorance, and a people who mean to be their own governors, must arm themselves with the power knowledge gives. A popular government without popular information or the means of acquiring it, is but a prologue to a farce or a tragedy or perhaps both.[12]

Some of the concerns identified by our founding fathers remain relevant in current times. Today, for the most part, the citizenry relies upon reporters, investigators, authors, and analysts to stay abreast of what is transpiring within the government and to raise the red flag when needed. In order to do this, such professionals and ordinary citizens alike need unfettered access to information and data regarding government operations and actions. In short, while the size, complexity, and diversity of our society continue to grow, the threat of governmental secrecy also grows, as does the need to stay vigilant about protecting the freedom of information.

2. The FOIA

2.1 General Overview

The FOIA[13] was enacted in 1966 and entered into force in 1967. Generally, the FOIA allows for broad rights of access to information held by government agencies. The FOIA also requires that government agencies publish material relating to their structure and functions, rules, decisions, procedures, policies, and manuals.

Since its initial passage, the FOIA has been substantially amended on several occasions. Significant amendments followed in 1974, 1986, 1996, and more recently 2007.[14] Among other changes, the 1974 amendments broadened the definition of agency, revised time limits for responding to FOIA requests, and required agencies to make indexes of information more readily available. In addition, they clarified Congressional intent to allow in camera judicial review of allegedly classified documents in FOIA litigation, required annual reports to Congress, and granted courts discretion to award attorney's fees and court costs for successful litigants.[15]

One of the most significant modifications came with the passage of the Electronic Freedom of Information Act[16] (EFOIA) in 1996. The main goal of the EFOIA was to address agency backlogs. However, it also mandated the electronic availability of many government records. To accommodate the societal changes ushered in by the Internet age, the 1996 amendments of the EFOIA required that agencies make information available electronically, including commonly requested documents.[17] In addition, the Department of Justice has issued guidance stating that documents requested three times or more be made available electronically in agency electronic reading rooms. These electronic resources provide a great initial resource for individuals who are commencing research into a particular area. However, one should not assume that they are a complete resource on any topic.

2.2 Exemptions

While the FOIA does have very broad coverage, it is also subject to a large number of discretionary exemptions that can arguably minimize the effectiveness of the access provisions. There are nine categories of discretionary exemptions that an agency can cite in refusing to disclose records, either in whole or in part.[18] Still, it must be emphasized that the FOIA also provides that any "reasonably segregable portion of a record" must be provided to the requester after "deletion of the portions which are exempt."[19] So, even if an agency has the right to withhold certain portions of a record due to an applicable exemption, it must provide the requesting party with access to those parts of the record that are not covered by the exemption. This is an issue that individuals requesting documents pursuant to the FOIA are likely to encounter again and again. Requesters should thus be prepared to fight claims of exemptions under certain circumstances and push for the disclosure of nonexempt portions of records in other scenarios.

The nine exemptions are exclusive and are to be construed narrowly.[20] The exemptions, to be discussed further, are:

1. National security,
2. Internal agency rules,
3. Information protection by other statutes,
4. Business information,
5. Inter- and intra-agency memos,
6. Personal privacy,
7. Law enforcement records,
8. Financial institutions, and
9. Oil wells data.

Exemption 1: Classified Secret Matters or National Defense or Foreign Policy. This exemption protects documents and records containing national security information concerning the national defense or foreign policy, provided that the information at issue has been properly classified in accordance with the substantive and procedural requirements of an executive order.

The Executive Order on Classified National Security Information (the "Order") sets standards for the classification and declassification of information.[21] The Order was issued by President Bill Clinton in 1995 and amended by President George W. Bush in 2003 to be more restrictive. The Order establishes three categories of classification: Top Secret, Secret and Confidential. The Order also requires that all information 25 years and older that has permanent historical value must be automatically declassified within five years unless it is exempted.[22] Individuals can make requests for mandatory declassification instead of using the FOIA to obtain the information. Decisions to retain classification are subject to the Interagency Security Classification Appeals Panel.

There has been a substantial expansion of classification in the past several years. In 2007, there were 23.1 million decisions for classification, up from 20.6 million in 2006, and nearly four times the 8.5 million in 2001. Inversely, the rate of declassification has slowed. Since 1995, more than a billion total pages have been declassified. In the past several years, declassification has decreased substantially, with only 37.2 million pages released in 2007. While that figure is down only slightly from 2006, the number of pages declassified in the past few years is but a fraction of the number of pages that were declassified each year in the late 1990s. For example, 204 million pages were declassified in 1997, while only 28 million pages were declassified in 2004. The Information Security Oversight Office (ISOO), a division of the National Archives, has policy oversight of the government-wide security classification system. A sample review by ISOO found that 56 percent of the classified documents examined were erroneously classified.[23]

Between 1995 and 2005, more than 25,000 publicly available records were reclassified at the National Archives under a secret agreement with the CIA, U.S. Army and other agencies. An ISOO audit of those files found that more than one-third were not eligible for classification.[24] It also found a "significant number of instances when records that were clearly inappropriate for continued classification were withdrawn from public access."

There has also been a large expansion in the creation of "sensitive but unclassified" categories of information, with more than 50 different categories currently being used by agencies. These categories are largely unregulated and have been used to justify withholding information even though they are not largely recognized in the FOIA as legitimate exemptions.

Specialist bodies have been created to review large numbers of classified documents on certain topics. For example, The John F. Kennedy Assassination Records Collection Act of 1992 ordered the creation of a special board to review and release information related to the assassination of President Kennedy.[25] More than 4 million pages were released, including thousands of previously classified records under the Act.[26] As another example of such a specialist body, The Nazi War Crimes Disclosure Act[27] created a board to review and release all classified information on Nazi war criminals. The Act was later amended to include classified information on the Japanese Imperial Government.[28] More than 8 million pages have been released under the Act.

In February 2005, the CIA agreed to release its own records on Nazi war criminals following Congressional pressure for such release.[29]

Notwithstanding these releases, Exemption 1 remains a particular challenge for individuals seeking information under the FOIA. It is an exemption that is often cited and is very difficult to fight.

Exemption 2: Internal Personnel Rules and Practices. Exemption 2 excludes from mandatory disclosure those records "that are related solely to the internal personnel rules and practices of an agency." Courts have interpreted the exemption to encompass two distinct categories of information:

a. internal matters of a relatively trivial nature—sometimes referred to as "low 2" information; and

b. more substantial internal matters, the disclosure of which would risk circumvention of a legal requirement—sometimes referred to as "high 2" information.

Exemption 3: Information Specifically Exempted by Other Statutes. The third exemption incorporates the disclosure prohibitions that are contained in various other federal statutes. As originally enacted in 1966, Exemption 3 was broadly phrased so as to simply cover information "specifically exempted from disclosure by statute." As amended, Exemption 3 allows the withholding of information prohibited from disclosure by another statute only if one or two disjunctive requirements are met. The statute either:

a. requires that the matter be withheld from the public in such a manner as to leave no discretion on the issue; *or*

b. establishes particular criteria for withholding or refers to particular types of matters to be withheld.

Thus, a statute falls within the coverage of the exemption if it satisfies any one of these requirements.

Exemption 4: Trade Secrets and Commercial or Financial Information. This exemption protects "trade secrets and commercial or financial information obtained from a person (that is) privileged or confidential." This exemption is intended to protect the interest of both the government and person and/or entity that submits the protected information.

Exemption 5: Privileged Inter-agency or Intra-agency Memoranda or Letters. This exemption protects "inter-agency or intra-agency memorandums or letters which would not be available by law to a party . . . in litigation with the agency." As such, it has been construed to "exempt those documents, and only those documents, normally privileged in the civil discovery context."

Exemption 6: Personal Information Affecting an Individual's Privacy. This exemption permits the government to withhold all information about individuals in "personnel and medical files and similar files" when the disclosure of such information "would constitute a clearly unwarranted invasion of personal privacy." This exemption cannot be invoked to withhold from a requester information pertaining to the requester. Accordingly, and quite logically, if an individual files a FOIA request demanding documents concerning him or herself, the government can't rightfully claim that it cannot release the documents due to concerns about that individual's privacy rights.

Exemption 7: Investigatory Records Compiled for Law Enforcement Purposes. As amended, this exemption protects from disclosure "records or information compiled for law enforcement purposes."

Exemption 7(A): Records or Information That Could Reasonably Be Expected to Interfere with Enforcement Proceedings. This exemption authorizes the withholding of "records or information compiled for law enforcement purposes, but only to the extent that production of such law enforcement records or information ... could reasonably be expected to interfere with enforcement proceedings."

Exemption 7(B): Disclosure Which Would Deprive a Person of a Fair Trial or an Impartial Adjudication. This exemption permits the government to withhold from disclosure "records or information compiled for law enforcement purposes (the disclosure of which) would deprive a person of the right to a fair trial or an impartial adjudication."

Exemption 7(C): Personal Information in Law Enforcement Records. This exemption provides protection for personal information in law enforcement records. This exemption is the law enforcement counterpart to Exemption 6, providing protection for law enforcement information, the disclosure of which "could reasonably be expected to constitute an unwarranted invasion of personal privacy."

Exemption 7(D): Identity of a Confidential Source. This exemption provides protection for "records or information compiled for law enforcement purposes (which) could reasonably be expected to disclose the identity of a confidential source —including a State, local, or foreign agency or authority or any private institution which furnished information on a confidential basis." It also protects information furnished by a confidential source "in the case of a record or information compiled by a criminal law enforcement authority in the course of a criminal investigation, or by an agency conducting a lawful national security intelligence investigation."

Exemption 7(E): Circumvention of the Law. This exemption affords protection to all law enforcement information which "would disclose techniques and procedures for law enforcement investigations or prosecutions, or would disclose guidelines for law enforcement investigations or prosecutions if such disclosure could reasonably be expected to risk circumvention of the law."

Exemption 7(F): Physical Safety to Protect a Wide Range of Individuals. This exemption permits the withholding of information necessary to protect the physical safety of a wide range of individuals. Whereas Exemption 7(F) previously protected records that "would endanger the life or physical safety of law enforcement personnel," the amended exemption provides protection to any individual when disclosure of information about him or her "could reasonably be expected to endanger (his/her) life or physical safety."

Exemption 8: Records of Financial Institutions. This exemption covers matters that are "contained in or related to examination, operating, or condition reports prepared by, on behalf of, or for the use of an agency responsible for the regulation or supervision of financial institutions."

Exemption 9: Geographical and Geophysical Information Concerning Wells. This exemption covers "geological and geophysical information and data, including maps, concerning wells."

The authority of the government to withhold information has been expanding since 9/11. For example, the Homeland Security Act[30] added a provision prohibiting the disclosure of voluntarily provided business information relating to "Critical Infrastructure." These issues will be discussed further in Chapter Eight.

2.3 Procedural Aspects of Making a FOIA Request

For all the advantages and disadvantages of the freedom of information laws, one thing is for certain: the laws cannot be effective if they are not being utilized. As such, it is essential to understand how to put these laws to work. The following sections examine some of the key procedural issues that should be taken into account by anyone seeking to make a request under the FOIA.

2.3.1 Who Can Make a Request Under the FOIA?

The FOIA allows any person or organization, irrespective of citizenship, to request records and information held by agencies of the federal government. A FOIA request can be made by "any person," a broad term that encompasses individuals (including foreign citizens), partnerships, corporations, associations, and foreign or domestic governments. Requests may also be made through an attorney or other representative on behalf of "any person." Although the statute specifically excludes federal agencies from the definition of a "person," states and state agencies can also make FOIA requests to the federal government.

2.3.2 To What Entities Does the FOIA Apply?

Agencies within the executive branch of the federal government, including the Executive Office of the President and independent regulatory agencies, are subject to the provisions of the FOIA. However, the FOIA does not apply to entities that "are neither chartered by the federal government [n]or controlled by it."[31] As a result, state governments, municipal corporations, the courts, Congress, and private citizens are not subject to the FOIA. Offices within the Executive Office of the President whose functions are limited to advising and assisting the President also do not fall within the definition of "agency." Such excluded offices include the Offices of the President and of the Vice President, and their respective staffs.[32] Under this definition of agency, however, executive branch entities whose responsibilities exceed merely advising and assisting the President generally are considered "agencies" under the FOIA.

2.3.3 What Are Agency Records?

The FOIA has a broad mandate, covering "agency records." The Supreme Court has articulated a basic, two-part test for determining what constitutes agency records under the FOIA: Agency records are records that are either created or obtained by an agency, and are under agency control at the time of the FOIA request.[33] When considering the control issue, it is important to note that courts have identified four relevant factors for an agency to consider when making such a determination:

a. the intent of the record's creator to retain or relinquish control over the record;

b. the ability of the agency to use and dispose of the record as it sees fit;

c. the extent to which agency personnel have read or relied upon the record;

d. the degree to which the record was integrated into the agency's record-keeping system or files.[34]

2.3.4 What Are the Requirements for a Proper FOIA Request?

The FOIA specifies only two requirements for an access request. First, the request must "reasonably describe" the records sought.[35] Second, it must be made in accordance with the agency's published FOIA regulations.[36] With respect to the requirement that the request reasonably describe the records sought, the legislative history of the 1974 amendments to the FOIA indicate that it is sufficient if the description of the requested record enables a professional agency employee familiar with the subject area to locate the record with a "reasonable amount of effort."[37] One FOIA request was held invalid because it required an agency's FOIA staff either to have "clairvoyant capabilities" to discern the requester's needs or to spend "countless numbers of personnel hours seeking needles in bureaucratic haystacks."[38] It is important to note that the fact that a FOIA request is very broad will not alone entitle an agency to deny the request. Rather, the key factor is the ability of an agency's staff to reasonably ascertain what records are being requested and then to locate them. With respect to the second requirement, obviously, it is essential to check the agency's published FOIA regulations and verify that one's request complies therewith.

2.3.5 What Are the Timing Requirements?

The FOIA requires agencies to respond to requests within 20 working days.[39] Agencies are not necessarily required to release the information requested within the statutory time limit, but access to releasable records should, at a minimum, be granted promptly thereafter.[40] In "unusual circumstances," an agency can extend the 20-day time limit for processing a FOIA request if it tells the requester in writing why it needs the extension and when it will make a determination on the request.[41] The FOIA defines "unusual circumstances" as the need to search for and collect records from separate offices, the need to examine a voluminous amount of records required by the request, and the need to consult with another agency or agency component.[42] If the required extension exceeds 10 days, the agency must allow the requester an opportunity to modify his or her request or to arrange for an alternative time frame for completion of the agency's processing.[43]

In many instances, though, agencies may fail to meet these time limits for a variety of reasons, including the lack of sufficient resources to respond promptly to all requests received. Agencies, therefore, have adopted the court-sanctioned practice of generally handling backlogged FOIA requests on a "first-in, first-out" basis. The EFOIA amendments expressly authorized agencies to promulgate regulations providing for "multitrack processing" of their FOIA requests—which allows agencies to process requests on a first-in, first-out basis within each track, but also permits them to respond to relatively simple requests more quickly than requests involving complex and/or voluminous records.

An agency's failure to comply with the time limits for either an initial request or an administrative appeal may be treated as a "constructive exhaustion" of administrative remedies. A requester may immediately thereafter seek judicial review if he or she wishes to do so.

New legislation recently enacted to reform FOIA administration provides new incentives to agencies to avoid processing delays. As discussed in more detail under section 5.1 of this chapter, the OPEN Government Act mandates tracking numbers for FOIA requests that take longer than 10 days to process and penalizes agencies that do not comply with the FOIA's time limits. These changes should provide incentives for federal agencies to respond more promptly.

2.3.6 What Does It Cost to Make a FOIA Request?

Agencies are authorized to charge certain fees associated with the processing of requests. Some categories of requesters cannot be charged these fees, and in some cases fees can be reduced or waived. To calculate the fees, an agency is required to determine the projected use of the records sought by the FOIA request and the type of requester asking for the documents.

Because the FOIA was intended to promote the public's access to information, news media organizations and educational institutions are excused from certain fees. The fee categories for FOIA are as follows:

1. **Commercial.** The commercial category applies to companies that or people who seek information for a purpose that furthers commercial, trade, or profit interests, including for use in litigation. Commercial requesters are required to pay for search, review, and duplication costs.

2. **Educational Institution.** Educational institutions include preschools, public or private elementary or secondary schools, and institutions of graduate higher education, undergraduate higher education, professional education, or vocational education that operate a program(s) of scholarly research. Educational institution requesters are required to pay duplication costs, but they are entitled to the first 100 pages without charge.

3. **Noncommercial Scientific Institution.** This category applies to noncommercially operated institutions that conduct scientific research not intended to promote any particular product or industry. Noncommercial requesters are required to pay duplication costs, but they are entitled to the first 100 pages without charge.

4. **Representative of the News Media.** People who actively gather news for entities organized and operated to publish or broadcast news to the public are required to pay for duplication, but they are entitled to the first 100 pages without charge.

5. **Other Requesters.** Requesters who do not fit into any of the above categories are required to pay search costs for more than two hours and duplication costs for more than 100 pages.

To demonstrate that you belong in an educational, news media, or noncommercial fee category, you must provide information about the intended professional scholarly or journalistic uses of the information you hope to receive. It is also advisable to list any relevant previous or pending publications, including books, articles, dissertations, publication contracts or letters of intent or interest, or similar information that shows your ability to disseminate the information you receive from the agency. In the request, you should also state that the materials are not requested solely for a private, profit-making commercial purpose. In addition, you should request that the agency notify you if any assessable fees will exceed an amount you specify.[44]

Actual search, review, and duplication fees vary by agency. Search/review fees can be anywhere from $8 to $45 per hour, and duplication fees can be from 10 cents to 35 cents per page. Agencies cannot require a requester to make an advance payment unless the agency estimates that the fee is likely to exceed $250 or the requester previously failed to pay proper fees. All fees are subject to change. Accordingly, you should verify fees in effect at the time you make your request.

2.3.7 Can I Get a Fee Waiver?

Under the FOIA it is possible to have all fees, including copying, waived by the agency if the material requested "is likely to contribute significantly to public understanding of the operations or activities of government and is not primarily in the commercial interest of the requester." If your request fits this statutory criterion, you should make your case for a fee waiver in your request letter as strongly as possible. To improve the likelihood of getting your request approved, be sure to describe the scholarly, historical, or current public interest in the material requested. You should also identify specific operations or activities of government to which the request relates and explain why the information will contribute to an understanding of those activities and operations. You should include a description of why the public in general would be interested and why the disclosure would be significant.

2.3.8 What Can I Expect After I Make My FOIA Request?

Ideally, the agency will promptly release everything you requested. Realistically, however, this is unlikely to occur. A discussion of more common agency responses—and suggested actions you can take—follow below.

You may receive an acknowledgment of your request and a statement that the request has been placed in the queue and will be processed in its turn. Agencies process requests on a first-come, first-served basis, and they may also process requests in separate queues depending on their complexity. If the agency has a backlog of requests (and most do), you may have to wait some time before you receive the materials you seek. In fact, this is one of the biggest complaints regarding the administration of the FOIA. Many seeking information will complain about the very long periods of time spent waiting for access to information. Still, you should feel free to call or write the FOIA office to follow up on requests that have been pending for an unreasonable period of time. Get the names of specific FOIA personnel you can contact about your request. If agencies fail to meet the response time provided by the FOIA, you are entitled to file an administrative appeal or a lawsuit. Please keep in mind that if your request is complex and/or of a sensitive nature, the agency will require a significant amount of time to search and review the responsive records. In practice, the reality is that it can take years to get a response to a FOIA request.

If you requested a fee waiver, your request may be acknowledged, but the agency may seek more information before processing the request. Sometimes the agency asks a series of questions, and sometimes a multi-page questionnaire is enclosed for you to fill out and return. The best way to avoid this response is to provide as much information as possible in your initial letter to support your request for a fee waiver.

When you do receive a response about the substantive nature of your request, the agency may state that no records were found in response to your request, or it may inform you that your request is too broad. If this happens, call or write the FOIA office and ask what additional information is needed from you to make your request more specific. You should also explain why you believe the agency has material relevant to your request and inquire about other places in the agency's files where pertinent records might be found. In addition, if no records were found, you may send an appeal questioning the adequacy of the agency's search.

Alternatively, information relevant to your request may be found, but the agency might withhold all or part of the information from disclosure to you. The FOIA allows an agency only nine exemptions from its obligation to provide information in response to a request. The citation of these exemptions, described earlier, can be appealed.

2.3.9 Can I Appeal an Adverse Response?

Individuals seeking information pursuant to the FOIA can be deterred by denials and/or delays. Appeals of denials and/or complaints about extensive delays can be filed with the agency to which the request was made. In addition, the federal courts can review *de novo* (without respect to agency decision) and overturn agency decisions. This is an area of frequent litigation, and the courts have heard thousands of cases in the 40-plus years of the FOIA's existence.[45]

It is worthwhile to file an administrative appeal if the agency's response is unsatisfactory. Appeals can be effective in successfully challenging excessive processing delays, fee waiver denials, and the improper full or partial withholding of documents. Agency regulations governing appeals do vary. Accordingly, it is important to take careful note of the instructions for filing an appeal in the agency's response to ensure that your appeal is timely. An appeal letter should state the grounds for appeal and reasons why the agency's response to the request was improper. If the rationale for the initial agency determination is unclear, you should request a more precise explanation of the agency's decision. In addition, in your appeal you should state that you expect a final ruling on the appeal within the 20-day statutory time limit. For illustration purposes, Appendix B contains a sample Appeal Letter.

Despite the existence of the legal right to appeal, the use of legal action is not a consistently effective means of acquiring the information that a governmental agency is withholding by claiming a FOIA exemption. This is particularly so when an agency exerts Exemption 1, which provides an exemption for reasons of national security and/or foreign policy. People attempting to do so will likely find courts to be very concerned about overstepping constitutionally separated powers, which reserve decisions regarding national security and foreign policy decisions to other branches of government; in particular, the executive branch.[46]

3. Other Laws Regarding Information Freedom

3.1 Other Federal Laws

While the FOIA is the most significant U.S. law concerning freedom of information, in the United States there are also other laws that help to protect certain aspects of information freedom. The Government in the Sunshine Act[47] requires the government to open the deliberations of multi-agency bodies, such as the Federal Communications Commission. The Federal Advisory Committee Act requires openness of committees that advise federal agencies or the President.[48] At the federal level, the Privacy Act of 1974 functions in conjunction with the FOIA to allow individuals to access their personal records held by federal agencies.[49]

There are also certain sector-specific laws. For example, the Emergency Planning and Community Right to Know Act[50] requires that industries produce an annual report of the toxins they release into the environment.[51] In addition, the Environmental Protection Agency (EPA) publishes this information annually in an online database known as the Toxics Release Inventory (TRI). In 2006, the EPA proposed reducing the amount of information available by making the report biannual and increasing the threshold for chemicals that need to be reported.[52]

In the end, the EPA agreed to continue producing the TRI annually, but it did increase the threshold for chemicals included in the report. A bill (S. 595) to return to the old reporting threshold, introduced by Senator Frank Lautenberg (D-N.J.), was proposed in late 2007. It is expected that further reform efforts may be proposed at the federal level. In the meantime, action occurs at the state level. The state of California restored the reporting threshold in October 2007 with the California Toxic Release Inventory Act of 2007, and 12 state attorneys general, led by New York's Andrew Cuomo, have sued the EPA over the rollback.[53]

3.2 State Laws

Significantly, in addition to the comprehensive system that is in place at the federal level, each state has some version of open government laws, and many have their own freedom of information laws.[54] The rights granted by these laws, and the applicable restrictions, tend to vary greatly from state to state. A number of states have information commissions or other review bodies that can issue opinions or review decisions.

Florida has among the most extensive state freedom of information laws.[55] The general policy of Florida's Open Records Law is that "all state, county, and municipal records shall be open for personal inspection by any person."[56] Despite the breadth of this general rule, Florida's Open Records Law is subject to a tremendous number of exemptions.

Like their federal counterpart, state laws on freedom of information have also been threatened since 9/11 due to terrorism concerns. In addition, there continues to be questions about the efficacy of such laws. In 2002, Investigative Reporters and Editors, together with the Better Government Association, conducted a comparison of the relative strengths of each state's open records laws. Their overall conclusion noted, "Unfortunately, state FOI laws have proven to be almost uniformly weak and easy to undermine."[57]

4. Problems and Criticisms

4.1 Difficulties with the Current FOIA

While the FOIA is commendable in many respects, there are also many aspects of the legislation and, more particularly, its administration that merit criticism and present cause for concern. Specifically, the FOIA has been hampered by a lack of central oversight and, as discussed earlier, long delays in processing requests. In some instances, requesters must wait years—or even decades for responses to their requests. The General Accounting Office (GAO) found in 2002 that "backlogs of pending requests government wide are substantial and growing, indicating that agencies are falling behind in processing requests."[58] In 2003, the National Security Archive conducted an audit of agency practices. This audit revealed a number of problems, including inaccurate or incomplete information regarding agency FOIA contacts, failure to acknowledge information requests, lost requests, and excessive backlogs.[59] A review of the FOIA's administration in the years 1998 through 2005, published by the Associated Press in 2006, found that nearly all executive departments had increasing delays ranging from three months to more than four years; national security-related agencies were releasing less information; and 30 percent of departments had not submitted their annual reports on time.[60] That same year, the National Security Archive found that the oldest request on record was 17 years old.[61] While the Archive noted that some agencies had reduced their backlogs since its 2003 review, many of the oldest requests had still not been resolved. The 2006 review also found an increase in withholding from 2003 to 2005 and noted that many agencies did not have adequate tracking systems, leading many to lose requests.

4.2 FOIA Under the Administration of George W. Bush

Like other freedoms, information freedom has proven vulnerable to shifts in political power, ideologies, and even current events. Recently, the FOIA system underwent momentous change under the leadership of President George W. Bush. The recent assaults on information freedom will be analyzed in detail in Chapter Eight, but a few aspects of the recent trends towards secrecy are worth introducing here. Over the course of the past few years, several policy decisions altered the landscape of the freedom of information. The events of September 11, 2001, provided some justification for these measures and helped to limit the public outcry that might have otherwise accompanied such a dramatic change in U.S. policy.

In October 2001, Attorney General John Ashcroft issued a memorandum stating that the Justice Department would defend in court any federal agency that withheld information requested under the FOIA, provided that the agency withheld the information on justifiable grounds.[62] The previous standard was to presume the disclosure, not the withholding, of information. However, surveys done by the National Security Archive and GAO found that for the most part the memo had not caused substantial changes in releases.[63] The administration has also refused to release information about the secret meetings of its energy policy task force; ordered federal Web sites to remove potentially sensitive information[64]; issued a controversial memo limiting access to records under the Presidential Records Act[65]; and refused to disclose information on the Patriot Act and the names of those arrested after 9/11. Many of these decisions have been successfully challenged in court, but they all show a pattern of secrecy in the Bush administration.

In addition, the National Security Archive has found a number of flaws in the FOIA under the Bush administration, including a complete centralization of agency FOIA operations that result in delays and lack of oversight, inconsistent practices regarding the acceptance of administrative appeals, further delays caused by the appeal of FOIA determinations, and a conflation of fee categories and fee-waiver standards.[66] Even after signing a FOIA reform bill into law, the Bush White House sought to dismantle its key oversight component through a budgetary maneuver, which will be explored in more detail in the next section.

When compared with prior administrations—including notable information freedom proponents such as Presidents Carter and Clinton—the entire culture regarding information flow seems to have transformed under the Bush administration. The problems and errors of the past few years have been instructive in showing that too much secrecy can breed irresponsibility and can, in turn, lead to a loss of trust and confidence among the public. Ultimately, excessive government secrecy can threaten even the most secure constitutional democracies.

5. The Future

5.1 Overview

There is reason to be hopeful about the future of the FOIA. As was expected, since assuming office President Obama has been making important changes to the administration of the FOIA, including a shift back towards a presumption of disclosure. In addition, recently enacted reform legislation is likely to have a positive impact on the administration of the FOIA. The next section analyzes some current trends and developments that suggest some optimism for the future may be in order.

5.2 OPEN Government Act of 2007

On December 31, 2007, President Bush signed into law the OPEN Government Act of 2007, a bill designed to reform the administration of the FOIA. It passed unanimously in both the House and the Senate earlier that month.[67] The OPEN Government Act of 2007 represents a bipartisan effort that has stretched over several years, spearheaded by Senators Patrick Leahy (D-Vt.) and John Cornyn (R-Tex.), the bill's original cosponsors, as well as Congressman Henry Waxman (D-Calif.) and Congressman William Lacy Clay (D-Mo.). The Senate bill was also cosponsored by Senator Jon Kyl (R-Ariz.), who originally opposed the bill and held up its passage via a secret hold. (He was outed by a crowd-sourcing effort led by the Society for Professional Journalists.) Efforts to amend the FOIA have faced stumbling blocks in part because of strong administration opposition to earlier versions of this FOIA reform bill in both the House and the Senate.

The OPEN Government Act is intended to fix some of the most persistent problems in the FOIA system, including excessive delay, lack of responsiveness, and litigation gamesmanship by various federal agencies. The measure mandates tracking numbers for FOIA requests that take longer than 10 days to process to ensure they will no longer fall through the cracks and provides incentives to agencies to avoid litigation and processing delays. Significantly, for the first time agencies that do not comply with the FOIA's time limits face penalties. Agencies are no longer permitted to charge requesters search fees (or, in the case of news media and educational requesters, duplication fees) when the agencies miss the 20-day deadline set out in the FOIA. Also, the attorneys' fees of requesters forced to go to court to obtain information under the FOIA are now eligible for reimbursement if the agency reverses its position after it is sued. These changes should provide incentives for federal agencies to respond more promptly and should also help to remove some of the financial obstacles that may have prevented some individuals from pursuing denied-access requests even when they felt the denial was incorrect.

The new law requires governmental agencies to report more accurately to Congress and the public on their FOIA programs. It also creates the Office of Government Information Services (OGIS) at the National Archives to mediate conflicts between agencies and requesters and review each agency's FOIA performance. The creation of this new ombudsman-type office is inspired in part by positive experiences a number of states have had providing mediation services for requesters. In addition, many countries around the world have established ombudsmen and/or information commissions as part of their FOI regimes. Research suggests that this has resulted in the successful resolution of many disputes without litigation, whether the body is given binding decision-making power or serves in a purely advisory capacity.

Unfortunately, this office currently remains in limbo due to a dispute between Congress and the Bush administration over its location. Just 35 days after signing the OPEN Government Act, President Bush eliminated the ombudsman job at the Archives in his proposed spending plan and transferred the responsibility to the Justice Department, which open government advocates criticized.[68] At a September hearing, William Lacy Clay (D-Mo.), the chairman of the House's Oversight and Government Reform Information Policy subcommittee, testified: "There has been no movement on establishing OGIS."[69]

Section 3 through Section 12 of the OPEN Government Act are discussed below, and the text of the FOIA, as amended by the OPEN Government Act, is set forth in Appendix A.

Section 3: Protection of Fee Status for News Media. The OPEN Government Act clarifies the definition of news media. Specifically, Section 3 amends § 552(a)(4)(A)(ii) of the FOIA by defining "a representative of the news media" directly in the statute. The provision (i) defines the term "news;" (ii) gives examples of news-media entities such as "television or radio stations broadcasting to the public at large;" (iii) recognizes the evolution of "methods of news delivery" through, for example, "electronic dissemination" and notes that news-media entities might make their products available by "free distribution to the general public;" and (iv) includes provisions for a "freelance journalist." The act codifies the definition currently used by most courts to determine which requesters are considered representatives of the news media and therefore entitled to reduced processing fees. The new law also includes a provision requiring agencies to inform requesters about the amount of information redacted from documents released under the FOIA and the exemption justifying each deletion.

Section 4: Recovery of Attorney Fees and Litigation Costs. Section 4 of the Open Government Act amends 5 U.S.C. § 552(a)(4)(E) by adding two new elements to the attorney fees provision of the FOIA. The FOIA's preexisting attorney fees provision provided that a court "may assess against the United States reasonable attorney fees and other litigation costs reasonably incurred" in cases in which the "complainant has substantially prevailed."[70] Section 4 of the OPEN Government Act first defines the circumstances under which a FOIA plaintiff can be deemed to have "substantially prevailed." It adds that a FOIA complainant has "substantially prevailed" in this arena if the complainant "obtained relief through either—(I) a judicial order, or an enforceable written agreement or consent decree; or (II) a voluntary or unilateral change in position by the agency, if the complainant's claim is not insubstantial." In addition, Section 4 of the act also changes the method by which attorney fees and costs are paid to plaintiffs under the FOIA. Such amounts will no longer be paid by the Claims and Judgment Fund of the United States Treasury. Instead, these fees and costs will be paid directly by the agency, using funds "appropriated for any authorized purpose."

Section 5: Disciplinary Actions for Arbitrary and Capricious Rejections of Requests. Section 5 of the OPEN Government Act amends 5 U.S.C. § 552(a)(4)(F) by adding reporting requirements for the Attorney General and the Special Counsel. The preexisting provision of the FOIA provides that where a "court orders the production of any agency records improperly withheld ... and assesses against the United States reasonable attorney fees and other litigation costs, and ... additionally issues a written finding that the circumstances surrounding the withholding raise questions whether agency personnel acted arbitrarily or capriciously with respect to the withholding, the Special Counsel shall promptly initiate a proceeding to determine whether disciplinary action is warranted against the officer or employee who was primarily responsible for the withholding." Section 5 also requires that the Attorney General notify the Special Counsel of each civil action described under this provision and submit a report to Congress on the number of such civil actions in the preceding year. The Special Counsel is also directed to submit a report to Congress "on the actions taken by the Special Counsel" under this provision.

Section 6: Time Limits for Agencies to Act on Requests. Section 6 of the OPEN Government Act has two provisions that address time limits for complying with FOIA requests, and the consequences of failing to do so. Significantly, this section did not take effect until one year after the date of enactment and applies to FOIA requests "filed on or after that effective date." Accordingly, agencies had until December 31, 2008, to take any necessary steps to prepare for the implementation of this section.

First, section 6(a) amends 5 U.S.C. § 552(a)(6)(A), which gives the statutory time period for processing FOIA requests and includes criteria for when that time period begins to run and when that time period may be suspended or "tolled." Specifically, section 6(a) provides that the statutory time period commences "on the date on which the request is first received by the appropriate component of the agency, but in any event not later than 10 days after the request is first received by any component of the agency that is designated in the agency's regulations under this section to receive requests." This provision addresses the situation where a FOIA request is received by a component of an agency that is designated to receive FOIA requests, but is not the proper component for the request at issue. In such a situation, the component that receives the request in error—provided it is a component of the agency that is designated by the agency's regulations to receive requests—has 10 working days within which to forward the FOIA request to the appropriate agency component for processing. Once the FOIA request has been forwarded and received by the appropriate agency component, the statutory time period to respond to the request commences.

Section 6(a) further provides for those circumstances when an agency may suspend, or "toll," the statutory time period. Specifically, an agency "may make one request to the requester for information and toll" the statutory time period "while it is awaiting such information that it has reasonably requested from the requester." The agency may also toll the time period "if necessary to clarify with the requester issues regarding fee assessment." There is no limit given for the number of times an agency may go back to a requester to clarify issues regarding fee assessments—which sometimes may need to be done in stages as the records are being located and processed. In both situations, section 6(a) specifies that the requester's response to the agency's request "ends the tolling period."

Second, section 6(b) addresses compliance with the FOIA's time limits by amending 5 U.S.C. § 552(a)(4)(A), the provision addressing fees. Section 6 (b) adds a clause to that provision providing that "[a]n agency shall not assess search fees (or in the case of a [favored] requester [i.e., one who qualifies as an educational or noncommercial scientific institution, or as a representative of the news media] duplication fees)—if the agency fails to comply with any time limit under paragraph (6), if no unusual or exceptional circumstances (as those terms are defined for purposes of (6)(B) and (C), respectively) apply to the processing of the request."

As noted in the language of the new provision, the terms "unusual circumstances" and "exceptional circumstances" are existing terms in the FOIA. "Unusual circumstances" occur when there is a need to search or collect records from field offices, or other establishments; when there is a need to search for and examine a voluminous amount of records; or when there is a need for consultation with another agency or with more than two components within the same agency. Unlike "unusual circumstances," "exceptional circumstances" are not affirmatively defined in the FOIA, but the FOIA does provide that "exceptional circumstances" cannot include "a delay that results from a predictable agency workload of requests—unless the agency demonstrates reasonable progress in reducing its backlog of pending requests." [71]

In addition, the statute provides that the "[r]efusal by a person to reasonably modify the scope of a request, or arrange an alternative time frame for processing the request ... shall be considered as a factor in determining whether exceptional circumstances exist." [72]

Section 6(b) therefore precludes an agency from assessing search fees (or in the case of "favored" requesters, duplication fees), if the agency fails to comply with the FOIA's time limits, unless "unusual" or "exceptional" circumstances "apply to the processing of the request."

Finally, section 6(b) amends 5 U.S.C. § 552(a)(6)(B)(ii), which discusses notifying requesters regarding the time limits and the option of arranging an alternative time frame for processing, by directing agencies "[t]o aid the requester" by making "available its FOIA Public Liaison, who shall assist in the resolution of any disputes between the requester and the agency." This provision incorporates an existing aspect of Executive Order 13392.

Section 7: Individualized Tracking Numbers For Requests and Status Information. Section 7 amends 5 U.S.C. § 552(a) by requiring agencies to assign a tracking number for each request that will require more than 10 days to process. This section further requires agencies to establish a phone number or a Web site to enable requesters to inquire about the status of their request. Like section 6, this section did not take effect until one year after the date of enactment of the OPEN Government Act and applies to requests "filed on or after that effective date."

Section 8: Reporting Requirements. Section 8 amends 5 U.S.C. § 552 (e)(1) by requiring that new statistics and data be included in the annual FOIA reports that agencies must submit to the Attorney General. The FOIA requires that agencies submit the reports to the Attorney General by February 1 of each year and that the reports "cover the preceding fiscal year."[73] In addition to reporting on the median number of days required to process requests, section 8 mandates that agencies provide the "average number of days for the agency to respond to a request beginning on the date on which the request was received by the agency, the median number of days for the agency to respond to such requests, and the range in number of days for the agency to respond to such requests."

Section 8 also requires agencies to provide an extensive breakdown of the time it takes to respond to requests. Specifically, agencies are now required to provide "the number of requests for records to which the agency has responded with a determination within a period up to and including 20 days, and in 20-day increments up to and including 200 days." All other requests must be grouped by number depending upon whether they were processed between 200 and 300 days, between 300 and 400 days, or greater than 400 days.

Additionally section 8 requires agencies to report "the average number of days for the agency to provide the granted information beginning on the date on which the request was originally filed, the median number of days for the agency to provide the granted information, and the range in number of days for the agency to provide the granted information."

Section 8 requires agencies to report their 10 oldest pending requests. Section 8 also sets forth a number of new reporting requirements for administrative appeals. Agencies are now mandated to provide "the median and average number of days for the agency to respond to administrative appeals based on the date on which the appeals originally were received by the agency, the highest number of business days taken by the agency to respond to an administrative appeal, and the lowest number of business days taken by the agency to respond to an administrative appeal." Likewise, agencies must now report on their ten oldest pending administrative appeals.

Section 8 also mandates that agencies report "the number of expedited review requests that are granted and denied, the average and median number of days for adjudicating expedited review requests, and the number adjudicated within the required 10 days." Similarly, agencies must also report "the number of fee waiver requests that are granted and denied, and the average and median number of days for adjudicating fee waiver determinations."

Finally, the reporting requirements shall be "expressed in terms of each principal component of the agency and for the agency overall." The data used to compile the reports must also be made "available electronically to the public upon request."

Section 9: Openness of Agency Records Maintained by a Private Entity. Section 9 amends 5 U.S.C. § 552(f), the definitions provision of the FOIA, by including in the definition of "record" any information "maintained for an agency by an entity under Government contract, for the purposes of records management." This provision makes clear that records managed by government contractors are considered agency records for purposes of the FOIA.

Section 10: Office of Government Information Services. Section 10 of the OPEN Government Act has four organizational elements. The first part of section 10 creates a new office, the Office of Government Information Services, within the National Archives and Records Administration. This new office has two main functions: to review agency FOIA activities and recommend changes to Congress and the President and to offer mediation services to FOIA requesters as a "nonexclusive alternative to litigation." This new office may also "issue advisory opinions if mediation has not resolved the dispute."

Second, section 10 directs the GAO to conduct audits "on the implementation of this section" and to issue reports.

Third, section 10 codifies many of the key provisions of Executive Order 13392, which are already in place across the government, and which directly address FOIA administration within each agency. Specifically, agencies are directed to designate a Chief FOIA Officer, and one or more FOIA Public Liaisons. Section 10 provides a detailed list of the various duties and responsibilities of the Chief FOIA Officer, who is charged with "agency-wide responsibility for efficient and appropriate compliance" with the FOIA. The Chief FOIA Officer is required to "monitor implementation" of the FOIA and recommend to the agency head "such adjustments to agency practices, policies, personnel, and funding as may be necessary to improve its implementation." The Chief FOIA Officers are to report to the Attorney General, through the head of the agency. The Attorney General, in turn, is given authority to direct the Chief FOIA Officers to submit reports on their agency's performance "at such times and in such formats" as he or she establishes.

Fourth, FOIA Public Liaisons are given the responsibilities of "assisting in reducing delays, increasing transparency" and also "resolving disputes."

Section 11: Report on Personnel Policies Related to the FOIA. Section 11 only applies to the Office of Personnel Management (OPM). This provision requires OPM to examine personnel policies and report to Congress on whether changes in those policies could be made to provide greater encouragement to, and "enhance the stature of," government employees involved in administering the FOIA. OPM is directed to file the report no later than one year after the date of enactment of the OPEN Government Act.

Section 12: Requirement to Describe Exemptions Authorizing Deletions of Material Provided Under the FOIA. Section 12 amends 5 U.S.C. § 552(b), the provision listing exemptions and generally requiring agencies to indicate directly "on the released portion of the record" the amount of information deleted, by adding the additional requirement that agencies also indicate "the exemption under which the deletion is made."

The OPEN Government Act addresses a range of administrative and procedural issues affecting FOIA administration. However, in some respects the measure did not arguably go far enough in reforming the administration of the FOIA. Contrary to some news reports, the OPEN Government Act of 2007 does not include a provision that was originally contained in legislation introduced in the House to reverse the presumption of secrecy applied by federal agencies pursuant to an October 2001 memorandum issued by former Attorney General John Ashcroft. However, the spirit of the new law does counter the government's tendency toward increased secrecy in recent years by providing greater oversight of agency decisions on FOIA requests through better reporting and a new independent body to which requesters can turn when agencies improperly withhold information. The long-term effects of the OPEN Government Act on the ability of individuals to access information requested under the FOIA remain to be seen.

5.3 The New Administration

Over the course of the past few years, lawmakers had been considering additional measures to reform the administration of the FOIA. One recent congressional proposal, the Faster FOIA Act,[74] would establish a 16-member commission to conduct a study on ways to reduce delays in processing requests submitted to federal agencies and to ensure the efficient and equitable administration of the FOIA. The bill would also require the commission to study whether FOIA fees and fee waivers need to be reformed.

The legislation, sponsored by Representative Brad Sherman (D-Calif.), was introduced in January 2007. It was referred to the House Committee on Oversight and Government Reform, where it was referred to the Subcommittee on Information Policy, Census, and National Archives. No action was taken on the bill. With a new administration that favors openness now firmly in place, it seems likely that additional reform measures may be proposed and eventually enacted.[75]

While the future of the FOIA remains to be seen, the election of Barack Obama as president brings cause to be hopeful about further reform. With tremendous focus placed on critical issues such as the economy and national security, neither presidential candidate placed much focus on FOIA issues during the 2008 campaign. Still, when compared with Senator John McCain, Obama appears more likely to implement an open and transparent government, and his early actions are certainly suggesting that this will be the case. However, it should be noted that even McCain—who has supported the release of Congressional Research Service reports to the public and who has spoken in favor of a federal shield law for reporters—would likely have taken the country down a far more open path than the Bush administration has.[76]

During his campaign, Obama outlined a transparency plan that incorporates technology to reverse the dynamic of Bush administration secrecy and create "a new level of transparency, accountability and participation for America's citizens."[77] Among the proposals in the plan are putting government data online in accessible formats; airing live Web casts of agency meetings; restoring scientific integrity; allowing people to track federal grants, contracts, earmarks, and lobbyist contacts online; and allowing five days for the public to review and comment on legislation online before it is signed.

In a 2007 speech, Obama also called for the creation of a "National Declassification Center" that would "turn the page on a growing empire of classified information, and restore the balance we've lost between the necessarily secret and the necessity of openness in a democratic society."[78] Obama also has a history of supporting open government issues. In the Senate, he was a cosponsor of the OPEN Government Act of 2007, and cosponsored (with Senator McCain) the Federal Funding Accountability and Transparency Act.[79] That act, which went into effect January 1, 2008, launched USASpending.gov, a Web site that gives people access to information on government contracts, grants, and other awards. In addition, as an Illinois state senator, Obama cosponsored what became known as the "verbatim record" bill,[80] which modified the state's Open Meetings Act to require public agencies to record (on video or audio) closed-door meetings. That law was the first of its kind enacted by any state.

Early indications are that the Obama administration is off to a very noteworthy start. Just one day after the inauguration, President Obama issued two important orders on the FOIA. The first memorandum instructs all agencies and departments of the federal government to "adopt a presumption in favor of FOIA requests." The second memo orders the director of the Office of Management and Budget to issue recommendations on measures to be implemented in order to make the federal government more transparent. Ultimately, time will tell just how open and transparent the federal government will be under the new administration. However, these initial early actions by the new president are very encouraging.

6. Conclusion

As demonstrated herein, freedom of information laws in the United States are rather complex. At their core, these laws provide for broad rights to access information held by government agencies. However, the litany of exemptions to the government's disclosure obligations can, at times, take the teeth out of the laws. Furthermore, delays and other administrative difficulties disrupt the proper functioning of the legislation. It is anticipated that the OPEN Government Act of 2007 will help to ease some of the delays and other administrative burdens that weigh down the proper functioning of our freedom of information laws. It is also expected that the new leadership of President Obama will help foster more open government.

The next chapter examines how the FOIA and other information access laws have facilitated public access to important information about issues impacting the environment. It shows how the FOIA can be an important tool in environmental protection.

Notes

1. Patricia M. Wald, "The Freedom of Information Act: A Short Case Study in the Perils and Paybacks of Legislating Democratic Values," 33 *Emory Law Journal* 649 (1984) for a detailed overview of the events and investigations leading up to the passage of the FOIA.

2. Harold L. Cross, *The People's Right to Know: Legal Access to Public Records and Proceedings* (Columbia University Press/Oxford University Press: 1953).

3. Archibald Cox, "Executive Privilege," 122 *University of Pennsylvania Law Review* 1383 (1974).

4. For a general history of the passage of the FOIA and Moss's role in this process, see George Kennedy, "How Americans Got Their Rights to Know: Getting Congress to Guarantee Access to Federal Information Through FOIA 30 Years Ago Was a Press Triumph," available at: http://www.johnemossfoundation.org/foi/kennedy.htm (last visited September 24, 2008).

5. See the current Wisconsin law at Wis. Stat. § 19.31-19.39 (2003). This policy statement of this legislation establishes a very broad mandate: declaration of policy. In recognition of the fact that a representative government is dependent upon an informed electorate, it is declared to be the public policy of this state that all persons are entitled to the greatest possible information regarding the affairs of government and the official acts of those officers and employees who represent them. Further, providing persons with such information is declared to be an essential function of a representative government and an integral part of the routine duties of officers and

employees whose responsibility it is to provide such information. To that end, ss. 19.32 to 19.37 shall be construed in every instance with a presumption of complete public access, consistent with the conduct of governmental business. The denial of public access generally is contrary to the public interest, and only in an exceptional case may access be denied. *Id.* at 19.31.

6. Administrative Procedures Act, U.S. Code at 5 U.S.C. §501 et seq.

7. *Id.* at §3.

8. "Attorney General's Manual on the Administrative Procedure Act, 1947," available at: http://www.law.fsu.edu/library/admin/1947cover.html (last visited September 10, 2008).

9. S. Rep. No. 89-813, at 3 (1965).

10. For general information about President Johnson's reluctance to sign the law, see: Ted Bridis, "The President Worried About Giving Up Secrets 40 Years Ago," *The Associated Press*, July 3, 2006.

11. "Statement by the President Upon Signing the Freedom of Information Act," 2 Pub. Papers 316 (July 4, 1966). Available at The American Presidency Project: http://www.presidency.ucsb.edu/ws/index.php?pid=27700&st=&st1= (last visited October 30, 2008).

12. Letter from James Madison to W. T. Barry (August 4, 1822), reprinted in *The Complete Madison: His Basic Writings* 337 (Saul K. Padover, ed., 1953).publisher?-MM

13. Freedom of Information Act, 5 U.S.C. 552, 1966.

14. Freedom of Information Act Amendments of 1974, Pub. L. No. 93-502, 4, 88 Stat 1564; Freedom of Information Reform Act of 1986, Publ. L. No. 99-570, tit. I Subtit. N. 1801, 100 Stat 3207-48, Electronic Freedom of Information Act Amendments (EFOIA) of 1996, Pub. L. No. 104-231, 2, 110 Stat 3048.

15. H.R. REP. NO. 93-876, at 6-7, reprinted 1974 U.S.C.C.A.N 6267, 6267-68.

16. Electronic Freedom of Information Act Amendments of 1996, Pub. L. No. 104-231, 110 Stat 3048 (1986).

17. Two major provisions of EFOIA require that form of the legal basis of these requirements are reproduced as follows: 1. Each agency, in accordance with published rules, shall make available for public inspection and copying . . . copies of all records, regardless of form or format, which have been released to any person under paragraph (3) and which, because of the nature of their subject matter, the agency determines have become or are likely to become the subject of subsequent requests for substantially the same records . . . § 4(5), 110 Stat. at 3049 (codified at 5 U.S.C. § 552(a)(2)(D) (2000)). 2. For records created on or after November 1, 1996, within one year after such date, each agency shall make such records available, including by computer telecommunications or, if computer telecommunications means have not been established by the agency, by other electronic means. § 4(7), 110 Stat. at 3049 [codified at 5 U.S.C. § 552(a)(2) (2000)].

18. 5 U.S.C. 552(b)(1)-(a).

19. *Id.* 552(b).

20. *Department of the Air Force v. Rose*, 425 U.S. at 361 (1976).

21. Executive Order 12958, as amended by Executive Order 13292, 68 Federal Register 15315 (March 28, 2003), available at: http://www.archives.gov/isoo/policy-documents/eo-12958-amendment.html.

22. Executive Order 12958-Classified National Security Information, as Amended, available at: http://www.archives.gov/about_us/basic_laws_and _authorities/appendix_12958.html.

23. Information Security Oversight Office 2007 Report to the President, May 30, 2008, available at: http://archives.gov/isoo/reports/2007-annual-report.pdf..

24. ISOO, Audit of the Withdrawal of Records from Public Access at the National Archives and Records Administration for Classification Purposes, April 2006, available at: http://www.archives.gov/isoo/reports/2006-audit-report.html.

25. President John F. Kennedy Assassination Records Collection Act of 1992.

26. Final Report of the Kennedy Assassination Records Review Board, 1998.

27. Nazi War Crimes Disclosure Act. Public Law 105-246.

28. Japanese Imperial Government Disclosure Act of 2000, December 6, 2000.

29. "C.I.A. Defers to Congress, Agreeing to Disclose Nazi Records," *The New York Times*, February 7, 2005.

30. Homeland Security Act of 2002, 116 Stat 2135 (2002).

31. H.R. Rep. No. 93-1380, at 14 (1974), reprinted in House Comm. on Gov't Operations and Senate Comm. on the Judiciary, 94th Cong., 1st Sess., Freedom of Information Act and Amendments of 1974 (P.L. 93-502) Source Book: Legislative History, Texts, and Other Documents at 231-32 (1975).

32. See *Nat'l Sec. Archive v. Archivist of the United States*, 909 F.2d 541, 544 (D.C. Cir. 1990) ("The Supreme Court has made clear that the Office of the President is not an 'agency' for purposes of the FOIA." [citing *Kissinger v. Reporters Comm. for Freedom of the Press*, 445 U.S. 136, 156 (1980)]; *Judicial Watch Inc. v. Nat'l Energy Policy Dev. Group*, 219 F. Supp. 2d 20, 55 (D.D.C. 2002) ("[T]he Vice President and his staff are not 'agencies' for purposes of the FOIA."), aff'd on other grounds, 334 F.3d 1096 (D.C. Cir.), cert. granted, 124 S. Ct. 958 (2003) (non-FOIA case).

33. *United States Dep't of Justice v. Tax Analysts*, 492 U.S. 136, 144-45 (1989) (holding that court opinions in agency files are agency records).

34. *Burka v. HHS*, 87 F.3d 508, 151 (D.C. Cir. 1996) [citing *Tax Analysts v. United States Dep't of Justice*, 845 F.2d 1060, 1069 (D.C. Cir. 1988)].

35. 5 U.S.C. § 552(a)(3)(A) (2000).

36. *Id.* § 552(a)(3)(A)(ii).

37. H. R. Rep. No. 93-876, at 6 (1974), reprinted in 1974 U.S.C.C.A.N. 6267, 6271.

38. *Devine v. Marsh*, 2 Gov't Disclosure Serv. (P-H) ¶ 82,022, at 82,186 (E. D. Va. August 27, 1981).

39. 5 U.S.C. § 552(a)(6)(A)(i).

40. 5 U.S.C. § 552(a)(6)(C)(i) (requiring that records be made available "promptly").

41. 5 U.S.C. § 552(a)(6)(B)(i).

42. 5 U.S.C. § 552(a)(6)(B)(iii)

43. 5 U.S.C. § 552(a)(6)(B)(ii)

44. For a court decision interpreting the fee provisions of the FOIA, see *National Security Archive v. Department of Defense*, 880 F.2d 1381 (D.C. Cir. 1989).

45. See Hammitt et al., Litigation Under the Federal Open Government Laws 2008 (2008), for an excellent review of the case law.

46. Tracey Colton Green, "Providing for the Common Defense Versus Providing for the General Welfare: The Conflicts Between National Security and National Environmental Policy," 65 *Southeastern Environmental Law Journal* 137 (1997).

47. Government in the Sunshine Act, 5 U.S.C. 552b.

48. Federal Advisory Committee Act, 1972, 5 U.S.C. App. II.

49. Privacy Act of 1974, 5. U.S.C. 552a.

50. Emergency Planning and Community Right-to-Know Act, 42 USC 11011-11050 (1986).

51. *Id*. at 11023.

52. OMB Watch, "EPA Proposes Rollback on Toxic Pollution Reporting," October 4, 2005, available at http://www.ombwatch.org/article/articleview/3117/1/241?TopicID=1 (last visited November 2, 2008).

53. OMB Watch, "States Sue EPA for Reduced Reporting on Toxics," December 4, 2007, available at http://www.ombwatch.org/article/articleview/4105/1/241?TopicID=1(last visited November 2, 2008).

54. For an overview, see the National Freedom of Information Coalition, available at: http://www.nfoic.org.

55. Open Meetings Law Fla. Stat. sec. 286.011 et seq.; Open Records Law Fla. Stat. sec. 119.01 et. seq.

56. *Id*. at 119.01(1).

57. "Investigative Reporters and Editors, Freedom of Information in the USA: Part 1," *The IRE Journal*, March-April 2002, available at http://www.ire.org/foi/bga/ (last visited November 2, 2008).

58. General Accounting Office, Update on Implementation of the 1996 Electronic Freedom of Information Act Amendments, GAO-02-493, August 2002, available at: http://www.gao.gov/new.items/d02493.pdf (last visited November 2, 2008).

59. National Security Archive, "The Ashcroft Memo: "Drastic" Change or "More Thunder than Lightning?" March 14, 2003, available at: http://www.gwu.edu/~nsarchiv/NSAEBB/NSAEBB84/index.html(last visited November 2, 2008).

60. "AP Review Finds Federal Government Missing Deadlines and Time Limits," *The Associated Press*, March 12, 2006.

61. National Security Archive, *A FOIA Request Celebrates its 17th Birthday: A Report on Federal Agency Backlog*, National Security Archive, March 2006, available at http://www.gwu.edu/~nsarchiv/NSAEBB/NSAEBB182/index.htm (last visited November 2, 2008).

62. New Attorney General FOIA Memorandum Issued, FOIA Post, October 15, 2001, available at: http://www.usdoj.gov/oip/foiapost/2001foiapost19.htm (last visited November 2, 2008).

63. *Id*.; General Accounting Office, Freedom of Information Act: Agency Views on Changes Resulting from New Administration Policy. GAO-03-981, September 3, 2003, available at http://www.gao.gov/cgi-bin/getrpt?GAO-03-981.

64. OMB Watch, "Access to Government Information Post September 11," April 25, 2005, available at http://www.ombwatch.org/article/articleview/213/1/1/ (last visited November 2, 2008).

65. Executive Order 13233 of November 1, 2001. http://www.fas.org/irp/offdocs/eo/eo-13233.htm.

66. National Security Archive, "The Ashcroft Memo: "Drastic" Change or "More Thunder than Lightning?" National Security Archive, March 14, 2003, available at: http://www.gwu.edu/~nsarchiv/NSAEBB/NSAEBB84/index.html (last visited November 2, 2008).

67. OPEN Government Act of 2007, Pub. L. No. 110-175, § 5 U.S.C.

68. *Bush Eliminates FOIA Ombudsman*, Cox Newspapers, February 4, 2008.

69. *Prolonged Dispute Keeps New FOIA Office Only on Paper*, Congress Daily, September 18, 2008.

70. 5 U.S.C. § 552(a)(4)(E).

71. 5 U.S.C. § 552(a)(6)(C)(ii).

72. *Id.* at § 552(a)(6)(C)(iii).

73. 5 U.S.C. § 552(e)(1).

74. The Faster FOIA Act of 2007, H.R. 541.

75. The Open FOIA Act of 2008, S. 2746.

76. Sunshine Week, "What the Candidates Are Saying About Open Government and FOI," June 10, 2008, available at http://www.sunshineweek.org/sunshineweek/candidates (last visited November 2, 2008).

77. BarackObama.com, "Science, Technology and Innovation for a New Generation," http://www.barackobama.com/issues/technology/#transparent-democracy (last visited November 2, 2008). Also see "Blueprint for Change: Obama and Biden's Plan for America," available at http://www.barackobama.com/pdf/ObamaBlueprintForChange.pdf.

78. BacakObama.com, Prepared Remarks for October 2, 2007, Speech, available at: http://www.barackobama.com/2007/10/02/on_fifth_anniversary_of_speech.php (last visited November 2, 2008).

79. Federal Funding Accountability and Transparency Act of 2006, Pub. L. No. 109-282, § 31 U.S.C.

80. Illinois Open Meetings Act Amendment, P.A. No. 93-0523, § 5 ILCS 120/2.06.

Chapter Three

Protecting the Environment with Freedom of Information

Secrecy, being an instrument of conspiracy, ought never to be the system of regular government.

—Jeremy Bentham

1. Overview

1.1 FOIA and Environmental Protection

Citizens have a right to know about what happens in their communities and workplaces. The FOIA can play an extraordinarily important role in ensuring that individuals have proper access to information about issues that can impact their environments. Armed with such information, individuals are better equipped to protect themselves, their families, and their communities. The 1984 chemical disaster in Bhopal, India, underscored the importance of understanding and working to minimize environmental risks in our communities before the worst happens.[1] Smaller-scale accidents occur regularly throughout the world, and serious environmental risks are present in a vast number of different areas. The environmental right to know also encompasses broader issues, like labeling consumer products and accessing information about pesticides, bio-monitoring, and other risks.

1.2 Recent Trends in Environmental Protection

In addition to the inherent motivation to protect our natural world, environmentalism is also prompted by self-centered needs, namely a drive to protect our own health and well-being. A failure to adequately protect our environment can lead ultimately to illness and death among human and animal populations. There are countless environmental hazards existing in our communities, and many have a negative impact on human health. Across the United States, numerous chemical plants, manufacturers, power plants, and other facilities store and utilize extremely hazardous materials that can injure or even kill employees and members of the local community. In fact, environmental hazards are responsible for a significant percentage of the total disease burden worldwide.

In recent years, a new level of attention has been directed towards efforts to protect the environment. From the success of Al Gore's slideshow-based documentary *An Inconvenient Truth,* to the mainstreaming of ideas such as ecotourism and carbon offsets, to corporate sustainability efforts, "green" has become the "new black," as many have put it. But beyond the ever-more-visible green culture, with its compact fluorescent light bulbs, Energy Star home appliances, and canvas grocery bags, as further highlighted below the environment still faces a number of critical problems, and there is much that freedom of information laws can do to ensure a clean and healthy earth moving forward.

1.2.1 Global Warming

Global warming continues to be a major concern for our planet. Over the past 35 years, demand for energy has more than doubled. Fossil fuels—coal and oil, mainly—have powered the explosive growth, but their use has raised carbon dioxide levels in the atmosphere by more than 35 percent from pre-industrial levels. As a result, the sun's rays no longer escape as easily from the atmosphere; some of their heat is radiated back, returning to the ground and the ocean, fueling global warming. In the next 40 years, average global temperatures are expected to rise by about 2 degrees Fahrenheit. It is expected that this increase in global temperatures will cause profound disruptions in rainfall patterns, agriculture, wildlife, and human activity. Furthermore, continued greenhouse gas emissions at or above current rates will continue to exacerbate the pace of global warming, inducing changes to the global climate system that will occur exponentially in the twenty-first century. The Intergovernmental Panel on Climate Change warns that in the next century carbon dioxide will continue to increase, ice caps will continue to melt, the acidity of our water will continue to rise, hurricanes and typhoons will become more intense, and heat waves and heavy precipitation events will continue to become more frequent.[2]

1.2.2 Threats to Our Water Supply

Globally, clean water supplies are in serious jeopardy. Consumption of water has been growing faster than the population has been increasing,[3] and the price of water is rising throughout the world.[4] More than 1 billion people worldwide lack access to safe drinking-water supplies, while 2.6 billion lack adequate sanitation; diseases related to unsafe water, sanitation, and hygiene result in an estimated 1.7 million deaths every year.[5] Inadequate access to sufficient quantities of clean water can also be a key factor in water-related disease and is closely related to ecosystem conditions. Access to a sufficient supply of clean water is such a crucial issue that it has even been the source of serious conflicts between different countries.[6] This problem is likely to grow in the near future as clean water supplies become more scarce and numerous countries might soon be caught up in water disputes.[7]

1.2.3 Dangerous Chemicals

The risk of toxic chemicals in the environment is a very real danger, with unintentional chemical poisonings claiming more than 355,000 lives each year.[8] Such poisonings are often linked to excessive exposure to toxic chemicals that are emitted directly into the soil, air, and water from various industrial complexes.[9] Of particular concern are many commonly used pesticides. Acute exposure to pesticides can lead to death or serious illness,[10] while long-term exposure can increase the risk of developmental and reproductive disorders, immune-system disruption, endocrine disruption, impaired nervous-system function, and the development of certain cancers.[11] The health risks of these chemicals are particularly dangerous for young children.

1.2.4 Threats to Animals

Environmental destruction also threatens animals. In particular, the world's largest land-based predator, the polar bear, faces an uncertain future due to several environmental factors. "Global climate change poses a substantial threat to the habitat of polar bears," the most recent Red List of Threatened Species report by the International Union for Conservation of Nature and Natural Resources (IUCN) found. "Due to their long generation time and the current greater speed of global warming, it seems unlikely that the polar bear will be able to adapt to the current warming trend in the Arctic." The IUCN also found that the polar bear was facing threats from "toxic contaminants, shipping, recreational viewing, oil and gas exploration, and development," as well as hunting.[12] When the polar bear was placed under the protection of the Endangered Species Act in May 2008, it became only the third species in the United States to be protected under the act due to global warming.[13]

The polar bear is but one example of the various animal species that have been impacted by our environmental conditions. Going forward, unless matters make a dramatic improvement, it is very likely that many more animal species will become threatened.

2. Notable Revelations

2.1 Overview

Given the environmental risks that we face, the importance of continued access to information held by the government and private industry is abundantly clear. Armed with this information, citizens will be better positioned to advocate for changes that will help to protect the environment. Over the years, the FOIA has allowed researchers to obtain information about a wide range of environmental risks. For example, the U.S. Public Health Service has disclosed that residents of Utah suffered an unusually high proportion of birth defects as a result of atomic bomb testing occurring between 1950 and 1964.[14] The Consumers Union and other groups have used the FOIA to report on unleaded gasoline additives, hazardous denture cleaners, dangerous home car repair ramps, and other unsafe products.[15] This section examines in closer detail some of the more significant stories that have been revealed through the FOIA.

2.2 Uncovering Environmental Threats

2.2.1 Water Pollution

Water pollution continues to be a major problem for many local communities and for our world at large. One of the greatest dangers of water pollution is that people are often not aware of the problem until after it impacts them. Various pollutants can contaminate water that is used for drinking, cooking, and bathing. Contaminates can also affect those who spend a significant amount of time within the water, such as beachgoers, including, in particular, surfers. Fortunately, the FOIA has proven to be a very useful mechanism for uncovering information about unsafe water conditions. For example, surfers in certain areas often find that they are plagued by similar illnesses that come from their exposure to the ocean.[16] These illnesses can and often do include viral meningitis; brachial neuritis; tonsillitis; trench fever; hepatitis C; and kidney, eye, ear, nose, and throat infections.[17] Surfers have used the FOIA to gather information about the water conditions of the oceans in which they surf and those who may be responsible for the pollutants that are contaminating the waters, ultimately harming their health.[18] There are many other instances when individuals and groups have used the FOIA to gather information about water pollution.

2.2.2 Industrial Pollution

Using documents obtained through the FOIA, the U.S. Public Interest Research Group (PIRG) reported in 2002 that nearly one-third of the country's major industrial facilities and government-operated sewage treatment plants had significantly violated pollution discharge regulations in the previous two years, but relatively few were prosecuted.[19] Through the FOIA, PIRG analyzed the behavior of industrial facilities, municipal treatment works, and federal installations by reviewing violations recorded in the permit compliance system database maintained by the Environmental Protection Agency (EPA). The report identified the most-polluted locations, singling out 10 states—Texas, Ohio, New York, Indiana, Tennessee, North Carolina, Alabama, Louisiana, Michigan, and Pennsylvania—as the states with the largest number of major facilities in "significant noncompliance" with discharge requirements during the period examined. In Texas, the study found that more than half of the 546 major facilities and plants violated the law at least once.[20]

A study such as this is extremely important not only for identifying areas of significant pollution, but also for suggesting reasons behind the pollution, and thereby, potentially helping to reduce it. "The continued dumping of hundreds of millions of pounds of toxic chemicals into our waterways and the significant violation of the Clean Water Act[21] by nearly 1,800 large facilities stems from several specific policy failures," the report said. Those failures, PIRG argued, included lax enforcement of the act by the EPA and state inspectors as well as a court system that has "eroded citizens' ability to file suits in order to enforce the Clean Water Act."[22] Such lax enforcement and lenient prosecution can combine to give companies little cause for concern that their polluting activities will be prosecuted.

2.2.3 Lead Contamination

The FOIA has also helped researchers uncover information about unsafe conditions in our water supply. For example, though the water supply of the District of Columbia suffered from elevated lead conditions,[23] authorities did not inform the public of the contamination for 15 months. The city's health department claimed that it didn't know of the lead problem until early 2004, but e-mails obtained by the *Washington Post* via the FOIA indicated that the department was aware of the contamination in October 2002.[24]

The lead problem was so severe that once it was revealed, the health department issued an advisory urging at-risk people to drink filtered water and get blood tests. Lead exposure can pose many health risks, including increased blood pressure, decreased brain function, decreased kidney function, and increased risks of birth defects and miscarriages among pregnant women.[25]

By exposing the problem, the FOIA helped to prevent ongoing contamination risks. In addition, by publicly revealing that local officials had information about the problem but concealed it from the public, the journalists who made this revelation may have caused other officials to think twice before suppressing information about environmental risks in which the community has a right to know.

2.2.4 Pollution from Local Facilities

In numerous cases the FOIA has proved to be very helpful in uncovering information about pollution. For example, in 1989 residents of Midlothian, Texas,[26] utilized the FOIA to further their quest for information about the burning of hazardous waste at two local cement manufacturing facilities.[27] The city's residents first became aware of the issue when one of the plants advertised in a local newspaper that they were seeking a permit that would allow them to store hazardous waste. Through a vigorous pursuit of FOIA requests with the EPA, the citizens were eventually able to determine what was being burned at the plants and what kinds of toxins might be released as a result of the incineration.[28] Through information gathered from public notifications and the FOIA, a group of citizens was able to make informed arguments against a project that could damage the local environment and potentially the health of the community.

2.3 Nuclear Safety

The FOIA has also helped to reveal information regarding projects that raise nuclear safety concerns. Particularly notable is the planned Yucca Mountain Repository in Nevada, which would be the country's first deep geologic repository for used nuclear fuel. The repository is set to be established in a desert on federal land about 80 miles from the Las Vegas metro area, inside the Yucca Mountain ridgeline, which is composed of volcanic materials. Its development has been stalled a number of times, but it is tentatively scheduled to commence operations in 2017.

As one might imagine, the establishment of a nuclear waste storage site is controversial, and concerns about safety have been raised by a number of individuals and organizations. Documents obtained by Nevada state officials through the FOIA have raised concerns regarding the possibility of an uncontrolled nuclear chain reaction inside the facility.[29] The documents appear to contradict Department of Energy (DOE) statistics cited in its final environmental impact statement.

According to the documents received by the state officials, canisters of radioactive waste could corrode inside the waste repository and cause up to 60 uncontrollable nuclear chain reactions, a phenomenon known as a criticality. By contrast, the DOE's final impact statement for the project claimed that there was a "very low probability" of a criticality occurring, pegging the chances at less than 2 in 10 million over 10,000 years.[30]

The information obtained by the state has been a very significant development in the battle over Yucca Mountain and may ultimately play a role in determining not only the future of the planned waste site but also the future of how nuclear waste is handled in the United States. At the time of this writing the future of the Yucca Mountain was still uncertain. In September 2008, the Nuclear Regulatory Commission (NRC) formally ruled that the DOE's construction application for the site was set to begin its full technical review, a process for which the NRC allows three years (with a one-year extension).[31]

However, the future of the site will largely be in the hands of President Barack Obama, who has said he's "always opposed using Yucca Mountain as a nuclear waste repository" and that he "believe[s] a better short-term solution is to store nuclear waste on-site at the reactors where it is produced, or at a designated facility in the state where it is produced, until we find a safe, long-term disposal solution that is based on sound science."[32]

2.4 Environmental Destruction

Through the FOIA, researchers and advocates have been able to gather information regarding a wide variety of issues contributing to environmental devastation. As one example, documents obtained though the FOIA have shown that the Bush administration ignored environmental concerns raised by government agency officials by permitting coal miners to continue the practice of "mountaintop removal," a process that levels mountaintops and discards the leftover rock into valleys and streams. Mountaintop removal is the subject of much controversy, as there are many concerns about how the practice impacts the environment. The practice is believed to be particularly devastating to streams, wildlife, and forests.[33]

In this instance, the government had prepared a statement in 1998 as part of a settlement of a lawsuit filed by people who live near mining operations in West Virginia. A draft environmental impact statement (EIS), prepared by the Clinton administration, addressed a proposal to possibly limit the filling of valleys through mountaintop removal. However, the document ultimately issued by the Bush administration included no new limitations. Instead, it suggested that the agencies involved better coordinate their efforts and develop better procedures to monitor the effects of mountaintop removal mining. Instead, the EIS issued by the Bush Administration suggested three alternative approaches, claiming all would improve environmental protections. According to a document obtained through a FOIA request by Trial Lawyers for Public Justice, however, the U.S. Fish and Wildlife Service said the administration's alternatives "cannot be interpreted as ensuring any improved environmental protection."[34]

Other documents revealed in this case highlight how the Bush administration disregarded and ignored findings of its own scientists, like when EPA official Ray George expressed concern that his agency's "science findings are not reflected in [the draft EIS's] conclusions/recommendations."[35] Unfortunately, the decision to ignore expert opinion and support a controversial program was also one that endorsed environmentally destructive practices.

2.5 Protecting Animals

Animal rights activists and others who care about animal welfare have found the FOIA to be a useful tool for gathering information about the treatment of animals in a variety of scenarios. The following sections examine some key examples of how information freedom laws have been used to protect animals.

2.5.1 Protecting the Polar Bear

In recent years, the polar bear has been a major victim of global warming. The number of polar bears has been dwindling due largely to a shrinking polar ice cap. Notwithstanding the clear jeopardy facing the bears, efforts to protect the polar bear from extinction have encountered various obstacles. By using the FOIA and state information freedom laws, however, researchers have been able to gather some insight into how and why efforts to protect the polar bear have stalled. Ultimately, this information may prove useful for those who are working hard to protect the future of the polar bear.

The Alaskan government has been particularly vociferous in arguing against greater protections for the polar bear, critiquing both the methods and the conclusions reached by federal and international scientists. Alaska's Department of Fish and Game has specifically challenged federal polar bear biologists who predicted the loss of two-thirds of the world's bears (and all of Alaska's polar bears) by 2050.[36]

But recently uncovered information calls into doubt the state's claims that the polar bear is not at risk. An e-mail obtained by University of Alaska professor Rick Steiner under state freedom of information laws shows that biologists employed by the state of Alaska were at odds with the administration of Governor Sarah Palin, which has consistently opposed any new federal protections for polar bears under the Endangered Species Act. The document was particularly important in that it appeared to have refuted subsequent statements by Palin that a "comprehensive review" of the federal science by state wildlife officials found no reason to support an endangered-species listing for the bears.[37] Notably, Palin also cited the state's "comprehensive review" while arguing against making the bears an endangered species in a *New York Times* op-ed.[38] (Arguably, Palin's opposition to an "endangered" designation for the bear may have much more to do with financial concerns than environmental ones. "State officials have expressed particular concern that a threatened-species listing gives environmentalists more leverage to oppose oil and gas development in Arctic Alaska and poses risks to Native subsistence," the *Anchorage Daily News* reported.[39])

What's more, the e-mail was only a small part of what was requested by Steiner. In a response to his request, the state said it generally withheld all substantive in-house comments on the bears, contending that these comments were private policy discussions among executive officials, a category exempt from release under state public records law. One can only speculate what other information may be contained in such other state documents.

Efforts to uncover information about the lack of protection for the polar bear have also been progressing at the federal level. For example, in early 2008 the National Resources Defense Council, the Centers for Biological Diversity, and Earthjustice filed a lawsuit under the FOIA for Department of Interior documents related to oil and gas development plans in a prime polar bear habitat. The groups wanted documents relating to the then-pending oil and gas lease sale of about 30 million acres of Alaska's Chukchi Sea.[40] The organizations, which had been requesting the documents for several months before filing suit, claimed the government had not disclosed documents that could show harmful effects to polar bears and other marine mammals. The Department of the Interior's sale went through in early February 2008, fetching $2.6 billion in bids, but the actual expansion of oil and gas industry in the area is still tangled up in several lawsuits.[41]

2.5.2 Circus Elephants

Many activists are busy at work behind the scenes, filing one FOIA request after another, attempting to obtain information about the treatment of animals in a variety of scenarios. However, some cases do receive a lot of public attention. This occurred in 2002, when the American Society for the Prevention of Cruelty to Animals (ASPCA) petitioned for the release of thousands of pages of documents from The U.S. Department of Agriculture (USDA) under the FOIA. The documents outlined actively alleged to have amounted to repeated abuse of elephants of the Ringling Brothers and Barnum & Bailey Circus by employees.[42]

The USDA has jurisdiction over animals that are used in circuses under The Animal Welfare Act.[43] Despite Ringling Brothers's repeated denials to the public, the USDA documents showed that Ringling Brothers employees routinely used force and pain to make elephants perform upon demand, and they consistently used a sharp instrument called an "ankus" or "bullhook" when working with the elephants. The bullhook is often used behind the ears of the elephant, an area that is particularly sensitive and the use of the bullhook is believed to cause the animal extreme pain.

Documents released to the ASPCA pursuant to its FOIA request disclosed several disturbing incidents, including those identified below:

- On July 26, 1999, a baby elephant named Benjamin mysteriously died while swimming in a pond in Texas, even though elephants are excellent swimmers by nature. USDA documents show that Benjamin's trainer had allowed him to go into the pond, but when he refused to come out the trainer went into the pond after him with an ankus. The use of the ankus against the baby elephant reportedly created "behavioral stress and trauma which precipitated in the physical harm and ultimate death of the animal."[44]

- In an unannounced inspection of Ringling Brothers's Florida breeding facility in January 1999, federal inspectors were shocked to find baby elephants with "large visible lesions" on their legs. The inspectors learned from Ringling Brothers employees that this was the result of the "routine separation process" that is used to take nursing babies away from their mothers so they can perform in the circus. This process uses ropes and chains around a baby elephant's neck and legs, and an official report from the inspectors noted that the company "routinely handles its baby elephants this way." In a letter to Ringling parent company Feld Entertainment, USDA officials stated this practice causes "unnecessary trauma, behavioral stress, and physical harm" to the elephants.

- In August 1999 in San Jose, California, San Jose Humane authorities and the police found bloody puncture wounds behind the left ears of many Ringling Brothers elephants. "The majority of the wounds documented are fresh, actively draining puncture wounds caused by an ankus or a hook," said Dr. Joel J. Parrott of the Oakland Zoo, according to a sworn affidavit obtained by the ASPCA. "It is in my professional opinion that there are far too many fresh wounds. It is apparent that Ringling Brothers is actively using an ankus that may be too sharp for the amount of force which is put behind it. It is apparent that the trainers and handlers may be using excessive force and poor techniques and controlling devices, to control and train their elephants."[45]

By obtaining these documents through the use of the FOIA, the ASPCA was able to bring to the public light crucial information concerning animal abuse. With such information, the public is in a better position to determine whether it wishes to patronize the Ringling Brothers circuses. Moreover, the information provides important evidence for those who work hard to bring an end to this kind of abuse.

2.5.3 Humane Society and the Department of Agriculture

In January 2005, The Humane Society of the United States (HSUS) filed a lawsuit against the USDA for failing to provide numerous documents that the animal protection organization had been requesting since 2001 under the FOIA. The suit also sought to compel the USDA to make annual reports from all registered animal research facilities available online through the Internet.[46]

In response to the lawsuit, the USDA's Animal and Plant Health Inspection Service (APHIS) announced in May 2005 that it would again post annual reports from registered animal research facilities on its Web site. In the past, APHIS posted the reports on its Web site, withholding only confidential business information and other material exempt under the FOIA, but at the request of research facilities, APHIS had stopped posting the documents and had pulled earlier reports. The HSUS lawsuit was able to reverse that trend.

Under the Electronic FOIA Amendment of 1996, the government must make available to the public information that has been released to any person that is likely to be requested again. The Justice Department advised APHIS to resume the annual report postings after reviewing the merits of the HSUS lawsuit and determining that the annual reports are regularly requested documents.

This was a very important result because the reports are crucial in determining whether the USDA is enforcing the standards of the Animal Welfare Act properly and effectively. The reports show the numbers of each species used in research, testing, and teaching per relevant pain and distress category. There are three categories: procedures that did not involve any pain or distress; those in which animals received anesthetic, analgesic, or tranquilizing drugs; and those when animals did not receive such relief. Any use of animals that involved unalleviated pain and/or distress must be accompanied by an explanation of the procedure(s) and the basis for withholding pain-relieving medications. Since animal research facilities are largely publicly funded, they should be held accountable to the people who support their work. These annual reports are an important way for taxpayers to monitor this research and keep on top of how the animals in such facilities are being treated.

Notwithstanding this partial victory, the decision of the APHIS to post annual reports did not settle the HSUS's lawsuit against the USDA. There are still unresolved issues between the agency and the HSUS, notably the large number of redacted pages in the annual reports so far provided. In addition, there are a number of annual reports that the agency says it must still vet with animal research facilities before releasing to the public.[47] The case and the claims of the HSUS are still pending in federal court. At the time of this writing, the USDA had neither agreed that it is legally obligated to post the annual reports online nor had it revised its withholdings to comply with the FOIA.

2.5.4 Wild Horses

The FOIA has also played an important role in the quest to protect America's wild horses. Specifically, the FOIA has been instrumental in exposing information about the slaughter of adopted wild horses, a practice that violates the law.[48] The adoption and slaughter of wild horses is related to a battle that has been brewing for decades between Western conservationists and ranchers over the estimated 46,000 wild horses and burros that roam remote ranges of 10 states from New Mexico to Oregon. Conservationists remain concerned about the welfare of these horses, but ranchers largely contend that the horses are a nuisance, competing with the ranchers' cattle and sheep for increasingly scarce grazing land.

The Bureau of Land Management (BLM) has largely sided with the ranchers, contending that the ranks of wild horses need to be reduced by half. As a result, the BLM has developed and implemented a plan to round up a number of the wild horses. Animal welfare advocates have criticized this plan, arguing that it favors rich and powerful ranching interests over the well-being of animals and contending that it may even place the horses at risk of extinction.

Under the plan, the rounded-up horses are to be adopted. Animal protection advocates, however, were concerned about the welfare of the animals and questioned whether the horses that were to be adopted by caring individuals truly were, or whether they were suffering a much more sinister fate. The Fund for Animals and the Animal Legal Defense Fund filed a lawsuit challenging the herd-reduction plan. The Fund for Animals also filed a second lawsuit under the FOIA in order to obtain information about horses going to slaughter. The BLM has maintained that most horses have been adopted, with only a small number inadvertently ending up in slaughterhouses.[49] However, animal welfare advocates have contended that many of the animals that were to be adopted into caring homes actually ended up being sold into slaughterhouses.[50]

3. Obstacles

3.1 General

The problems that plague the effective administration of freedom of information laws in the area of environmental protection are largely the same problems that plague the proper administration of information access in other areas, namely access fees, administrative delays, the culture of secrecy, and the overuse of secrecy classifications.

This section examines some of the issues that are having the most profound impact on the ability of individuals to use the FOIA and other information freedom laws to obtain information that can be useful in halting activities that devastate the environment.

3.2 Too Much Information? Too Little Organization

A number of factors complicate efforts to use FOIA and other laws to achieve information about environmental hazards. For one, the sheer volume of information complicates the quest for the production of meaningful information. There are a multitude of different federal and state laws and regulations addressing different aspects of environmental protection, including water cleanliness, air pollution, pesticides, hazardous waste, emission control, and related issues. Each year, numerous reports are filed with the EPA, either directly or through state agencies. This means that different agencies may collect different reports on a particular facility's environmental compliance at different times and in different formats and may then store that information in different ways—some storing it in various databases, some in file cabinets, some even in boxes that are stacked in storage facilities. In practice, this may mean that individuals seeking information regarding the polluting substances released by a particular factory may have great difficulty locating it.

3.3 Over-Reliance on the Exemptions

Individuals seeking information about certain environmental situations may find themselves stymied by government reliance on the exemptions, particularly the exemption concerning national security and foreign policy. There are a number of cases that demonstrate this reality. Consider, for instance, Weinberger v. Catholic Action of Hawaii/Peace Education Project.[51] In this case, the Supreme Court affirmed that the requirements of the National Environmental Policy Act[52] to prepare environmental impact statements for projects "significantly affecting the quality of the human environment"[53] extended to the Department of Defense (DoD). However, the Court ruled that due to the FOIA exemption for national security, the DoD had no obligation to disclose such statements and assessments. In this case, Catholic Action had reason to believe that nuclear weapons were stored at a particular site but could not prove it with publicly available records and documentation. Concerned about the health and safety effects of possible nuclear weapon storage, Catholic Action sought to secure the release of necessary documents and informatin. Due to what it claimed to be reasons of national security, the DoD would neither confirm nor deny that nuclear weapons were located at the site. In finding for the DoD, the Court maintained that since Catholic Action could not prove that the nuclear weapons were located at the site, it could not prove that an environmental impact statement was even necessary, let alone that it needed to be disclosed under the FOIA.

3.4 Delay, Delete, and Deny

As in other areas, journalists, activists, and other researchers seeking information about environmental issues may encounter problems with government agencies delaying the provision of information and with key information being deleted or denied outright. As the following section will show, the problems associated with delays, deletions, and denials became more pronounced after the terrorist attacks of September 11.

3.4.1 Removal of Information from the Internet Post 9/11
3.4.1.1 Removal of RMP Data

As will be discussed in further detail in Chapter Nine, subsequent to the terrorist attacks of September 11, 2001, a good deal of government information that was once available for public consumption online and in databases was removed and made inaccessible. Due to its potential for being used in acts of terrorism, certain information that could also be useful for environmental protection (e.g., information about certain chemicals and pollutants) was also made less available for public consumption.

One example is the EPA's removal of certain risk management plan data (RMP) from the Internet. RMPs contain information about chemicals used in plants and include a hazard assessment, a prevention program, and an emergency response plan. The following notice was posted by the EPA: "In light of the September 11 events, EPA has temporarily removed RMP Info from its Web site. EPA is reviewing the information we make available over the Internet and assessing how best to make the information publicly available. We hope to complete that effort as soon as possible."[54]

The RMP data was removed despite the fact that statutory directives provided clearly that only the Offsite Consequence Analyses (OCA) portions of the RMPs were exempted from Internet posting. In fact, in a 2004 round of rulemaking, the EPA even acknowledged that Internet disclosure of RMPs that did not include the OCA information presented no unique increased threats of terrorism.[55]

"Does a terrorist really need to know about a facility's plans to improve safety or respond to an accident?" the government accountability group Office of Management and Budget (OMB) Watch wondered in a January 2002 article on the RMP removal. "Even for the more controversial [worse-case scenario information] how is a terrorist uniquely advantaged? It is hardly difficult to find chemical facilities located near large populations."[56] While the removal of such information does not do much to reduce the terrorist threat, it *does* diminish the ability of the public to be informed about —and take action against—community dangers. Instead of such wholesale deletion of information that can be of great use to researchers, activists, communities, and individuals, environmental groups have called for "mandatory security restrictions such as establishing anti-terrorist technology standards and a general duty clause for responsible, anti-terrorist chemical storage and handling."[57] If followed, these suggestions would allow for a much more targeted and appropriate response to the potential risks of RMP access by would-be terrorists.

3.4.1.2 Removal of Data by FERC

The EPA was not the only agency to remove data from the Internet in the wake of 9/11. The Federal Energy Regulatory Commission (FERC) also reconsidered its Internet access policies and removed tens of thousands of documents regarding dams, pipelines, and other energy facilities.[58] Public requests for information about Critical Energy Infrastructure Information (CEII) are now channeled to a special request page that requires registration (and the requestor's social security number) and agreement with limitations on the use and disclosure of any information provided. For example, members of the public—and journalists—are bound by nondisclosure agreements to "only discuss CEII with another recipient of the identical CEII," and face civil or criminal sanctions if they do otherwise.[59]

At first consideration, the removal of such information from public Web sites may seem well-reasoned due to the potential harm that terrorists and others with ill intent could do using the information. However, a 2003 investigation by journalists from *US News & World Report* showed the removal of such information might be motivated more by a desire to advance the economic interests of favored industries and to keep executive actions from being scrutinized than to prevent terrorism. The *US News* investigation revealed a great number of examples of critical information that was either removed from public view or never even posted in the first place.[60] The article detailed missing energy information, tire and safety information, environmental information, transportation information, and the potential for misuse of critical infrastructure information laws to shield private industry.

3.4.2 Regulation Under the Clean Air Act

Problems resulting from delays, deletions, and denials have plagued information access in the area of environmental protection. For example, agency delays, deletions, and denials have had a negative impact on the ability of journalists, activists, and other individuals to obtain information about government policies regarding climate change, including, in particular, the role of pollution in causing global warming.

In April 2007, the U.S. Supreme Court ruled in *Massachusetts, et al v. U.S. Environmental Protection Agency, et al.*[61] that greenhouse gas emissions are eligible for regulation under the Clean Air Act if they do indeed endanger public health.[62] This important development affirmed a position previously rejected by the Bush administration. As a result, the EPA would have to either regulate greenhouse gases under the Act or prove that emissions are not a risk to public health and welfare, and therefore not in need of regulation.

In May 2007, the White House ordered the EPA, along with other agencies, to prepare regulatory responses by the end of the year. According to EPA officials, the agency's draft finding and recommendation on CO_2 emissions, which found that they were dangers that must be controlled, was sent to the White House OMB in December 2007. But officials at the OMB reportedly refused to even open the EPA's draft document, knowing that it could trigger regulatory action on climate change under the Supreme Court ruling.[63]

Investigations conducted by two committees in the House of Representatives found that the administration delayed acting on the EPA findings. In fact, despite repeated requests for the EPA information, the White House refused to share any related documents until the records were subpoenaed in April 2008 by the House Select Committee on Energy Independence and Global Warming.

After reviewing the subpoenaed records, committee chair Edward Markey (D-Mass.) charged the administration with discarding the EPA's science and legally based recommendations to address climate change.[64] Markey reported that the EPA documents supported scientific conclusions that greenhouse gas emissions may "endanger public welfare" and that motor vehicle emissions do contribute to global warming.

Rep. Henry Waxman (D-Calif.), chair of the House Oversight Committee, proclaimed the administration's lack of action to be "in violation of the Supreme Court's directive."[65] According to his committee, the draft was the product of about 500 comments from internal EPA review, external federal expert review, and other interagency comments.

The *Wall Street Journal*, claiming to have a copy of the original documents, reported that the White House had done more than delay the EPA information. The administration had apparently attempted to remove entire findings, the paper found.[66] According to anonymous officials quoted by the *Journal*, the White House pressured the EPA to remove conclusions that greenhouse gases endanger public welfare, information on how to regulate the gases, and an analysis of the cost of regulating greenhouse gases. The draft of the EPA's findings affirmed "the agency's authority to tackle climate change, and suggest[ed] a variety of regulatory avenues" and concluded that the "net benefit to society" of regulating automobile emissions "could be in excess of $2 trillion." However, the White House allegedly reworked the EPA's findings to indicate that the Clean Air Act is a flawed vehicle for regulating greenhouse gas emissions and that separate legislation is needed.

On July 11, 2008, the EPA released an Advanced Notice of Proposed Rulemaking (ANPR)[67] on climate change that appeared to confirm that the White House changes had been made. The ANPR included conclusions that differed starkly from those reported by the *Journal* and congressional committees. For instance, the ANPR states that the "net present value to society [of regulating emissions] could be on the order of $340 to $830 billion." Despite the Supreme Court ruling that the administration has the authority to regulate greenhouse gas emissions, the administration continues to deny the Clean Air Act should be used. Unlike the original draft, the ANPR was accompanied by 85 pages from other department secretaries aimed at attacking the Act and included no finding of endangerment or regulatory recommendations. For example, the Department of Energy called the Clean Air Act a flawed vehicle for regulating greenhouse gas emissions.

The ANPR marked the opening of a 120-day public comment period, when the EPA solicited views on the current state of climate science, regulatory options for curbing greenhouse gas emissions, and the appropriateness of developing greenhouse gas regulations under the authority of the Clean Air Act. Rep. Markey called the ANPR "a plan for no-action," and his committee charged the White House of handing off the responsibility of addressing urgent emissions regulations to the next administration due to special interest influence. Thus far, no action has been taken on the ANPR. As of fall 2008, President-elect Barack Obama asserted that his administration will have to implement the Court's decision. His energy advisor told Bloomberg News in October 2008 that an Obama administration would tell the EPA that it may use the Clean Air Act to regulate greenhouse gas emissions.[68] While as of this writing it seems like the lengthy debacle may be near its end, it is highly indicative of a larger struggle between appointed officials and agency career staff that may remain a part of government culture.

3.4.3 Climate Change Policy

The Bush Administration has also attempted to censor the climate change information that reaches the public and the Congress, such as in the highly publicized case of NASA climatologist James Hansen.[69] Most recently, we have learned that not only did the White House pressure the EPA to make changes to its regulatory process regarding climate change, but that Vice President Dick Cheney's office was responsible for suppressing key sections of congressional testimony from a high-level Centers for Disease Control and Prevention (CDC) official. In July 2008, a former climate adviser at the EPA said the CDC official's report went from 14 pages to 6 pages after the vice president's office pushed to delete "any discussion of the human health consequences of climate change."[70]

The removed sections declared climate change a serious public health concern due to its influence on the spread of disease. While it had been known that the testimony was altered, the public was not aware that the interference had come from so high in the administration.[71]

While this evisceration was shocking in and of itself, the *Washington Post* revealed that Cheney's alterations were indicative of a larger pattern of high-level administration officials exercising influence over expert recommendations by withholding information.[72] These incidents indicate a pattern of censorship targeting the scientific community and the government's career staff. Given the crucial nature of the matters at issue, one could rightfully argue that the actions have been placing the health and safety of the American people in jeopardy.

4. Conclusion

Clearly, the FOIA has an important role to play in the area of environmental protection. The public has a right to know about human health and environmental issues that affect it. Ensuring that environmental information is available to the public allows communities to develop plans to make their residents safer and creates incentives for industry to improve its environmental performance (and save money by doing so). Additionally, access to environmental information allows individuals to make better-informed choices about things such as what they eat and drink, where they live, and how they invest their money. Ultimately, the most effective choice informed citizens can make is to take action and help ensure their environment is protected. Time and again citizens empowered with information about environmental hazards have written letters, called officials, protested companies, boycotted products, and used many other methods to make their informed opinions heard.

Proper access to information about environmental issues is continually at risk from attacks from corporations and legislators that are friendly to certain industries. It is important that citizens, public interest groups, community groups, unions, heath care officials, and others continue to promote and protect environmental right-to-know laws and programs. The public should not have to demonstrate a need to know information, nor should it have to face obstacle after obstacle to obtain information about threats to its health and safety. While the important information revealed through the use of freedom of information laws highlights the necessity of protecting and defending the FOIA, the struggles and obstacles that environmental journalists, activists, and community members continue to face show that we have more work to do in this area.

The next chapter shifts focus to a discussion on human health. Chapter 4 examines how the FOIA and other freedom-of-information laws have helped to break stories about important issues impacting human health. It will also show the obstacles that individuals sometimes encounter when attempting to obtain information about health issues using the FOIA.

Notes

1. For a background on the Bhopal disaster, see Dominique Lapierre and Javier Moro, *Five Past Midnight in Bhopal* (Warner Books, 2002).

2. Intergovernmental Panel on Climate Change, Summary for Policymakers, 2007, available at: http://ipcc-wg1.ucar.edu/wg1/Report/AR4WG1_Print _SPM.pdf (last visited November 11, 2008).

3. Elizabeth Mygatt, "World's Water Resources Face Mounting Pressure, Earth Policy Institute," July 26, 2006, available at http://www.earth-policy.org/Indicators/Water/2006.htm (last visited November 12, 2008).

4. Edwin H. Clark II, "Water Prices Rising Worldwide, Earth Policy Institute," March 7, 2007, available at http://www.earth-policy.org/Updates/2007/ Update64.htm (last visited November 12, 2008).

5. World Health Organization, "The World Health Report 2002: Reducing Risks, Promoting Healthy Life, 2002," available at http://www.who.int/entity/whr/ 2002/en/whr02_en.pdf (last visited November 11, 2008).

6. Peter H. Gleick, *Water and Conflict: Fresh Water Resources and International Security* (Cambridge, MA: The MIT Press, 1993).

7. Sandra L. Postel and Aaron T. Wolf, "Dehydrating Conflict," *Foreign Policy*, No. 126 (September–October 2001), 60–67.

8. World Health Organization, "The World Health Report 2003: Shaping the Future, 2003," available at http://www.who.int/entity/whr/2003/en/whr03 _en.pdf (last visited November 11, 2008).

9. Leticia Yáñez, et al. "Overview of Human Health and Chemical Mixtures: Problems Facing Developing Countries," *Environmental Health Perspectives*, December 2002, available at http://www.ehponline.org/members/2002/suppl-6/901- 909yanez/ehp110s6p901.pdf (last visited November 11, 2008); and The World Bank, Toxics and Poverty, August 1, 2002.

10. World Health Organization, Public Health Impact of Pesticides Used in Agriculture. Geneva, World Health Organization, 1990.

11. The United Nations Environment Programme, Childhood Pesticide Poisoning, May 2004, available at http://www.who.int/entity/ceh/publications/ pestpoisoning.pdf(last visited November 11, 2008).

12. The International Union for Conservation of Nature and Natural Resources, 2008 Red List: *Ursus maritimus*, 2008, available at http://www.iucnredlist.org/ details/22823 (last visited November 11, 2008).

13. Felicity Barringer, "Polar Bear Is Made a Protected Species," *The New York Times*, May 15, 2008, http://www.nytimes.com/2008/05/15/us/15polar.html? fta=y (last visited November 11, 2008).

14. Freedom of Information Act: Hearings Before the Subcomm. on the Constitution of the Senate Comm. On the Judiciary, 97th Cong., 1st Sess. 604, 775 (1981).

15. *Id.*

16. Tina Adler, "Marine Science: Surf's Yuck," *Environ Health Perspective*, (August 2004) 112(11): A614.

17. "SwellNet Dispatch, Words from Clean Ocean," June 16, 2006, available at: http://www.swellnet.com.au/dispatch.php?dispatch=Clean_Ocean_160606.php (last visited November 5, 2008).

18. *Id.*

19. Eric Pianin, "Widespread Water Violations Decried," *The Washington Post*, August 7, 2002.

20. *Id.*

21. The Clean Water Act, 33 U.S.C. § 1251 (1972).

22. The U.S. Public Interest Research Group Education Fund, "Permit to Pollute: How the Government's Lax Enforcement of the Clean Water Act Is Poisoning Our Waters," August 2002, available at http://www.pennenvironment.org/uploads/ Nd/7s/Nd7sho0FW_ZmWKPNJrqOeg/PermittoPolute.pdf (last visited November 3, 2008).

23. The problem of lead in drinking water in Washington D.C. has been documented by a number of researchers. SeeTee L. Guidotti, Thomas Calhoun, John O. Davies-Cole, Maurice E. Knuckles, Lynette Stokes, Chevelle Glymph, Garret Lum, Marina S. Moses, David F. Goldsmith, and Lisa Ragain, "Elevated Lead in Drinking Water in Washington, D.C., 2003–2004: The Public Health Response," *Environmental Health Perspectives*, May 2007, available at http://www.ehponline.org/ members/2007/8722/8722.html (last visited November 1, 2008).

24. Carol D. Leonnig and David Nakamura, "D.C. Knew of Lead Problems in 2002; Timing of E-Mails Contradicts Claims," *The Washington Post*, March 29, 2004.

25. D. Stöfen, "The Health Dangers of Lead in Drinking Water," *Social and Preventive Medicine*, January 1971; and Dixie Farley, "Dangers of Lead Still Linger," *FDA Consumer* magazine, January/February 1998, available at http://www.fda.gov/FDAC/features/1998/198_lead.html (last visited November 1, 2008).

26. "National Citizens Cement Kiln Coalition, Downwinders At Risk," available at http://www.cementkiln.com/DARNCCKCHotSpots.htm#TEXAS(last visited on September 24, 2008); see also the Web site of Toxic Texas, available at http://www.txpeer.org/toxictour/txi.html (last visited on September 24, 2008).

27. Mike Ward, "How Citizens Make the Act Work," *Quill*, October 1996.

28. *Id.*

29. Keith Rogers, "Documents Say 60 Nuclear Chain Reactions Possible," *Las Vegas Review-Journal*, November 26, 2003.

30. Department of Energy, "Final Environmental Impact Statement for a Geologic Repository for the Disposal of Spent Nuclear Fuel and High-Level Radioactive Waste at Yucca Mountain, Nye County, Nevada," *DOE/EIS-0250*, February 2002, available at: http://www.ocrwm.doe.gov/documents/feis_2/vol_1/indexv1.htm (last visited November 8, 2008).

31. "Yucca Mountain Application Docketed," *World Nuclear News*, September 9, 2008, available at http://89.151.116.69/WR-Yucca_Mountain_application_docketed-0909087.html (last visited November 8, 2008).

32. "Barack Obama, Letter to the Editor," *Las Vegas Review-Journal*, May 20, 2007, available at http://www.lvrj.com/opinion/7598337.html (last visited November 8, 2008).

33. Erik Reece, "Moving Mountains," *Grist*, February 16, 2006, available at http://www.grist.org/news/maindish/2006/02/16/reece/ (last visited October 30, 2008).

34. Elizabeth Shogren, "Federal Coal-Mining Policy Comes Under Fire," *The Los Angeles Times*, January 7, 2004, available at http://articles.latimes.com/2004/jan/07/nation/na-mining7(last visited November 12, 2008).

35. E-mail from Ray George, EPA West Virginia/Western Pennsylvania State Liaison Officer, to Kathy Hodgkiss, EPA Region 3 Acting Director, Environmental Services Division (December 29, 2002, at 1:37 PM), available at http://www.tlpj.org/briefs/wvhc-ovec.exhibits44-75.pdf (page 31).

36. Tom Kizzia, "E-mail Reveals State Dispute Over Polar Bear Listing," *Anchorage Daily News*, May 25, 2008, available at: http://www.adn.com/polarbears/story/416432.html (last visited November 3, 2008).

37. *Id.*

38. Sarah Palin, "Bearing Up," *The New York Times*, January 5, 2008, available at http://www.nytimes.com/2008/01/05/opinion/05palin.html?_r=2&oref=slogin&oref=s login (last visited October 29, 2008). In the piece, Palin wrote: "This month, the secretary of the interior is expected to rule on whether polar bears should be listed under the Endangered Species Act. I strongly believe that adding them to the list is the wrong move at this time. *My decision is based on a comprehensive review by state wildlife officials of scientific information from a broad range of climate, ice and polar bear experts.*" (emphasis added).

39. Kizzia, *supra* note 34.

40. Center for Biological Diversity, Natural Resources Defense Council, and Earthjustice joint press release, "Conservation Groups File Suit for Suppressed Polar Bear Documents," January 28, 2008, available at: http://www.commondreams.org/news2008/0128-16.htm (last visited October 29, 2008).

41. Derek Sands, "DOI Sued for Sanctioning Chance Harm to Polar Bears in Chukchi Sea Drilling," *Inside Energy with Federal Lands*, July 14, 2008.

42. American Society for the Prevention of Cruelty to Animals, "USDA Documents Provide Proof of Circus Abuse of Elephants," March 12, 2002, available at http://www.charitywire.com/charity17/02845.html (last visited September 7, 2008).

43. Animal Welfare Act, 7 U.S.C. 2131, et seq.

44. American Society for the Prevention of Cruelty to Animals, *supra* note 40.

45. *Id.*

46. Humane Society of the United States, "HSUS Files Suit Against USDA Over FOIA Delays," January 27, 2005, available at http://www.hsus.org/animals_in_research/animals_in_research_news/hsus_files_suit_against_usda_over_foia_delays .html (last visited September 23, 2008).

47. Humane Society of the United States, "USDA Agrees to Provide Online Animal Research Reports in Wake of HSUS Suit," May 6, 2005, available at http://www.hsus.org/animals_in_research/animals_in_research_news/usda_agrees_to _provide_online_reports.html (last visited September 23, 2008).

48. Evelyn Nieves, "A Roundup of Wild Horses Stirs Up a Fight in the West," *The New York Times*, February 25, 2002, available at http://query.nytimes.com/gst/fullpage.html?res=9806E7D91F3EF936A15751C0A9649C8B63 (last visited November 4, 2008).

49. For background on the challenges claimed by the Bureau of Land Management, see "Bureau of Land Management, Fact Sheet on Wild Horse and Burro Management Challenges," October 2008, available at http://www.blm.gov/wo/st/en/prog/wild_horse_and_burro/new_factsheet.html (last visited October 31. 2008).

50. There have been many documented cases of the wild horses being sold into slaughterhouse. See, for example, Maryann Mott, "Wild Horses Sold by U.S. Agency Sent to Slaughter," *National Geographic News*, May 5, 2005, available at http://news.nationalgeographic.com/news/2005/05/0505_050505_wildhorses.html (last visited October 3, 2008).

51. *Weinberger v. Catholic Action of Hawaii/Peace Education Project*, 454 U.S. 139 (1981).

52. National Environmental Policy Act, 42 U.S.C. 4321 (1970).

53. Requirements of NEPA, 40 C.F.R. 1506.6, 1506.10 (2004); noting, however, that if an environmental assessment shows no adverse effect, a full environmental impact assessment does not have to be completed.

54. Susan Nevelow Mart, "Let the People Know the Facts: Can Government Information Removed from the Internet Be Reclaimed?" LLRX.com, available at: http://www.llrx.com/features/reclaimed.htm (last visited November 11, 2008).

55. Environmental Protection Agency, "Accidental Release Prevention Requirements," April 9, 2004, available at http://www.epa.gov/EPA-AIR/2004/April/Day-09/a7777.htm (last visited November 8, 2008).

56. OMB Watch, "Benefits of Chemical Information Should Not Be Forgotten," January 16, 2002, available at http://www.ombwatch.org/article/articleview/394/1/39 (last visited November 8, 2008).

57. Timothy R. Henderson, "September 11th: How It Has Changed a Community's Right to Know," *The Maryland Bar Journal*, July/August 2002.

58. OMB Watch, "Access to Government Information Post September 11th," Federal Energy Regulatory Commission, April 25, 2005, available at http://www.ombwatch.org/article/articleview/213/1/104/#FERC (last visited November 8, 2008).

59. Federal Energy Regulatory Commission, "File a CEII Request," available at http://www.ferc.gov/help/filing-guide/ceii-request.asp (last visited November 8, 2008).

60. Christopher H. Schmitt and Edward T. Pound, "Keeping Secrets," *US News & World Report*, December 22, 2003, available at http://www.usnews.com/usnews/news/articles/secrecy/22secrecy.htm (last visited November 4, 2008).

61. 549 U.S. 118 (2007).

62. 42 U.S.C.' 7401-7671q.

63. Felicity Barringer, "White House Refused to Open Pollutants E-Mail," *The New York Times*, June 25, 2008, available at http://www.nytimes.com/2008/06/25/washington/25epa.html?_r=1&adxnnl=1&oref=slogin&adxnnlx=1216983823-z6z/aCL/aiwzML4yaNbLXA (last visited November 4, 2008).

64. House Select Committee on Energy Independence and Global Warming, Letter to President George W. Bush, June 24, 2008, available at http://globalwarming.house.gov/tools/2q08materials/files/0064.pdf (last visited November 10, 2008).

65. House Committee on Oversight and Government Reform, Letter to EPA Administrator Stephen L. Johnson, March 12, 2008, available at http://oversight.house.gov/documents/20080312110250.pdf (last visited November 10, 2008).

66. Stephen Power and Ian Talley, "Administration Releases EPA Report, Then Repudiates It," *The Wall Street Journal*, July 12, 2008, available at http://online.wsj.com/article/SB121578600530545953.html (last visited November 4, 2008).

67. EPA, "Advance Notice of Proposed Rulemaking: Regulating Greenhouse Gas Emissions under EPA-HQ-OAR-2008-0318," July 11, 2008, available at http://www.epa.gov/climatechange/anpr.html.

68. Jim Efstathiou Jr., "Obama to Declare Carbon Dioxide Dangerous Pollutant," *Bloomberg News*, October 16, 2008, available at http://www.bloomberg.com/apps/news?pid=newsarchive&sid=alHWVvGnkcd4 (last visited November 8, 2008).

69. Andrew C. Revkin, "Climate Expert Says NASA Tried to Silence Him," *The New York Times*, January 26, 2006, available at http://www.nytimes.com/2006/01/29/science/earth/29climate.html (last visited November 8, 2006).

70. Elana Schor, "Cheney Accused of Suppressing Testimony on Climate Change's Risks," *The Guardian*, July 8, 2008, available at http://www.guardian.co.uk/world/2008/jul/08/dickcheney.usa (lasted visited November 4, 2008).

71. The original testimony is available at: http://www.climatesciencewatch.org/file-uploads/Draft_CDC_testimony_23oct07.pdf, and the final testimony, available at: http://epw.senate.gov/public/index.cfm?FuseAction=Files.View&FileStore_id=7c34e37a-8a6f-4753, lacked such statement.

72. Juliet Eilperin, "Cheney's Staff Cut Testimony on Warming Health Threats at Issue, Ex-EPA Official Says," *The Washington Post*, July 9, 2008, available at http://www.washingtonpost.com/wp-dyn/content/article/2008/07/08/AR2008070801442.html (last visited November 4, 2008).

Chapter Four

Protecting Human Health with Freedom of Information

We seek a free flow of information ... we are not afraid to entrust the American people with unpleasant facts, foreign ideas, alien philosophies, and competitive values.

—John F. Kennedy

1. Overview

This chapter examines the role that freedom of information and open government can play in protecting human health. It explores significant instances when journalists and other individuals were able to gather information about various health risks and issues through freedom of information laws. Finally, it provides strategies for obtaining information about health issues from the government.

2. Notable Revelations

The FOIA has been a very effective tool for journalists and public interest groups seeking to obtain government and industrial reports regarding various health issues. Researchers have used the FOIA to obtain information about contaminated food supplies,[1] the use of injured and sick cows in meat production,[2] the mercury levels in fish consumed by pregnant women[3], and contaminated drinking water on Marine bases,[4] among other things. This section highlights several examples in the area of health in which freedom of information laws have proven to be particularly useful.

2.1 Drug Safety

2.1.1 FDA and Drug Testing Overall

The FOIA has been very helpful in generating information about drug safety. Using the FOIA, researchers have found that many Food and Drug Administration (FDA) scientists felt pressure not to call into question the safety of certain drugs and medical devices. A survey conducted in 2002 by the inspector general of the Department of Health and Human Services found that almost one-fifth of the FDA scientists indicated that they had been pressured or intimidated into recommending the approval of a drug, despite their own misgivings about the drug's safety or effectiveness. Moreover, more than one-third of the scientists were not confident in the FDA's ability to assess the safety of any particular drug. The FDA initially released a report based on the survey results, but it did not include any voices of dissent found in the survey and did not release the entire findings. The survey, obtained in 2004 via the FOIA by the Union of Concerned Scientists and Public Employees for Environmental Responsibility, supports the criticism—leveled by some—that the FDA is ineffective at keeping unsafe drugs off the market.[5]

2.1.2 Uncovering the Risks of the Birth Control Patch

The FOIA has also helped researchers to learn about specific drugs that may pose safety risks, like the birth control patch. According to drug safety reports obtained by the Associated Press under the FOIA, at least a dozen women died in 2004 from blood clots apparently caused by use of a new birth control patch, Ortho Evra.[6] In addition, according to the research, dozens more women, most in their late teens and early twenties, suffered strokes and other clot-related problems after using the patch.

Lawsuits have been filed on behalf of an estimated 4,000 women since the documents were released, alleging that both the FDA and Johnson & Johnson subsidiary Ortho McNeil, the company that makes the patch, knew of possible problems with the patch before it came on the market. Despite claims by the FDA and Ortho McNeil that the patch was as safe as using birth control pills, the reports appear to indicate that the risk of dying or suffering a blood clot was about three times higher than with birth control pills. In October 2007, Johnson & Johnson settled the first such lawsuit scheduled to go to trial, paying $1.25 million to the family of Alycia Brown, who died in 2004 when she was 14 years old.[7] As of October 2008, Bloomberg News estimated that the company had paid about $68 million to victims and their families thus far, and that "several hundred" cases had been settled.[8]

2.1.3 Investigating the Connection Between Vaccines and Autism

The FOIA has also been instrumental in uncovering information about the potential connections between vaccines and autism. This complex developmental disability is being diagnosed in numbers far higher than ever before, suggesting to some that a non-genetic cause may be partly to blame, and parents and activists have become increasingly suspicious of the link between vaccines and autism.

New scientific research and documents recently released under the FOIA bring into question the safety of thimerosal, a mercury-containing preservative that is found in small amounts in several vaccines commonly administered to American children. Safe Minds, an advocacy group of parents who believe that their autistic children were damaged by thimerosal, used the FOIA to obtain records showing that as early as December 1999 the Centers for Disease Control and Prevention (CDC) had reason to believe that thimerosal caused developmental delays in some children.[9] The documents showed that the amount of mercury contained in the preservative for vaccines given in the first three months of life would dramatically increase the risk of autism in children who received those vaccinations. As many as 30 million American children may have been exposed to mercury in excess of Environmental Protection Agency (EPA) guidelines—levels of mercury that, in theory, could have killed enough brain cells to alter brain functioning.[10]

2.2 Food Safety

The FOIA has also proven to be an effective tool for gathering information about food safety. Contamination and other safety issues have threatened certain aspects of our food supply. Unfortunately, all too often this information has failed to become public knowledge until brought to light by journalists or activists, often through the use of freedom of information laws. This section examines some notable information about the safety of our food supply that has been obtained via the FOIA.

2.2.1 Seafood Safety

FDA documents received in 2002 by a nongovernmental organization, the Environmental Working Group, pursuant to a FOIA request revealed that the commercial tuna industry had placed tremendous pressure on the FDA as it was issuing its recommendations regarding the consumption of certain seafood by pregnant women. In January 2001, the FDA recommended that pregnant women avoid eating shark, swordfish, tilefish, and mackerel because of high levels of mercury contamination that could cause brain defects or delays in mental development in their unborn children. "Mysteriously absent from the list was one of the most significant sources of mercury in the American diet, tuna," *New York Times* food writer Marian Burros noted.[11]

While tuna does not have the highest level of mercury of all seafood (that honor goes to swordfish), it is still a major concern because Americans eat so much of it. "Americans eat nearly three pounds of canned tuna per capita every year, making it the nation's second most popular seafood (behind shrimp)," Stephanie Mencimer reported in *Mother Jones*. "The government promotes it via school lunch programs, WIC (the federal food program for poor women and children), and even in the FDA and U.S. Department of Agriculture dietary recommendations."[12]

Back in the 1970s, the FDA appeared to take some interest in the safety of tuna and conducted occasional tests of store-bought tuna fish, but thereafter there was a lull in activity at the FDA level. After facing criticism from environmental groups and scientists, however, the FDA in 2001 released an advisory that warned pregnant women about mercury. The original draft reportedly listed canned tuna as a high-mercury product. This notice led to three private meetings, uncovered through a FOIA request, between several tuna industry representatives and the FDA where the industry representatives expressed their concerns about massive losses in sales and the potential for class action lawsuits.[13] When the FDA advisory was issued on January 12, 2001, it did not include tuna.[14] The process rightly raised serious questions about the influence the tuna industry had over the FDA's determination and recommendations.

The failure of the FDA to include tuna in its 2001 recommendations did not end concerns about mercury levels in fish, however. After the federal authorities declined to regulate tuna, some states stepped up with more stringent warnings. For example, the state of Washington warns that children under six should eat no more than half a can of albacore a week.[15] A number of other states have also issued their own advisories on tuna.[16] In addition, scientists, doctors, and environmental groups continued to urge the FDA to adopt more stringent federal warnings based on the EPA's reference dose for safe mercury exposure.

The FDA did revisit its mercury advisory in 2004, putting fish into high-mercury and low-mercury categories[17], but a FDA official told the agency's Food Advisory Committee that commercial concerns remained. Clark Carrington said that agency staffers had crafted the boundaries so that canned light tuna—which makes up 75 percent of the U.S. tuna market—would fall in the low-mercury group "in order to keep the market share at a reasonable level."[18]

The 2004 advisory, issued jointly with the EPA, warned pregnant and nursing women to eat no more than six ounces of albacore, and no more than 12 ounces of chunk light tuna, per week. The FDA recommended that children follow the same guidelines, but simply eat "smaller portions" of the fish. A 44-pound child following the guidelines would consume four times the mercury the EPA considers safe, according to *Mother Jones*.

2.2.2 Documenting the Risks of Mad Cow Disease

Data gathered through the FOIA suggests that government officials may have vastly underestimated the risks of mad-cow disease. In arguing that the risk of the disease was very low, the USDA often cited a November 2001 Harvard Center for Risk Assessment report. But the *Denver Post*, using documents obtained via the FOIA, found that experts who examined the Harvard report in a peer-review process said it ignored important issues and focused on insignificant details. The USDA had not made public those critical comments from scientists until the newspaper and others filed FOIA requests in 2004. The peer review said that even with the flaws in the Harvard report, the risk of a mad cow epidemic could still be very low. However, it noted that it is impossible to know due to the report's problems.[19]

2.2.3 Plant Processing Safety

Food processing plants are a vital link in the modern American food chain, and it is of utmost importance that they remain safe and clean in order to not pass on disease to food consumers. In several instances, the FOIA has helped to highlight unsafe conditions in these plants and has raised important questions as to whether the government is doing enough to ensure food safety.

In 2006, the Minneapolis *Star Tribune* reviewed safety-testing results it obtained using the FOIA for 22 plants where the world's largest turkey processor, Jennie-O Turkey Store, produces ground turkey.[20] At the largest Jennie-O plant, in Willmar, Minnesota, federal inspectors found that half of the ground turkey it tested contained salmonella bacteria—more than twice the national average. This level, dangerously close to the permissible federal maximum of 55 percent, led food safety advocates to challenge federal oversight of ground turkey processing. Although no illnesses have been reported from the Jennie-O plants, an epidemiologist who investigates food-borne illness told the newspaper that it is often difficult to trace where the pathogen came from, and that many illnesses also go unreported. Each year, salmonella infects more than 40,000 Americans and kills as many as 500.

In a lengthy story published in 2003, the *New York Times* detailed Food Safety and Inspection Service reports obtained by consumer groups through the FOIA that found contaminants on food as it was processed at meat-packing plants—even after it had gone through a plant's safety processes. The meat inspectors also reported cases when meat had been condemned, but not subsequently marked or removed from production. Congressional critics, consumer groups, and some government inspectors argue that revelations such as the ones in the *Times* article illustrate the weakness in the food safety system the USDA phased in from 1998 to 2000. Senator Tom Harkin (D-Iowa) told the paper that the USDA "really doesn't have good enforcement procedures, and they don't have any clear standards for judging whether a company's plan is adequate or not."[21]

The FOIA has also led to significant revelations about the health and safety of poultry. Internal USDA documents, obtained by the Scripps Howard

News Service through a FOIA request in 2001, detailed a widespread problem with chickens being processed at plants participating in an experimental "science-based" inspection program. Nearly 40 percent of these chickens heading to supermarket shelves were contaminated with sores, scabs, and other "defects" that should have been detected on the processing line. In addition, 1.1 percent of the chickens examined were diseased, 18.8 percent were contaminated with material from the chicken's digestive tract, and 98.6 percent had "other defects involving feathers, hair, or oil glands that weren't properly removed on the processing line."[22]

2.3 Hospital-Related Health and Safety

Using California's freedom of information legislation, a reporter at the *Sacramento Bee* obtained statistics that showed that a growing number of California paramedics, under stress with easy access to medication, were abusing drugs and alcohol and putting patients at risk. By reviewing enforcement records obtained under the California Public Records Act,[23] the *Bee* reported that between 2005 and 2007, "the state agency charged with monitoring and prosecuting substance abuse by paramedics has logged more than 65 drug and alcohol cases—up from only eight cases in 1999–2000." In addition to some paramedics being incompetent, "[i]n the worst cases, they are committing crimes, too: Driving drunk or high. Getting into hit-and-run accidents. Abusing patients. Stealing. Even injecting the powerful morphine they carry, replacing it with a saline solution, and giving that to victims in pain."[24] These are extremely important records for the journalist to have researched and brought to light. While 65 may not seem like a very high number, given the issues at hand the stakes couldn't be any higher.

2.4 Military Health and Safety

Using the FOIA, Salt Lake City newspaper *The Deseret News* in 1995 obtained documents revealing a U.S. Army project known as Project Shipboard Hazard and Defense (Project SHAD). This project's experiments sprayed nerve, germ, and chemical agents on a variety of ships and their crews in the 1960s to gauge how quickly the toxins could be detected and how rapidly they would disperse. In 2002, the Pentagon officially acknowledged using actual chemical and biological warfare agents in the tests, including the nerve agents VX and sarin and deadly staphylococcal enterotoxin, and publicly released the documents first reported on by the newspaper seven years earlier. This revelation did more than highlight how the Army was essentially using human guinea pigs to test out hazardous chemicals; it also allowed hundreds of affected veterans to receive disability and health benefits previously denied them.[25]

3. Challenges

3.1 Tracking Needles in Haystacks

One of the main challenges with seeking information in the health and medical sector arises from the fact that there are a plethora of sources from which information can be sought and requested. Individuals seeking information about health-related issues through the FOIA will have a number of different points of contact. Each FOIA office in the Department of Health and Human Services has a FOIA Requester Service Center that processes relevant requests, including the following:

1. Administration on Aging;
2. Administration for Children and Families;
3. Agency for Healthcare Research and Quality;
4. Centers for Disease Control and Prevention;
5. Centers for Medicare & Medicaid Services;
6. Food and Drug Administration;
7. Health Resources and Services Administration;
8. Indian Health Service;
9. National Institutes of Health;
10. Office of Inspector General;
11. Program Support Center;
12. Public Health Service;
13. Substance Abuse and Mental Health Services Administration. Points of contact for each of these and other relevant government agencies are set forth in Appendix C.

3.2 Overcoming Delays

Individuals using the FOIA to seek information about health issues are likely to experience obstacles similar to individuals seeking information in other areas, such as processing delays. A recent tally of unfilled information requests to the FDA totaled 20,365. Significantly, 1,925 of those requests were more than three years old. The FDA has more backlogged requests than both the Defense Department and the Justice Department.[26]

There are no signs that these problems are going to improve any time soon. While delays and backlogs have been increasing, the FDA has actually decreased the resources it devotes to the administration of the FOIA. It has, for instance, cut back on the number of workers who handle FOIA requests. The equivalent of 88 full-time staffers worked on filings in 2006, down from 123 in 1995.[27]

In a recent study done by the Association of Health Care Journalists and Northwestern University's Medill School of Journalism, only one-third of the health reporters surveyed said they'd received responses from the FDA within 20 days of filing a request under the FOIA. Many of these journalists waited months or years to receive the requested information, if they ever received it at all.[28]

The delays of the FDA in responding to FOIA requests are of great concern, as they limit the ability of researchers, consumer groups, and individuals to alert the public to food and drug dangers and to hold the FDA accountable when it fails to detect and warn the public of health dangers.

Delays have also been a problem at the Department of Health and Human Services (HHS). The department's 2006 FOIA Report shows a growing backlog, as HHS received more requests than it processed in that year, which resulted in a net gain in pending requests from 24,484 to 26,063.[29] HHS has been focusing on strategies for reducing the delays, however, and in early 2007 it posted an updated FOIA Implementation Status Report in which it established goals to reduce backlog and improve both processing and public awareness.[30] The department says it achieved the great majority of its goals, and its 2007 FOIA Report bears fruit: The number of backlogged FOIA requests actually decreased in that year, as the department processed more cases than it received, even though the number of requests received rose by more than 30,000 from the previous year.[31] So while HHS seems to be improving the speed at which it processes FOIA requests, a large backlog remains.

4. Conclusion

The FOIA and other freedom of information laws can be helpful to researchers, activists, journalists, and individuals seeking to gather information about medical and health-related issues. As demonstrated throughout this chapter, the FOIA has been an instrumental tool for those seeking important data about such issues. While history shows a number of important revelations have come to light through the use of the FOIA, it is also clear that the administration of the FOIA can—and should—be improved. As is the case in other areas, the proper functioning of the FOIA has been adversely affected by delays in the provision of information. Given the critical nature of many health issues and the importance of obtaining timely information about matters that can place individuals at risk, it is essential that improvements be undertaken to ensure that these delays and other problems can be mitigated.

The next chapter examines the impact of the FOIA and related legislation in promoting better protection in various areas. It will show how journalists and other individuals were able to use the FOIA to uncover information about dangerous conditions, potentially impacting safety.

Notes

1. Melody Peterson and Christopher Drew, "The Slaughterhouse Gamble," *The New York Times*, October 10, 2003, available at http://query.nytimes.com/gst/fullpage.html?res=9502E1DC143FF933A25753C1A9659C8B63 (last visited November 5, 2008).

2. Donald G. McNeil, Jr., "Where the Cows Come Home," *The New York Times*, January 2, 2004, available at http://query.nytimes.com/gst/fullpage.html?sec=health&res=9C03E3DB1631F931A35752C0A9629C8B63&n=Top%2FNews%2FScience%2FTopics%2FLivestock (last visited November 6, 2008).

3. Marian Burros, "Second Thoughts on Mercury in Fish," *The New York Times*, March 13, 2002, available at http://query.nytimes.com/gst/fullpage.html?res=9E07E7DC1539F930A25750C0A9649C8B63 (last visited November 5, 2008).

4. Manuel Roif-Franzia and Catharine Skipp, "Tainted Water in the Land of Semper Fi," *The Washington Post*, January 28, 2004, available at http://www.washingtonpost.com/ac2/wp-dyn?pagename=article&node=&contentId=A54143-2004Jan27&notFound=true (last visited November 6, 2008).

5. Marc Kaufman, "Many FDA Scientists Had Drug Concerns, 2002 Study Shows," *The Washington Post*, December 16, 2004, available at http://www.washingtonpost.com/wp-dyn/articles/A3135-2004Dec15.html (last visited November 6, 2008).

6. Martha Mendoza, "Birth Control Patch Appears Riskier Than Pill," *The Associated Press* via the *Los Angeles Times*, July 17, 2005, available at http://articles.latimes.com/2005/jul/17/news/adna-patch17 (last visited November 5, 2008).

7. David Voreacos and Patricia Hurtado, "J&J Pays $1.25 Million to Settle Suit Over Death of 14-Year-Old," *Bloomberg News*, October 24, 2007, available at http://www.bloomberg.com/apps/news?pid=newsarchive&sid=aTTqmPEzxr9U (last visited November 6, 2008).

8. David Voreacos, "J&J Paid $68 Million to Settle Birth-Control Cases," *Bloomberg News*, October 10, 2008, available at http://www.bloomberg.com/apps/news?pid=20601109&sid=amZT0X84_8zU&refer=home (last visited November 6, 2008).

9. Arthur Allen, "The Not-So-Crackpot Autism Theory," *The New York Times*, November 10, 2002, available at http://query.nytimes.com/gst/fullpage.html?res=9B03EFD7153EF933A25752C1A9649C8B6 (last visited November 5, 2008).

10. Margaret Cronin Fisk, "Suit Targets Mercury-Laced Vaccinations," *The Recorder* (American Lawyer Media), March 26, 2002.

11. Marian Burros, "Second Thoughts on Mercury in Fish," *The New York Times*, March 13, 2002, available at http://query.nytimes.com/gst/fullpage.html?res=9E07E7DC1539F930A25750C0A9649C8B63 (last visited November 5, 2008).

12. Stephanie Mencimer, "Why Mercury Tuna Is Still Legal," *Mother Jones*, September/October 2008, available at http://www.motherjones.com/news/feature/2008/09/exit-strategy-tuna-surprise.html (last visited November 5, 2008).

13. *Id.*

14. Food and Drug Administration, "FDA Announces Advisory on Methyl Mercury in Fish," January 12, 2001, available at http://www.cfsan.fda.gov/~acrobat/hgadv5.pdf (last visited November 5, 2008).

15. Washington State Department of Health, Fish Facts for Healthy Nutrition, available at http://www.doh.wa.gov/ehp/oehas/fish/fishadvmerc.htm (last visited October 10, 2008).

16. Maine Center for Disease Control and Prevention, "The Maine Family Fish Guide," available at: http://www.maine.gov/dhhs/eohp/fish/documents/MeFFGuide.pdf; Massachusetts Department of Environmental Protection, "Fish Consumption Advisories," available at: http://www.mass.gov/dep/toxics/stypes/hgres.htm#fish; New Hampshire Department of Environmental Services, "Statewide Mercury Fish Consumption Advisory Update," available at: http://des.nh.gov/organization/commissioner/pip/factsheets/ard/documents/ard-ehp-25.pdf; Wisconsin Department of Natural Resources, "Mercury in Wisconsin Fish," available at: http://dnr.wi.gov/org/caer/cea/mercury/fish.htm; California Office of Environmental Health Hazard Assessment, "Methylmercury in Sport Fish," available at: http://oehha.ca.gov/fish/hg/index.html; Rhode Island Department of Health, "Fish Is Good, Mercury is Bad!," available at: http://www.health.state.ri.us/environment/risk/Fishisgood-english.pdf; and Hawaii Department of Health, "A Local Guide to Eating Fish Safely," available at: http://www.hawaii.gov/health/about/family-child-health/wic/pdf/fishsafety.pdf.

17. Environmental Protection Agency and Food and Drug Administration, "What You Need to Know About Mercury in Fish and Shellfish," March 19, 2004, available at http://www.cfsan.fda.gov/~dms/admehg3.html (last visited November 5, 2008).

18. Mencimer, supra note 12.

19. Anne C. Mulkern, "Experts Say USDA Officials Underestimate Mad-Cow Risk," *The Denver Post*, February 13, 2004.

20. Dave Shaffer, "Salmonella Rates High at State Plants," *Star Tribune*, April 14, 2006.

21. Melody Peterson and Christopher Drew, "The Slaughterhouse Gamble," *The New York Times*, October 10, 2003, available at http://query.nytimes.com/gst/fullpage.html?res=9502E1DC143FF933A25753C1A9659C8B63 (last visited November 5, 2008).

22. Lance Gay, "Store Chicken Filled with 'Defects.' " *Scripps Howard News Service* via the *Chicago Sun-Times*, March 2, 2001.

23. 23 Public Records Act, Calif. Stat. §§ 6250-6276.48 (1968).

24. Andrew McIntosh, "Special Report: Some Rescuers Pose Threat," *Sacramento Bee*, January 28, 2007, available at: http://www.sacbee.com/797/story/114035.html (last visited November 6, 2008).

25. Lee Davidson, "Sailors Exposed to Deadly Agents", *The Deseret News*, May 24, 2002.

26. Justin Blum, "Drug, Food Risks Stay Secret as Inquiries to U.S. FDA Pile Up," Bloomberg.com, June 19, 2008, available at: http://www.bloomberg.com/apps/news?pid=20601103&sid=a91FU255oQBM&refer=news (last visited November 1, 2008).

27. *Id.*

28. The Association of Health Care Journalists, "FOIA survey: FDA's slow response means stories go unpublished," April 10, 2008, available at http://

www.healthjournalism.org/about-news-detail.php?id=50 (last visited November 6, 2008).

29. Department of Health and Human Services, *HHS Fiscal Year 2006 Freedom of Information Annual Report*, 2007, available at http://www.hhs.gov/foia/reports/06anlrpt.html (last visited November 6, 2008).

30. Department of Health and Human Services, *Updated Status Report on Executive Order 13392 Review Plan*, 2007, available at: http://www.hhs.gov/foia/reference/updatedstatus.html (last visited November 6, 2008).

31. Department of Health and Human Services, *HHS Fiscal Year 2007 Freedom of Information Annual Report*, 2008, available at http://www.hhs.gov/foia/reports/07anlrpt.html (last visited November 6, 2008).

Chapter Five

Protecting Safety with Freedom of Information

Liberty cannot be preserved without a general knowledge among the people, who have a right and a desire to know.

—President John Adams

1. Overview

This chapter examines how freedom of information laws can protect safety in a number of different ways and explores instances in which researchers, journalists, consumer advocates, and ordinary citizens were able to use such laws to obtain information about important safety issues. This chapter will also offer tips and recommendations on how to gather information about issues that are relevant to the protection of safety.

2. Notable Revelations

2.1 Overview

The FOIA has helped researchers uncover important information about products and services that threaten human safety. For example, in February 2007 the *Associated Press* and other news agencies obtained documents from the Army Corp of Engineers that revealed that 122 levees across the country are in jeopardy of failing.[1] In another example, the *Marine Corps Times* used the FOIA to reveal that the Marine Corps issued to nearly 10,000 troops in Iraq body armor that ballistics experts rejected because tests revealed life-threatening flaws in the vests. The Corps recalled 5,277 vests made by Point Blank Body Armor when faced with the imminent publication of an eight-month probe into the purchase and distribution of the vests.[2] This section examines several additional notable revelations that were achieved through the use of the FOIA.

2.2 Safety of Methods of Transportation

2.2.1 Swissair Crash

Using the FOIA, *USA Today* obtained more than 1,000 pages of documents from the government concerning the September 2, 1998, crash of Swissair Flight 111. After reviewing those documents, along with tens of thousands of pages of other government documents, the newspaper connected the crash with the airplane's flight entertainment system. The system, which employed personal consoles to allow passengers to watch movies, shop, and play computer casino games, was made by Interactive Flight Technologies (IFT), a Las Vegas company that was formed only four years before the crash.

The Federal Aviation Administration (FAA) banned all use of IFT technologies a year after the crash, but it received heavy criticism for not catching the problems sooner. The documents obtained by *USA Today* revealed that no one directly employed by the FAA had ever reviewed IFT's design or installation plans, supervised the installation, or signed off on any work. Instead, that work was all done by a company that the FAA authorized to work on its behalf. After the Swissair crash, the FAA tightened oversight of such private companies and individuals, but problems remain.[3]

2.2.2 Marine Corps' Harrier Jet

Using the FOIA, *The Los Angeles Times* was able to obtain maintenance, safety, and combat records exposing the troubled history of the Marine Corps' Harrier attack jet. The Harrier has the highest major accident rate of any Air Force, Army, Navy, or Marine plane currently in service, having killed 45 Marines in 143 noncombat accidents since the Marines began using the jet in 1971.[4] More than one-third of the fleet has been lost to crashes.

Known as the "widow maker" among military aviators, the Harrier was originally developed by the British to take off and land vertically like a helicopter, yet fly like a conventional fighter jet. Congressional hearings prompted by the *Times*'s story have found that the recurring malfunction of the craft is linked to the same innovative technology that allows the plane to lift straight off the ground. Failures of the engine, wing flaps, and ejection systems, along with inexperienced mechanics and insufficient flight time for pilots, have all contributed to the plane's high accident rate. Military officials have previously stated that accidents are often the price of technological progress, but the *Times* investigation found that the plane rarely performed missions that could not have been handled by safer and more conventional aircraft.[5]

After the 2003 Congressional hearings, the Marine Corps pledged to allocate additional resources to improve the Harrier's safety record. Marine officials stated they would increase pilots' flight time to the minimum 17 to 20 hours needed to remain proficient in the challenging aircraft. In the past, the plane was grounded so often that pilots could not get enough flight time, averaging only 8.2 hours a month. In addition to pilot training, the Marines worked with Rolls Royce, the maker of the plane's engine, to overhaul nearly half of the 154-aircraft fleet. The Marines also reported they increased spending on spare parts and hired more seasoned mechanics.[6]

Pilot safety is not the only concern, as Harrier jet accidents have taken place in suburban areas during training. In 2005, a Harrier pilot ejected from his plane over Yuma, Arizona, and watched it nosedive into the yards of several suburban homes.[7] The plane was carrying four 500-pound bombs and 300 rounds of ammunition. Fortunately the explosives did not detonate, but the crash damaged several houses and landed a few feet from the bedroom of a 21-year old nursing student, leaving the resident with partial hearing loss.

2.2.3 Critical Flaws in Space Shuttle

Using the FOIA, the *Orlando Sentinel* researched nearly 2,000 NASA hazard-evaluation studies and malfunction reports from 113 past shuttle missions. The reports identified a number of critical shuttle flaws, including the misfiring of explosive bolts used to attach the shuttle to the launch pad, faulty wiring, fuel leaks, thruster failures, and foam damage from external fuel tanks.

To begin with, NASA used explosive bolts to attach the shuttle to the launch pad anchoring system before takeoff. According to the *Sentinel's* evaluation, the explosive bolts have malfunctioned and prematurely detonated in at least 16 flights, as in the case of the 2002 Atlantis launch. Fortunately, backup explosives were triggered and the shuttle was able to takeoff, but something could have gone terribly wrong. The explosive bolts have been a recurring problem throughout NASA's history, but the agency has chosen "to live with it" since they believe the shuttle will wrench itself free from the launch pad.

Additional NASA reports illustrate dozens of electrical problems due to faulty wiring. During the July 1999 launch of the Columbia shuttle, a pair of computers controlling two of Columbia's three main engines were knocked out due to electrical "arcing," and backup computers had to take over. A disaster was averted, and the shuttle had to be grounded for nearly five months. Inspections following the incident revealed damaged, chafed, and exposed wiring.

Launches have also been cancelled due to fuel leaks. NASA has been criticized for being unable to prevent highly explosive hydrogen gas leaks from the external tank, shuttle, and ground system that accumulates on the launch pad before blast off. The *Sentinel*'s research discovered that errors, malfunctions, and leaks of hydrogen occurred at least 56 times, and in 2002 tiny cracks were found in the hydrogen fuel line of the Atlantis shuttle.

The *Sentinel*'s investigation also pointed to thruster failures that could leave astronauts unable to steer a shuttle effectively. A shuttle is guided through space by 44 jet thrusters mounted on its nose and tail that allow the craft to steer through space. In many cases these failing thrusters have to be shut off due to leaks while in orbit, as in the 1995 Discovery space station mission. Much to the alarm of the Russians inside, damaged thrusters aboard the Discovery spewed hazardous fuel and had to be shut off as the craft approached the Mir space station.

All seven crew members were killed during the 2003 Columbia shuttle disaster, illustrating the consequences of NASA's inability to acknowledge and permanently fix shuttle defects. Investigators concluded that a 1.67-pound chunk of foam flew off the external tank 82 seconds after liftoff and smashed a hole in the thermal armor along Columbia's left wing, allowing hot gases to penetrate and destroy the shuttle during reentry. Furthermore, foam that insulates a shuttle's external fuel tank is regularly ripped loose during takeoff and reentry, causing damage to the craft's thermal armor. Prior to the Columbia shuttle, foam debris had damaged thermal armor in all 112 previous launches.[8]

2.3 Chemical Safety

2.3.1 The Risks of Rat Poison

Using the FOIA, researchers from the National Resources Defense Council (NRDC) were able to obtain documents that show that rat-poison companies had special access and behind-the-scenes influence over the Environmental Protection Agency (EPA) as it drew up health and safety rules for their product.[9] The pesticide industry had been fighting off or stalling regulatory initiatives designed to protect children and wildlife from becoming unintended victims of rat poison.

In August 1998, the EPA published a proposal for new child safety regulations, approving the use of rat poisons, but only if certain precautions were taken. The report found that rat poisons "pose a significant risk of accidental exposure to humans, particularly children, household pets, and non-target animals," but contended that the products should remain on the market because they helped contain disease.[10] However, the EPA contended that the poisons should only remain available if two new safeguards were implemented: adding an agent to make the poison taste more bitter and using a dye that would make it more obvious if a child accidentally ingested the poison.[11]

Three years later the EPA reversed course, electing not to include either safeguard, saying its scientists had reached a consensus that new measures would do more harm than good by making the rat poisons less effective against a creature responsible for spreading serious disease.[12] However, the documents obtained via the FOIA by the NRDC challenge this assertion and show that behind-the-scenes industry influence may have had an impact. The documents show that the EPA consulted heavily with representatives from rat-poison companies before seeking comment from opponents. The documents also suggest that "manufacturers got officials to tone down their assessment of the risks associated with rat poison."

By September 2001, the agency was finalizing a document outlining the environmental risks inherent in nine rat poisons. It had just one stage of the procedure left: sending a copy of the report to the industry for an "error only" review that was supposed to take 30 days, giving manufacturers a chance to weigh in before the public did. Over the next 15 months, according to the documents obtained by the NRDC, the agency did more than make technical corrections. At the behest of the industry, the EPA made broad changes to play down the dangers posed by rat poison, including rewriting a section about the fatal poisoning of seven deer. While refusing to meet with consumer and environmental groups, the agency held five closed-door meetings with members of the Rodenticide Registrants Task Force, whose members include a number of companies doing business in this area.

While the documents received by the NRDC demonstrate that the pesticide industry had unprecedented access to regulators, the facts suggest what effect the access had. A federal judge argued that the industry access corrupted the scientific mission of the EPA. In August 2005, U.S. District Judge Jed Rakoff ruled that the agency failed to justify its agreement with pest control companies. "In short, the EPA lacked even the proverbial 'scintilla of evidence' justifying its reversal of the requirement it had imposed, after extensive study, only a few years before," Rakoff wrote.[13]

Using the FOIA, the NRDC was able to obtain information about this incredibly important issue and bring it to the public's attention. Poison control center data indicates that in 2004 alone, more than 15,000 children under the age of six accidentally ingested rat poison.[14] Wildlife organizations contend that each year, numerous endangered animals die from ingesting rat poison that is spread outside to protect crops from rodents. Because rat poison is a blood thinner, other animals occasionally bleed to death when they consume the poison directly or eat an animal that has been killed by it.

2.3.2 Identifying the Dangers of "Safe" Pesticides

The chemical pesticides known as pyrethrins and their synthetic relatives, pyrethroids, were developed as a safer alternative to organophosphates, compounds that were derived from Nazi nerve gases. Organophosphates were commonly found in products such as Dursban, which was banned by the

EPA in 2000. The agency found that Dursban and related products posed a risk to children because of potential effects on the nervous system and brain development.[15]

In 2008, however, the Center for Public Integrity (CPI) used the FOIA to obtain an EPA database of pesticide incidents that showed these "safe" alternatives "accounted for more than 26 percent of all fatal, 'major,' and 'moderate' human incidents in the United States in 2007, up from 15 percent in 1998." The CPI analyzed the more than 90,000 "adverse-reaction" reports filed by manufacturers to the EPA and found that the supposedly "safe" pesticide compounds—found in consumer products like Hartz Dog Flea & Tick Killer and Raid Ant and Roach Killer—led the list of poisonings.[16] The database, which had never before been made public, was considered one of the "Ten Most Wanted Government Documents" by the Center for Democracy and Technology, a watchdog group.[17]

2.4 The Dangers of Certain Plastics

There has been growing concern about the safety of plastics containing phthalates, which are substances that make plastics flexible and are found in a wide variety of products used by consumers, including infant products and children's toys, packaging, flexible tubing, and some adhesives. Government researchers even found such plastics in human bodies.[18]

The effects of phthalates on human health have not been well established, but there have been some concerning studies involving animals. For example, in male rodents exposed to phthalates before or soon after birth, many rodent pups showed a variety of developmental and reproductive abnormalities, including undescended testes, feminized reproductive organs, and hypospadias (failure of the penis to form a fully closed tube). Children may be especially vulnerable to the impact of phthalates, which is particularly concerning given the fact that the substance is found in many toys and other items accessed by children and by the fact that children have a propensity for putting toys in their mouths.[19]

Even retailers recognize the risks of phthalates and are taking action on their own accord. In early 2008, Wal-Mart, Toys "R" Us, and Babies "R" Us told their suppliers that they would no longer carry products containing phthalates as of January 1, 2009.[20] This led to progress on the legislative front. Later in the year, the Senate voted 89-3 for the Consumer Product Safety Improvement Act of 2008 (the CPSIA).[21] The House passed the bill 424-1, a reflection of the national outcry over a recent rash of recalls of toys and children's products contaminated by lead and other dangerous elements. The administration objected to parts of the bill, but President George W. Bush did sign it into law in August 2008. While the measure is not perfect, it does represent a good first step in protecting society, especially children, against the health risks of phthalates and other dangerous substances.

With respect to the current discussion, the most relevant component of the CPSIA is Section 108. This section of the law establishes a prohibition on the sale of certain products containing specific phthalates. Section 108(a) provides: "Beginning on the date that is 180 days after the date of enactment of this Act, it shall be unlawful for any person to manufacture for sale, offer for sale, distribute in commerce, or import into the United States any children's toy or child care article that contains concentrations of more than 0.1 percent of di-(2-ethylhexyl) phthalate (DEHP), dibutyl phthalate (DBP), or benzyl butyl phthalate (BBP)."[22]

The provisions of the CPSIA concerning phthalates also call for the establishment of a chronic hazard advisory panel that is charged with studying the effects on children's health of all phthalates and phthalate alternatives as used in children's toys and child care articles.[23] The panel is asked to:

a. examine all of the potential health effects (including endocrine disrupting effects) of the full range of phthalates;

b. consider the potential health effects of each of these phthalates both in isolation and in combination with other phthalates;

c. examine the likely levels of children's, pregnant women's, and others' exposure to phthalates, based on a reasonable estimation of normal and foreseeable use and abuse of such products;

d. consider the cumulative effect of total exposure to phthalates, both from children's products and from other sources, such as personal care products;

e. review all relevant data, including the most recent, best-available, peer-reviewed, scientific studies of these phthalates and phthalate alternatives that employ objective data collection practices or employ other objective methods;

f. consider the health effects of phthalates not only from ingestion but also as a result of dermal, hand-to-mouth, or other exposure;

g. consider the level at which there is a reasonable certainty of no harm to children, pregnant women, or other susceptible individuals and their offspring, considering the best available science, and using sufficient safety factors to account for uncertainties regarding exposure and susceptibility of children, pregnant women, and other potentially susceptible individuals; and

h. consider possible similar health effects of phthalate alternatives used in children's toys and child care articles.

While the risks of phthalates are now receiving attention by government and industry alike, not everyone has supported a ban on the dangerous chemicals. One opponent was Exxon Mobil, which "spent a chunk of its $22 million lobbying budget in the past 18 months to try to prevent any ban," according to the *Washington Post*.[24]

For years, the NRDC had been seeking information from the Consumer Product Safety Commission (CPSC) about phthalates, especially regarding the CPSC's communication with industry about the chemicals. The NRDC filed a FOIA request in April 2007 but did not receive any information. Recently, the NRDC filed a lawsuit against the CPSC for its failure to hand over its communications, contending that the public has a right to know about them.[25] Clearly, such communications will be extremely important for determining what, if any, influence private industry has had on the failure of the CPSC to protect the public against dangerous chemicals.

3. Challenges

3.1 Overview

While the FOIA can be a useful tool for gathering information about matters that may impact personal safety, obtaining such information is not always easy. As is the case in other areas examined in this book, individuals attempting to use the FOIA to obtain information about safety concerns are likely to be troubled by delays. Delays are particularly disturbing in this area, as they affect information about dangerous products, vehicles, and other items, which when withheld can result in injuries or even death.

3.2 Defining the Appropriate Resource

While most of the challenges that are likely to be encountered in this field are similar to those encountered in other areas, there are some unique challenges to be addressed and strategies that can be employed. One challenge to overcome is determining what resource(s) to contact for the information. When facing an environmental problem, for example, one's first resource is likely to be the EPA. Likewise, when wishing to obtain information about drug issues, the Food and Drug Administration (FDA) will be an excellent initial resource. When investigating issues of safety, however, the determination of the appropriate source is less clear-cut. With respect to product safety, a useful starting point will be the CPSC, which has jurisdiction over most consumer products, from home appliances to toys to lawn mowers. However, other federal agencies have jurisdiction over certain items that may commonly be considered consumer products. For example, the Department of Transportation regulates automobiles, trucks, and motorcycles, and the FDA regulates products such as food, drugs, and cosmetics. Table 1 summarizes resources for information about particular consumer products.

Even within the CPSC, it will be helpful if you have a sense of the specific databases that may house the particular information you want to obtain. If you are able to file a specific request, even identifying particular databases that are to be consulted, you may be able to receive more of the information that you are seeking. The CPSC operates several essential databases, as follows:

National Electronic Injury Surveillance System (NEISS). This database contains vast quantities of occurrences and incidents associated with any of

Product/Issue	Government Agency	Web site
Motor vehicle, motor vehicle equipment, and car seat performance in protecting children when riding in on-road vehicle	National Highway Traffic Safety Administration, within the Department of Transportation	www.nhtsa.dot.gov
Food, drugs, cosmetics, radiation, medical devices, and veterinary medicines	Food and Drug Administration	www.fda.gov
Pesticides, rodenticides, fungicides	Environmental Protection Agency	www.epa.gov
Boats and other watercraft (including personal watercraft)	United States Coast Guard	www.uscg.mil
Work-related incidents	Occupational Safety and Health Administration, within the Department of Labor National Institute for Occupational Safety and Health, within the Centers for Disease Control and Prevention, Department of Health and Human Services	www.osha.gov www.cdc.gov/niosh/
Deceptive or unfair trade practices	Federal Trade Commission	www.ftc.gov
Firearms	Bureau of Alcohol, Tobacco and Firearms, within the Department of the Treasury	www.atf.treas.gov
Chemical Safety	U.S. Chemical Safety and Hazard Investigation Board	www.chemsafety.gov

hundreds of consumer products. If you want to see how the information is stored or obtain a complete list of products in the database, ask CPSC for a copy of the NEISS Coding Manual. If you are aware of the parametric codes, you can be much more precise when asking the CPSC for what you require. This, in turn, is likely to save you much more time in the long run.

Death Certificate File. This is a database of death certificates (personal names removed) for fatal injuries associated with nearly any product. These records can help to add details to the dangers you may want to describe.

In Depth Investigation File (INDP). This file contains lengthy investigations of specific cases associated with nearly any product.

Injury/Potential Injury Incident File (IPII). This file lists more data on injuries and potential injuries associated with nearly any product you designate.

Regulated Product Comprehensive Plans. These plans are published by CPSC for any product for which regulatory or industry volunteered action is taken.

Being able to identify one or more relevant databases may facilitate and speed up your research.

4. Conclusion

The role of the FOIA in protecting safety cannot be understated. Unfortunately, we cannot rely fully upon government and/or industry to keep us aware of products and services that may be dangerous. The work of journalists and advocacy groups acting in the public interest can improve our knowledge about the safety of various goods and services, such as consumer products, chemicals, and methods of transportation. At the same time, as in other areas analyzed in this book, ordinary citizens can also use the FOIA as a means of obtaining information about issues impacting their safety.

Notes

1. Beverley Lumpkin, "Corps of Engineers Lists 122 Levees at Risk from Coast to Coast," *Associated Press*, February 2, 2007.

2. Christian Lowe, "Marine Corps Issued Flawed Armor," *Marine Corps Times*, May 9, 2005.

3. Gary Stoller, "Doomed Plane's Gaming System Exposes Holes in FAA Oversight," *USA Today*, February 16, 2003, available at http://www.usatoday.com/money/biztravel/2003-02-16-swissair-investigation_x.htm (last visited November 22, 2008).

4. Alan C. Miller and Kevin Sack, "The Vertical Vision/Part I: The Widow Maker," *The Los Angeles Times*, December 15, 2002.

5. Alan C. Miller and Kevin Sack, "Congressional Hearings Will Focus on Marine Harrier Jet," *The Los Angeles Times*, January 8, 2003, available at http://www.latimes.com/news/nationworld/nation/la-na-harrier8jan08,0,5634215.story (last visited November 22, 2008).

6. Alan C. Miller and Kevin Sack, "Accident-Prone Harrier Jet Faces Further Investigation," *The Los Angeles Times*, January 21, 2003, available at http://www.latimes.com/news/nationworld/nation/la-na-harrier21jan21,0,3075887.story (last visited November 22, 2008).

7. Alan C. Miller and Kevin Sack, "North Carolina Crash Is Second in a Month for Marine Harrier Jet," *The Los Angeles Times*, July 16, 2005, available at http://www.latimes.com/news/nationworld/nation/la-na-harrier8jan08,0,5634215.story (last visited November 22, 2008).

8. Kevin Spear and Jim Leusner, "Critical Flaws in Shuttles Loom as Potential Disaster," *Orlando Sentinel*, August 17, 2003, available at (last visited November 22, 2008).

9. Juliet Eilperin, "Rat-Poison Makers Stall Safety Rules; EPA Had Drafted Regulations To Protect Children, Animals," *Washington Post*, April 15, 2004, at A03.

10. *Id.*

11. Environmental Protection Agency, "EPA Takes Action to Reduce Accidental Exposures to Rat Poisons," October 16, 1998, available at http://yosemite.epa.gov/opa/admpress.nsf/b1ab9f485b098972852562e7004dc686/81eac9505e72832a85 25669f0074f188?OpenDocument (last visited November 22, 2008).

12. Environmental Protection Agency, "Amendment to the Rodenticide Cluster and Zinc Phosphide Reregistration Eligibility Decision (RED) Documents," November 28, 2001, available at http://www.epa.gov/EPA-PEST/2001/November/Day-28/p29557.htm (last visited November 22, 2008).

13. Juliet Eilperin, "Judge Rebukes EPA on Rat Poison Reversal," *The Washington Post*, August 9, 2005, available at http://www.washingtonpost.com/wp-dyn/content/article/2005/08/08/AR2005080801225.html (last visited November 22, 2008).

14. *Id.*

15. "EPA Bans Pesticide Dursban, Says Alternatives Available," CNN.com June 8, 2000, available at http://archives.cnn.com/2000/HEALTH/06/08/dursban.ban.02/index.html (available at November 22, 2008).

16. M. B. Pell and Jim Morris, " 'Safe' Pesticides Now First in Poisonings," The Center for Public Integrity, July 30, 2008, available at http://www.public integrity.org/investigations/pesticides/pages/introduction (last visited November 4, 2008).

17. Center for Democracy and Technology, "Ten Most Wanted Government Documents," available at http://www.cdt.org/righttoknow/10mostwanted/ (last visited November 4, 2008).

18. Manori J. Silva, Dana B. Barr, John A. Reidy, Nicole A. Malek, Carolyn C. Hodge, Samuel P. Caudill, John W. Brock, Larry L. Needham, and Antonia M. Calafat, "Urinary Levels of Seven Phthalate Metabolites in the U.S. Population from the National Health and Nutrition Examination Survey (NHANES) 1999–2000," *Environmental Health Perspectives*, March 2004, available at http://www.ehponline.org/members/2003/6723/6723.html (last visited November 5, 2008).

19. Environment and Human Health Inc., "Plastics That May be Harmful to Children and Reproductive Health, June 12, 2008," available at http://www.ehhi.org/reports/plastics/ehhi_plastics_report_2008.pdf (last visited November 22, 2008).

20. Lyndsey Layton, "Lawmakers Agree to Ban Toxins in Children's Items," *The Washington Post*, July 29, 2008, available at http://www.washingtonpost.com/wp-dyn/content/article/2008/07/28/AR2008072802586.html (last visited November 22, 2008).

21. Consumer Product Safety Improvement Act of 2008, Public Law No: 110-314.

22. *Id.* at Section 108(a).

23. *Id.* at Section 108(b)(2).

24. Layton, *supra* note 20.

25. Jennifer Sass, "NRDC Sues Consumer Product Safety Commission for Withholding Industry Correspondence," NRDC Switchboard, July 30, 2008, available at http://switchboard.nrdc.org/blogs/jsass/nrdc_sues_consumer_product_saf.html (last visited November 22, 2008).

Chapter Six

Fighting Corruption and Government Waste with Freedom of Information

Every thing secret degenerates, even the administration of justice; nothing is safe that does not show it can bear discussion and publicity.

—Lord Acton

1. Overview

In this chapter, attention shifts to examining the impact that the FOIA has had in achieving important revelations about government waste and corruption. Since its entry into force, the FOIA has been a key instrument in helping to expose governmental waste and corruption and other malfeasance by government actors. Using the FOIA, various public interest groups, journalists, and individuals have brought public attention to wasteful and otherwise questionable governmental spending. For example, researchers and organizations have used the FOIA to highlight suspect government spending on matters such as unnecessary road-building and timber giveaways,[1] the awarding of defense and reconstruction contracts following the Iraq war[2], and the antitrust litigation against Microsoft.[3] The FOIA has also helped to expose various instances of misconduct and crime by law enforcement and other representatives of government.

This chapter shows how the FOIA and other open government initiatives help to expose government corruption, waste, and malfeasance and thereby also limit it in the future. Using actual examples, it also shows how researchers have used freedom of information laws to obtain important details about significant acts of impropriety undertaken by various government actors. Lastly, it discusses the obstacles that researchers, activists, and others seeking information about issues in this area may encounter and offers suggestions on how to overcome or mitigate some of those obstacles.

2. Notable Revelations

2.1 Government Waste and Loss

Despite certain obstacles that have been highlighted in this book and will be further discussed in this chapter, the FOIA has been instrumental in helping researchers uncover important data about government waste. This kind of information is of great importance to the public. When the government acts wasteful with, or otherwise mismanages, tax dollars that are entrusted to it, the public loses out, as such funds could have been directed to programs or individuals in need—or perhaps even refunded to taxpayers. In short, when the government engages in such activity, it betrays the public trust. Accordingly, it is of the utmost importance that journalists and other researchers have the ability to use the FOIA and other information-access laws to obtain details about the government's conduct in this area. When journalists and others are able to bring these issues to light, those who are responsible can be called to task and steps can be taken to ward off further waste.

2.1.1 Loss of Weapons

The press is replete with examples proving that government can be very poor at managing property, funds, and other resources. For example, documents obtained from the Pentagon by the *St. Petersburg Times* pursuant to a FOIA request indicate that since the 1991 Persian Gulf War, thousands of pounds of explosives; hundreds of mines, mortars, grenades, and firearms, and dozens of rockets and artillery rounds have been lost or stolen from U.S. stockpiles and have possibly been misused. Losses were reported throughout the military, with the exception of the Air Force. The Army reported the most losses, releasing 223 incident reports. The Navy and Marines each made public 15 reports of lost munitions, and the Department of Defense released four.

Oversight was so lax at a few bases that it was easy to steal almost anything designed to cause death or serious battlefield injuries; in one case, classified guidance systems for three Stinger missiles disappeared somewhere between Fort Bliss, Texas, and Tucson, Arizona, in 1998 or 1999. The documents also revealed that more than half of the thefts were inside jobs involving military personnel, National Guardsmen, or civilian employees of the military. This story has a clear significance far beyond the value of the missing items (and taxpayer money). Given the lethal nature of the misplaced items, their loss raises serious concerns about public safety.[4]

A more recent report revealed that over a five-year period, the Bureau of Alcohol, Tobacco, Firearms and Explosives (ATF) lost 76 weapons and hundreds of laptops that contained sensitive information.[5] A Justice Department report, spurred by a regular audit of the ATF, also revealed that the Bureau's rate of loss for weapons was nearly double that of other agencies, such as the FBI and the DEA.

2.1.2 Millions Lost at NASA

The military has not been the only part of government that has been losing valuable property. Data gathered through the FOIA by a San Antonio TV station revealed that between 1998 and 2002, NASA lost about $34 million in government property. Among the lost or missing property: about 200 computers, an ice machine valued at $1,000, a $30,000 mock-up of an international space station module and a $69,000 stand to support it; an optical disk drive valued at $170,000; a spectrum analyzer worth nearly $23,000, and a $300,000 robot. The equipment losses occurred throughout NASA's 10 centers, but Maryland's Goddard Space Flight Center led the pack with $16.8 million lost during the period.

The information uncovered by this research brought much attention to the issue of waste at NASA and may have applied enough public pressure for the agency to focus on tracking down misplaced items and implementing measures to minimize the risk of future loss. According to the *Houston Chronicle*, in the two years after the major loss was revealed, NASA's loss rate fell back below the goal of 0.5 percent. In addition, many of the items that were reported as missing subsequently turned up after NASA employees tracked them down or verified incorrect paperwork.[6]

2.2 Hurricane Fraud

Unfortunately, history suggests that there is a strong tendency for fraud to occur after hurricanes and other natural disasters. In the chaos and devastation that follow such events, those with nefarious and/or profit-seeking intent may attempt to take advantage of the situation. Journalists using the FOIA have been very effective in revealing information about such fraudulent acts. The horror of the Katrina debacle is still fresh in the minds of many, when the Federal Emergency Management Agency (FEMA) was roundly criticized for its actions during the hurricane. FEMA was also found to have issued between $600 million and $1.4 billion worth of improper or fraudulent disaster assistance payments for Hurricanes Katrina and Rita, which was 16 percent of the total payout of more than $6 billion at the time.[7] However, FEMA's poor track record with hurricane response predates Katrina by many years.

During Labor Day weekend 2004, Hurricane Frances hit the Florida coast about 100 miles north of Miami-Dade County, but that didn't stop the federal government from approving $31 million in claims for that county's residents. Using the FOIA, journalists from Florida's *Sun-Sentinel* found that FEMA approved claims for new furniture, clothes, televisions, microwaves, refrigerators, cars, and even funerals, despite the fact that the Medical Examiner recorded no deaths there resulting from the hurricane.[8] The *Sun-Sentinel*'s reporting led to a Senate investigation, a change in FEMA procedures, and the indictment of more than a dozen Miami-Dade residents on charges of fraudulently obtaining FEMA money.[9]

Similarly fraudulent activity occurred during prior hurricanes. Using FOIA requests, the *Washington Post* learned that dozens of wealthy beach towns and coastal communities that sustained little damage from 2003's Hurricane Isabel received millions of dollars in taxpayer-funded relief from FEMA. The *Post* reported that while some of the money paid for emergency worker overtime and debris clearing, it also funded tennis court lights, bicycle path repairs, and, alarmingly, $15 million worth of sand.[10]

2.3 Waste in the Medicare System

In 2005, reporters with the *Washington Post* used the FOIA to conduct an in-depth, long-term investigation into the provision, quality, and efficiency of Medicare services. The reporters obtained records of hospital visits by Medicare patients and additional data, ultimately revealing that Medicare officials knew of a number of health care facilities that were out of compliance with applicable requirements and, further, that conditions at some facilities put patients at serious risk.

For example, at Palm Beach Gardens Medical Center, a Florida hospital that handles many Medicare patients, there was a high rate of recurring infection in heart patients. "State inspectors in 2002 found 'massive post operative infections' in the heart unit, requiring patients to undergo more surgery and lengthy hospital stays," the *Post* reported. "In a four-year period, 106 heart patients at Palm Beach Gardens developed infections after surgery, according to lawsuits and government records." While this alone is disconcerting, the newspaper showed that such recurring infections actually benefited the hospital, which was reimbursed equally for new cases and for patients readmitted with complications from medical errors or poor care. "Under Medicare's rules, each time a patient comes back for another treatment, a hospital qualifies for an additional payment," the *Post* noted. "In effect, Palm Beach Gardens was paid a bonus for its mistakes."

This report provided further evidence for Medicare's critics, who have argued that one of the main problems with the system is that it provides incentives for providers to charge for additional services and to focus on receiving greater payments, rather than on patient needs and prevention. As a result of the research and other studies, Medicare began to work on ways to improve the system and began requiring hospitals to report on their performance. Clearly, the significance of the research conducted by this journalist using the FOIA went far beyond highlighting the economic loss that was sustained by the government from waste and mismanagement in the Medicare system. By highlighting patients who were subject to unclean environments that fostered recurrent infection, the *Post* also helped highlight an important public health concern.[11]

2.4 Other Instances of Loss and Mismanagement

The FOIA has been a very effective tool for uncovering details regarding mismanaged funds. In many instances, the mismanagement of such funds has resulted in poor communities being deprived of money that was to be allotted to them. This section examines some notable examples.

2.4.1 Mismanagement Post 9/11

As we saw earlier in the chapter, fraud and hurricanes have a sordid shared history, but sadly it seems that fraud and mismanagement follows many other major tragedies as well. History is replete with many instances when government funds intended for recovery were used for the benefit of those not impacted by the disaster. This was the case with the 9/11 terrorist attacks. The *Associated Press*, for example, used the FOIA to demonstrate that economic-recovery money intended for small businesses was mismanaged, with businesses far-removed from New York City and Washington, D.C. receiving the vast majority of the $5 billion in funds. "While some at New York's Ground Zero couldn't get assistance they desperately sought, companies far removed from the devastation—a South Dakota country radio station, a Virgin Islands perfume shop, a Utah dog boutique, and more than 100 Dunkin' Donuts and Subway sandwich shops—had no problem securing the loans," the *Associated Press* reported. Of the 19,000 loans approved by the Small Business Administration (SBA) for the government's two recovery programs, fewer than 11 percent went to companies in New York and Washington. The report found several examples of small businesses that received the loans unknowingly, and government officials told the *Associated Press* that they believed banks assigned loans to the terror relief program without telling borrowers.[12]

2.4.2 Buffalo's Poor Lose Out on $556 Million in Federal Community Grants

Oftentimes it is society's most vulnerable who suffer from government waste or fraud, whether it is the hurricane victim, the sick patient, or the poor. These people put a certain amount of faith in the government to help them, and the government usually obliges. However, corruption, fraud, or waste somewhere along the way often trips things up.

Such was the case in Buffalo, a poor city abandoned by industry that receives a substantial amount of government aid for its residents. Using the FOIA, the *Buffalo News* obtained documents that showed that some $556 million in federal community grant money received by the city over 30 years to revitalize neighborhoods and combat poverty was not spent to improve neighborhoods, but rather "frittered away" by City Hall "through parochial politics and bureaucratic ineptitude." Among other things, the money was used to pay City Hall employees' salaries, repay bad loans, restore an arcade, and develop an industrial park.[13]

In breaking this story, the *Buffalo News* did far more than just show how federal funds are misused. Rather, using the FOIA, the *News* broke a major scandal and showed how the poor were being deprived of money that was specifically dedicated to them. At the time, the city received more federal Community Development Block Grant aid per resident than all but one city in the country because of its pervasive poverty, but there was little evidence of that money on the city's streets. "When you consider the millions and millions of dollars that have flowed into this city over the years and you look at the conditions in the neighborhoods, it's a disgrace," the director of the University of Buffalo's Center for Urban Studies told the *News*. "It's the shame of this city."

Revelations such as this are extraordinarily important. The community was granted federal funds because the town was populated with people who were in great need of such money. However, the people who needed this money never benefited from it. When journalists and activists are able to use freedom of information laws to shed light on such waste and abuse, it may help in two ways: It may help pressure the local authorities who are receiving such funds to get their act together, and it may also prevent other communities from engaging in such waste.

2.5 Use of Paid Pundits

In 2005, the FOIA was instrumental in exposing that a number of writers, commentators, and freelance journalists were on the Bush administration payroll. The scandal started when *USA Today* used the FOIA to obtain a contract that showed prominent pundit Armstrong Williams had been paid $240,000 by the Department of Education to promote the No Child Left Behind Act[14] (NCLB) on his nationally-syndicated TV show and to urge other black journalists to also champion the act.[15] This was part of the Bush administration's effort to build support in the black community for the controversial legislation. Over the next weeks and months, several other writers and commentators were revealed to be on the Bush administration payroll, including syndicated columnists Maggie Gallagher[16] and Michael

McManus[17] and freelance writer Dave Smith, who was paid by the USDA to tout federal programs in magazine articles.[18] None of the published articles by any of the journalists disclosed that they had been paid by the federal government. Accordingly, there was no reason for anyone reading the articles to have assumed that they were anything other than neutral new stories. Unfortunately, given the financial consideration that was paid to these authors, this was not the case.

2.6 Misconduct by Law Enforcement

2.6.1 Overview

Journalists, community activists, and other individuals have used the FOIA and other freedom of information laws to obtain information about misconduct by law enforcement authorities. The following sections examine some notable examples in this area.

2.6.2 Wrongful Arrests and/or Imprisonments

In 2005, students at New York University School of Law released a study of federal immigration law enforcement for the Migration Policy Institute that used data uncovered via the FOIA to reveal that thousands of people had been wrongly identified as immigration violators. Data from the National Crime Information Center database between 2002 and 2004 showed that 42 percent of people who had been identified as immigration law violators were later determined to be "false positives," meaning that the Department of Homeland Security was subsequently unable to confirm that the identified individuals had indeed violated any immigration laws. The report was significant in that it provided the first public glimpse of how a new post-9/11 crime policy was affecting on-the-ground policing strategies across the country, and it offered a ringing example of how new tools implemented to fight terrorism were impacting the lives of many Americans.[19]

2.6.3 Uncovering Cover-Ups

The FOIA has been instrumental in uncovering information about various cover-ups. As one example, evidence gathered from documents obtained from the Department of Justice (DOJ) through the FOIA helped overturn the conviction of former Central Intelligence Agency (CIA) operative Edwin Wilson in 2003. Wilson was convicted in 1983 of arms dealing with Libya, but he claimed the activities were part of his cover. The CIA and the DOJ both claimed in court that this was not true, and that Wilson "was not asked or requested, directly or indirectly, to perform or provide services, directly or indirectly, for CIA" after his retirement in 1971. But official documents told a different story, showing that both agencies knew about Wilson's work post-retirement and that they had offered false testimony in his trial. Wilson himself amassed these documents over the years by filing many FOIA requests, and for his efforts, a federal judge in Houston overturned his conviction after 20 years, stating that "one would have to work hard to conceive of a more fundamentally unfair process with a consequentially unreliable result than the fabrication of false data by the government, under oath by a government official, presented knowingly by the prosecutor in the courtroom with the express approval of his superiors in Washington."[20]

2.6.4 Unlawful FBI Activities

FOIA documents obtained by the *San Francisco Chronicle* in 2002 after a 17-year legal battle showed the FBI had conducted unlawful intelligence activities at the University of California (Berkeley), the nation's largest public university, in the 1950s and 1960s. The activities included covert support for Ronald Reagan's first successful campaign for state governor, during which he had pledged to suppress student protests.[21] According to the documents, the FBI also secretly campaigned to get University of California at Berkeley President Clark Kerr fired, conspired with the director of the CIA to pressure the university's Board of Regents to "eliminate" liberal professors, mounted a covert operation to manipulate public opinion, and infiltrated agent provocateurs into nonviolent student dissent groups. The documents also showed that FBI Director J. Edgar Hoover maintained a secret and unauthorized "Security Index," which listed citizens deemed potentially dangerous to national security who would be detained without warrant during a national emergency.[22]

The *Chronicle* report prompted an apology from the FBI director at the time, Robert Mueller, who called the Bureau's actions "wrong and anti-democratic."[23] It also prompted an internal investigation into whether or not the FBI stonewalled the *Chronicle* reporter. Over the course of the 17 years the paper tried to get the documents, the FBI spent more than $1 million fighting three lawsuits filed under the FOIA by the reporter. Mueller said he ordered the FBI's Records Management Division "to determine whether the FBI redacted information in order to shield the FBI from embarrassment or to cover up unlawful activities."[24]

While this was an incredible revelation, showing the breadth and depth of a decades-long FBI campaign, as well as a seemingly coordinated effort to stonewall the press, it was clearly not the only instance where the Bureau was identified as engaging in questionable monitoring activities. More recently, the American Civil Liberties Union (ACLU) obtained hundreds of pages of documents using the FOIA that showed the FBI had gathered information about antiwar and environmental protestors and other activists in Colorado and other states. The documents showed that the monitoring program, undertaken as part of the fight against terrorism, encompassed a wide range of different activist groups. As one example, the documents revealed that the FBI had opened an inquiry into environmental activists planning a lumber industry protest because an activist training camp was to be held on "nonviolent methods of forest defense."[25]

2.6.5 Exposing Taser Dangers

A massive 2006 study by journalists and students in Texas revealed the dangers of Tasers, electrical pulse weapons that are increasingly used by police. Journalists from *Fort Worth Weekly* and graduate students issued information access requests under the state's Public Information Act[26] to 254 separate sheriff's offices around Texas and found that many officers were not waiting for a possible life-or-death crisis before using a Taser against a suspect. Rather, officers were more likely to use the weapon as "a first-choice persuader—like a high-tech baton."

The story's revelations are particularly troubling given the risks and dangers of the use of Tasers, which the United Nations Committee Against Torture said "constituted a form of torture" in 2007.[27] The Taser problem is especially prevalent in Texas. Figures published in the *Weekly* showed that Texas accounted for 12 of the approximately 170 known Taser-related deaths between 2001 and 2006. Although Tasers are often thought of as being nonlethal, they have been associated with a number of deaths, often when they are used against victims who are on drugs.

While the project can certainly be considered an information freedom success story, it also shows the difficulty that journalists and citizens face in attempting to wrangle information from governments, especially from smaller offices. "About a fourth of the state's 254 sheriff's offices failed to respond at all to the records requests" issued by the students, the *Weekly* reported. What's more, some sheriff's offices "said they could not find the records requested, or they demanded hundreds or thousands of dollars for records that other law enforcement officials provided free of charge."[28]

2.7 Mismanagement of the Foster Care System

Children who are in the government-run foster care system are another example of an extremely vulnerable group. While government policies and actions should protect these wards of the state, several revelations prompted by the use of the FOIA show this isn't always the case.

In 2003, the Illinois Department of Children and Family Services (DCFS) was forced to admit that 462 children had been "lost" in the foster care system after the *Chicago Sun-Times* filed a FOIA request. Interestingly, the number initially given by DCFS to the newspaper was 214 children missing, but a task force set up to investigate found, among other things, that officials and staff at DCFS had sought to cover up the larger number by altering their record-keeping.[29]

A few years later, the *Orange County Register* spent more than a year litigating in Juvenile Court to gain access to information regarding children who died since January 2000 and who had been under the Court's protection. Orange County fought to keep the details under wraps, citing confidentiality issues and a "chilling effect" such information would have on social workers who are expected to candidly evaluate what went wrong in case files.[30]

When a judge finally ruled to release the documents to the newspaper in 2006, the *Register* found that 23 abused or neglected children under the Court's protection died since 2000, with the majority of the deaths being of natural causes. However, others died by accident, suicide, or abuse, and many had been visited repeatedly by social workers before dying.[31]

In the fall of 2006, two different reporters at the *Cincinnati Enquirer* requested records relating to foster providers from the Ohio Department of Jobs and Family Services (ODJFS). One reporter was requesting a full database of foster care providers, while another was petitioning for the records of one specific provider who was accused of molesting two foster children in his care. The requests came on the heels of a highly publicized case of a three-year-old foster child who died when his foster parents left him tied up in a closet while they took a weekend trip to Kentucky.[32]

However, ODJFS denied both requests, arguing that those were not public records. According to court documents, ODJFS counsel told the reporter seeking the database that the paper was welcome to sue if it disagreed, noting that he "believe[d] the Department will fight it and we will win, and you can have that precedent on the books."[33] The paper did sue in December 2006, and 16 months later the Ohio Supreme Court sided with the *Enquirer*, ruling that the Ohio Public Records Act entitled the paper to the names and addresses of foster parents.[34]

The paper's victory was bittersweet, though, as legislation passed a few months earlier declared that identifying information about foster providers was confidential, only to be released when a provider is charged with a crime or loses his certification.

2.8 Undue Influence by the Government

In January 2002, New York's *Daily News* obtained documents from the Department of Energy revealing that Vice President Dick Cheney had tried to help Texas-based energy giant Enron collect a $64 million debt from an energy project in India by raising the subject with an Indian political leader during a Washington, D.C., meeting. This is significant because the White House had maintained that neither the President nor the Vice President bestowed any special favors and/or concessions upon the now-bankrupt Enron.[35] Significantly, Enron's founder had contributed more than $600,000 to President Bush's political campaigns over the years, and a report by Rep. Henry Waxman (D-Calif.) charged that the Bush administration's energy plan, masterminded by Cheney, included 17 corporate welfare give-aways aimed at helping Enron. Cheney's task force on the energy plan met with Enron officials six times while crafting the strategy.[36]

3. Challenges

Gathering information about government waste and corruption can be challenging. Logically, this is exactly the kind of information that government agencies may be less than inclined to share with information seekers. When seeking information about issues concerning government corruption, waste, mismanagement, and other improper actions, one should be prepared for delays and possible claims of exemptions. In some cases, litigation may be required to obtain the requested information. Nonetheless, as the examples discussed herein illustrate, it is possible to obtain information about these issues using the FOIA and other freedom of information laws.

4. Conclusion

Government corruption, waste, and mismanagement remain a serious problem for taxpayers and our society in general. Furthermore, as demonstrated in this chapter, government loss and mismanagement can also result in risks to public health and safety. The important revelations made possible by virtue of the FOIA, some examples of which were discussed herein, emphasize the need to protect, defend, and use the FOIA vigorously.

Chapter Seven examines the impact that the FOIA has had on efforts to protect human rights and civil liberties. It also shows the challenges that researchers face when attempting to acquire information about such pressing issues and make suggestions for a means to overcome these challenges.

Notes

1. Taxpayers for Common Sense, "Road Woes at the Forest Service," March 29, 2002, available at http://www.taxpayer.net/search_by_tag.php?action=view& proj_id=323&tag=Forest%20Service&type=Project (last visited November 17, 2008).

2. James Cox, "Study: Bush Donors Rake in Contracts," *USA Today*, October 30, 2003, available at http://www.usatoday.com/money/companies/2003-10-30-contracts_x.htm (last visited November 17, 2008).

3. Joel Brinkley, "U.S. Versus Microsoft: The Reaction," *The New York Times*, November 7, 1999, available at http://query.nytimes.com/gst/fullpage.html? res=9F06E5DC143AF934A35752C1A96F958260 (last visited November 17, 2008).

4. Sydney P. Freedberg and Connie Humburg, "Wandering Weapons: America's Lax Arsenal," *St. Petersburg Times*, May 11, 2003, available at http://www .sptimes.com/2003/05/11/Worldandnation/Wandering_weapons__Am.shtml (last visited October 13, 2008).

5. Holly Watt, "ATF Lost Guns, Computers," *The Washington Post*, September 18, 2008, available at http://www.washingtonpost.com/wp-dyn/content/article/ 2008/09/17/AR2008091703662.html (last visited November 15, 2008).

6. Patty Reinert, "NASA Can't Find Millions in Property," *The Houston Chronicle*, February 27, 2004.

7. US Government Accountability Office, "Hurricanes Katrina and Rita Disaster Relief," June 14, 2006, available at http://www.gao.gov/cgi-bin/getrpt?GAO-06-844T (last visited November 15, 2008).

8. Sun-Sentinel Investigation: FEMA, *Sun-Sentinel*, available at http://www.sun-sentinel.com/news/sfl-femacoverage,0,6697347.storygallery?coll=sfla-news-utility (visited August 4, 2008).

9. Sally Kestin and Megan O'Matz, "FEMA Disaster Aid Operations Tightened After Frances," *Sun-Sentinel*, August 6, 2005, available at http://www.sun-sentinel. com/news/local/southflorida/sfl-fema06aug06,0,4025655.story (last visited November 13, 2008).

10. Gilbert M. Gaul, "Emergency Funds Spent to Replace Beach Sand," *The Washington Post*, May 30, 2004, available at http://www.washingtonpost.com/ wp-dyn/articles/A1111-2004May29.html (last visited August 5, 2008).

11. Gilbert Gaul, "Inefficient Spending Plagues Medicare," *The Washington Post*, July 24, 2005.

12. "9/11 Recovery Loans Went to Many Far From Attacks," *Associated Press*, September 9, 2005, available at: http://www.sptimes.com/2005/09/09/ Worldandnation/911_recovery_loans_we.shtml (last visited November 17, 2008).

13. James Heaney, "The Half-Billion-Dollar Bust," *Buffalo News*, November 14, 2004, at A01.

14. No Child Left Behind Act of 2002, U.S. Public Law 107-110 (2002).

15. Greg Toppo, "Education Dept. Paid Commentator to Promote Law," *USA Today*, January 7, 2005, available at http://www.usatoday.com/news/washington/ 2005-01-06-williams-whitehouse_x.htm (last visited August 31, 2008).

16. Howard Kurtz, "Writer Backing Bush Plan Had Gotten Federal Contract," *The Washington Post*, January 26, 2005, available at http://www.washingtonpost .com/wp-dyn/articles/A36545-2005Jan25.html (last visited November 13, 2008).

17. Jim Drinkard and Mark Memmott, "HHS Says It Paid Columnist for Help," *USA Today*, January 27, 2005, available at http://www.usatoday.com/news/ washington/2005-01-27-hhs_x.htm (last visited November 13, 2008).

18. Christopher Lee, "USDA Paid Freelance Writer $7,500 for Articles," *The Washington Post*, May 11, 2005, available at http://www.washingtonpost.com/ wp-dyn/content/article/2005/05/10/AR2005051001593.html (last visited August 30, 2008).

19. New York University School of Law and the Migration Policy Institute, Blurring the Lines: A Profile of State and Local Police Enforcement of Immigration Law Using the National Crime Information Center Database, 2002–2004, December 2005, available at http://www.migrationpolicy.org/pubs/MPI_report _Blurring_the_Lines_120805.pdf (last visited November 15, 2008).

20. Dana Priest, "False Evidence Cited in Overturning Arms Dealer's Case," *The Washington Post*, October 30, 2003.

21. Seth Rosenfeld, "Reagan, Hoover and the Red Scare," *San Francisco Chronicle*, June 9, 2002, available at http://www.sfgate.com/cgi-bin/article.cgi?f=/chronicle/archive/2002/06/09/MNCFINTRO.DTL (last visited November 15, 2008).

22. Seth Rosenfeld, "Feinstein Demands Answers from FBI," *San Francisco Chronicle*, June 23, 2002, available at http://www.sfgate.com/cgi-bin/article.cgi?file=/c/a/2002/06/23/MN135007.DTL (last visited November 15, 2008).

23. Seth Rosenfeld, "FBI Chief Admits '60s Spying on UC 'Wrong,' " *San Francisco Chronicle*, February 16, 2003, available at http://www.sfgate.com/cgi-bin/article.cgi?f=/c/a/2003/02/16/MN162401.DTL (last visited November 15, 2008).

24. "Reynolds Holding, Inquiry into FBI's Conduct," *San Francisco Chronicle*, February 16, 2003, available at http://www.sfgate.com/cgi-bin/article.cgi?f=/chronicle/a/2003/02/16/MN8819.DTL (last visited November 15, 2008).

25. Nicolas Riccardi, "FBI Keeps Watch on Activists," *Los Angeles Times*, March 27, 2006, available at http://articles.latimes.com/2006/mar/27/nation/na-fbi27 (last visited November 15, 2008).

26. The Public Information Act, Texas Government Code, Chapter 552 (1993).

27. The United Nations Office at Geneva, Committee Against Torture Concludes Thirty-Ninth Session, November 23, 2007, available at http://www.unog.ch/unog/website/news_media.nsf/(httpNewsByYear_en)/D3DD9DE87B278A87C125739-C0054A81C?OpenDocument (last visited November 15, 2008).

28. "A Stunning Toll," *Fort Worth Weekly*, March 8, 2006, available at: http://www.fwweekly.com/content.asp?article=3743 (last visited September 24, 2008).

29. Chris Fusco, "Number of Missing DCFS Wards Doubles," *Chicago Sun-Times*, April 29, 2003.

30. Jenifer B. McKim, "County fights release of details," *Orange County Register*, September 15, 2006, available at http://www.ocregister.com/ocregister/news/article_1274522.php (last visited November 16, 2008).

31. Jenifer B. McKim, "Lost Lives," *Orange County Register*, September 15, 2006, available at http://www.ocregister.com/ocregister/news/article_1274888.php (last visited November 16, 2008).

32. Randy Ludlow, "Legislators Move More Records Off Table," *Columbus Dispatch*, January 31, 2008, available at http://blog.dispatch.com/know/2008/01/lawmakers_moving_more_records.shtml (last visited November 16, 2008).

33. *State, Ex Rel. The Cincinnati Enquirer v. Barbara Riley*, Memorandum In Support Of Complaint For Writ Of Mandamus, Case 06-2239, available at; http://www.sconet.state.oh.us/tempx/584576.pdf.

34. Randy Ludlow, "Foster Parent Records Were Public, Court Rules," *Columbus Dispatch*, April 17, 2008, available at http://blog.dispatch.com/know/2008/04/foster_parent_records_were_public_court_rules.shtml#more (last visited November 16, 2008).

35. Timothy J. Burger, "Veep Tried to Aid Firm: Key Role in India Debt Row," (New York) *Daily News*, January 18, 2002, available at http://www.nydaily

news.com/archives/news/2002/01/18/2002-01-18_veep_tried_to_aid_firm_key _r.html (last visited November 17, 2008).

36. Kenneth R. Bazinet, "Veep Tried to Aid Firm: Prez Raps Probes of Enron," (New York) *Daily News*, January 18, 2002, available at http://www.nydaily news.com/archives/news/2002/01/18/2002-01-18_veep_tried_to_aid_firm _prez_.html (last visited November 17, 2008).

Chapter Seven

Protecting Human Rights and Civil Liberties with Freedom of Information

Secrecy, being an instrument of conspiracy, ought never to be the system of a regular government.

—Jeremy Bentham

1. Introduction

In this chapter, attention is directed to how the FOIA has been used and can be used to obtain information on human rights and civil liberties. It discusses examples of where individuals have used the FOIA to gather data about very significant issues impacting individual rights and liberties, and it comments upon the challenges that people may face when attempting to gather information about these highly controversial issues.

2. Notable Revelations

2.1 Overview

The FOIA has been an effective mechanism for securing the disclosure of important data regarding human rights violations and other instances of governmental abuse. The few examples discussed in this chapter are but a mere illustrative selection of cases where freedom-of-information laws led to the revelation of tremendous, history-altering facts. On the Web site of George Washington University's National Security Archive[1] you can read Central

Intelligence Agency (CIA) manuals from the 1960s and the 1980s specifying approved methods of prisoner abuse, as well as one of the last major pieces of the puzzle explaining the roles of the United States and the United Kingdom in the August 1953 coup against Iranian Premier Mohammad Mossadeq.[2] This site, which is a tremendous resource of information regarding the FOIA, also features telephone conversations of former U.S. Secretary of State Henry Kissinger berating high-level subordinates for their efforts in 1976 to restrain human rights abuses by military dictators in Chile and Argentina.[3] The following sections examine in greater detail a few examples of important revelations achieved through the FOIA.

2.2 War Conduct

2.2.1 Vietnam War

In 2005, the National Security Agency (NSA) released many key documents about U.S. conduct in the Vietnam War after the press publicly criticized the agency's reluctance to declassify the information pursuant to FOIA requests filed by the National Security Archive and other groups. The NSA ended up releasing hundreds of documents concerning Vietnam, including the Gulf of Tonkin incident.

Among the most significant documents released by the NSA was a 2001 article in which an agency historian argued that intelligence officers "deliberately skewed" the evidence passed on to policy makers and the public to falsely suggest that North Vietnamese ships had attacked American destroyers on August 4, 1964. This was an extremely significant revelation, as it was on the basis of these reports that President Lyndon Johnson ordered air strikes against North Vietnam and Congress broadly authorized military action supporting the South Vietnamese. Some intelligence officials told the *New York Times* they believed the article's release was delayed because of parallels that could be drawn between flawed intelligence in the Vietnam and Iraq Wars, but a NSA spokesperson denied any political calculation behind the delay.[4]

2.2.2 Mass Graves in Afghanistan

Concerns about improper conduct during wartime is not only a historical matter. Such concerns continue to the present day. The FOIA could help shed light on the issue of suspected mass grave sites in Afghanistan, but thus far FOIA requests have been improperly denied, according to the advocacy group Physicians for Human Rights (PHR).

At issue are mass graves reported to contain more than 2,000 Taliban fighters at Dasht-e-Leili. According to news reports, near the end of November 2001, hundreds of Taliban fighters died of asphyxiation while being transported in shipping containers to Sheberghan prison following their surrender. PHR personnel visited the site in 2002 and said they found recently buried remains in the graves, but there has not yet been any official accounting from the Afghan government, the Department of Defense (DoD), or other U.S. agencies as to how and why the prisoners died.

This silence led the PHR on a six-plus year investigation during which it has tried to use the FOIA to uncover more information about the mass graves and possible human rights violations. In June 2006, the PHR used the FOIA to request all DoD records relating to any investigation of the matter. The DoD failed to release the documents, and PHR filed administrative appeals, but the DoD still would not release any information. The PHR had no choice but to turn to litigation.

In February 2008, PHR filed a lawsuit in the U.S. District Court for the District of Columbia against the DoD, claiming that the department had improperly withheld public records under the FOIA. The PHR is asking the court to disclose the records in their entirety. It is hoped that the sought-after records could help PHR to determine how and why the prisoners died and whether anyone should be held accountable. The PHR is seeking documents from the DoD relating to the department's investigations of human rights violations and the mass deaths of hundreds of captured Taliban fighters in Afghanistan by soldiers of the Northern Alliance in November 2001.[5]

2.3 Crime and Punishment

2.3.1 Criminal Acts by the U.S. Military

The FOIA has helped researchers to investigate the conduct of American military personnel overseas. Documents obtained using the FOIA by the *Denver Post* provided hard evidence to back up anecdotal claims of victimized female soldiers, who said their complaints were met with incomplete investigations and lenient treatment of offenders. The *Post*'s documents showed that soldiers in Iraq and Afghanistan accused of rape and other sex crimes received light administrative punishments for their crimes, such as demotions in rank, fines, or discharge, and, sometimes, no punishment at all.[6] Military commanders have broad discretion in determining how to deal with accused soldiers and have the freedom to determine whether or not to recommend criminal prosecution. The documents uncovered by the *Post* confirmed that, for the most part, soldiers serving overseas were getting slaps on the wrists for committing sex crimes. In this instance, the FOIA proved to be useful in getting the word out about atrocious conduct occurring at the hands of some of our military personnel based overseas.

2.3.2 Detainee Abuse Cases

The FOIA has been instrumental in revealing information about detainee abuse in the so-called global war on terror. Various organizations have been successful in persuading courts to release information that reveals the mistreatment of a number of individuals by government agents.

The FOIA has, for instance, played a role in helping to uncover the Iraqi prisoner abuse scandal. On September 29, 2005, Judge Alvin Hellerstein ordered the DoD to disclose redacted versions of prisoner abuse photos taken at Iraq's Abu Ghraib prison by reservist Joseph Darby. "Suppression of information is the surest way to cause its significance to grow," Hellerstein wrote, rejecting the government's claim that the photos were protected under Exemption 7(F) of the FOIA (which concerns physical safety). "Clarity and openness are the best antidotes, either to dispel criticism if not merited or, if merited, to correct such errors as may be found." Finding that the invocation of Exemption 7(F) had no relation to law enforcement, but was instead being used to suppress a debate about speech, Hellerstein observed that "my task is not to defer to our worst fears, but to interpret and apply the law, in this case the Freedom of Information Act, which advances values important to our society, transparency and accountability in government."[7]

Further information about detainee abuse was revealed pursuant to the FOIA in 2006, when three leading human rights organizations found that hundreds of military and civilian personnel were implicated in abuse charges in Iraq, Afghanistan, and Guantánamo Bay, Cuba. The Detainee Abuse and Accountability Project, a joint project of New York University's Center for Human Rights and Global Justice, Human Rights Watch, and Human Rights First, also discovered that few of those implicated faced disciplinary action.

The 27-page report produced by the groups, titled "By the Numbers," was released two years after the prisoner abuse scandal at Iraq's Abu Ghraib prison. It documented 330 cases since late 2001 in which U.S. military and civilian personnel were alleged to have abused or killed detainees. The cases involved more than 600 U.S. personnel and over 460 detainees; about two-thirds of the abuse occurred in Iraq.

The report showed that of the 600 personnel implicated in detainee abuse, only 54 had been convicted by a court-martial, only 40 had spent any amount of time in jail, and only 10 received sentences of more than one year. The report found that the highest-ranking service member to be charged in connection to an abuse case was a staff sergeant and concluded that low-ranking soldiers made up a majority of those convicted and punished.[8]

The Pentagon said in response to the report that more than 250 service members, including two officers, had been held accountable in 600 abuse investigations. Following the report's release, the Army said it planned to press charges against the chief of the interrogation center at Abu Ghraib prison, making him the highest-ranking officer at the prison to face charges.[9]

2.3.3 Arrests and Convictions

The FBI's COINTELPRO (COunterINTELligencePROgram) targeted civil-rights and antiwar activists in the 1960s and early 1970s and was reportedly behind thousands of civil-rights abuses. During this time, the FBI kept a file on Cleveland Mayor Carl Stokes and tried to stop him from granting $20,000 to a so-called "black extremist" group, the Afro Set, which ran community outreach and antidrug programs.[10] Harlell Jones was a leader of the Afro Set and an active political organizer in Cleveland. He and his group "were targets of the FBI's ... COINTELPRO."[11] Jones was convicted and sentenced to life in prison for second-degree murder in 1972, based largely upon the testimony of an informer.

Jones initiated FOIA litigation against the FBI to help him discover facts to win a retrial of his case.[12] The documents he received formed the basis of a successful habeas corpus petition, and eventually his conviction was reversed and he was released in 1978, partly on the basis of FBI documents that outlined an attempt to frame him for the killing.[13]

Jones's release from prison did not terminate his FOIA litigation. In 1992, nearly 20 years after commencing the FOIA request, the district court granted the FBI's motion for summary judgment without conducting an in camera review of the documents.[14] Jones appealed, claiming that the FBI's COINTELPRO actions and the withholding of evidence from his 1972 trial constituted bad faith and required in camera review. The Sixth Circuit agreed. "Even where there is no evidence that the agency acted in bad faith with regard to the FOIA action itself there may be evidence of bad faith or illegality with regard to the underlying activities which generated the documents at issue," the judgment read.[15]

The court further added:

> COINTELPRO went beyond the detection and prevention of criminal activity; the program's infringements of civil liberties seem well documented; and because the FBI worked closely with local law enforcement and supplied the key prosecution witness, the program is tied to the tainted prosecution of plaintiff for murder. This does not mean that the FBI acted in bad faith with regard to the FOIA request, but it does mean that the courts of this circuit should not process the case in the same manner as they would a request for documents regarding a routine FBI investigation.[16]

2.3.4 Overestimated Terrorist Arrests

The *Los Angeles Times* used the Freedom of Information Act in 2003 to obtain internal Department of Justice (DOJ) documents detailing the cases of the 286 suspected terrorists investigated by the FBI and arrested in the period following 9/11. The cases were components of a list used by the Bush Administration and the DOJ as a public-relations tool in promoting the War on Terror, but the *Times*'s review discovered that many of the individuals cited on the list were arrested and charged for much smaller crimes, such as purchasing fraudulent hazardous waste permits and commercial drivers licenses, or accepting stolen boxes of cereal. These people were kept on the anti-terror list even after prosecutors admitted publicly that they had no connection to terrorism.[17]

A similar investigation by *The Washington Post* in 2005 concluded that in the DOJ's list of terrorism prosecutions, "the numbers are misleading at best." The *Post*'s analysis determined that only 39 of the suspects listed were convicted of terrorism or national security-related crimes, as opposed to the 200 convictions previously inferred by Justice. The newspaper concluded that the median sentence for all suspects named in the DOJ's list was a mere 11 months.[18]

The *Post* investigation also revealed that only 14 people convicted on the Justice Department's list had clear links to al Qaeda and that many more of those named were linked to Colombian drug cartels, Rwandan war leaders, or other groups with no relation to al Qaeda or Osama bin Laden. Reports based on DOJ documents by the Center for Law and Security at New York University have similarly concluded that the majority of cases appeared to include no link to terrorism once the case reached court.[19]

In a separate report, the *Post* found that about 10 percent of the names on the Justice Department's list were involved in a fraudulent drivers license scandal in Pennsylvania. The men involved in the scandal were mostly Iraqi political refugees from the first Gulf War, and none were found to have links to terrorist cells, but the DOJ continued to name them on its list of anti-terrorist investigations, and the group of men made up the largest single investigation on the list. In the meantime, the lives of the suspects involved were severely disrupted following the charges; one Iraqi man living in Pittsburgh was forced to move to a different neighborhood after his auto repair shop was destroyed in an arson fire two days after he was initially charged with having links to terrorists.[20]

2.3.5 Prisoner "Suicide"

The family of Kenneth Trentadue used the FOIA to obtain Bureau of Prisons and DOJ records in a nearly 10-year investigation of Trentadue's death in an Oklahoma federal prison. Trentadue had been awaiting a sentencing hearing in Oklahoma City in 1995 following a years-long period of prison sentences for bank robbery and drug possession. In a shock to his family and lawyers, he committed suicide in his cell late at night using a ripped bed sheet, according to prison officials. The intense bruising and scarring on Trentadue's body, visible at his wake, led his family to believe he had in fact been murdered in prison and prompted them to begin an investigation into his death.

Through the FOIA they obtained evidence of a missing prison videotape relating to Trentadue's death; records stating that Trentadue's cell had been cleaned prior to the arrival of the FBI, counter to standard procedure; and inconsistent statements from guards, including evidence of mud on Trentadue's prison shoe. The Trentadue family was awarded $1.1 million for emotional damages by a federal judge, and the DOJ reopened the investigation under its Public Integrity department.[21]

A 1999 DOJ report deemed the response to Trentadue's death by Bureau of Prisons employees "significantly flawed." While maintaining that his death was a suicide, the report determined that prison officials present at Trentadue's death responded inappropriately by delaying entry into his cell, not examining him properly, and neglecting to provide immediate medical attention. The report also states that the FBI assigned the case an insufficient amount of attention for several months and mismanaged important evidence. Also included in the report was evidence that three Bureau of Prisons employees and one FBI employee lied to their supervisors or to investigators in the aftermath of Trentadue's death.[22]

2.4 Other Civil Rights Issues

2.4.1 FBI Searches

In 2004, the American Civil Liberties Union (ACLU) used the FOIA to obtain documents proving the FBI's use of the most controversial and contested search measure contained in the USA Patriot Act, one month after former Attorney General John Ashcroft publicly denied using the search provision at all.[23]

The measure in question, Section 215, allows the FBI to secretly access individuals' business materials in investigations, including travel, doctor, or library records. The ACLU—along with the Electronic Privacy Information Center (EPIC), the American Booksellers Foundation for Free Expression, and the Freedom to Read Foundation—uncovered 383 pages of DOJ documents, many containing a significant amount of blacked-out information.[24]

One of the documents uncovered was an FBI memorandum seeking permission from the DOJ to use Section 215 in a search dated less than one month after Attorney General John Ashcroft denied any FBI usage of the section and accused critics of the measure of spreading "baseless hysteria." At that time Ashcroft also declassified a document proving that the measure had been used. The report did not specify how many times the DOJ invoked Section 215 in the month following Ashcroft's comments.

An e-mail uncovered in the report also acknowledged that Section 215 could be used in certain cases to obtain physical objects, such as apartment keys; the DOJ had previously acknowledged the section could be used to obtain computer files and genetic information.[25]

The FBI initially responded to the ACLU's request for information by attempting to classify the documents for at least one more year. In a lawsuit filed by the ACLU, the United States District Court for the District of Columbia ordered the FBI to turn the documents over earlier, over a period of six weeks.

2.4.2 Civil Rights Complaints

Hundreds of DOJ records uncovered via a series of FOIA requests in 2004 by the Transactional Records Access Clearinghouse at Syracuse University (TRAC) revealed that federal enforcement of civil rights laws dropped sharply during George W. Bush's first term as president. The group's report found that 84 criminal civil rights defendants were prosecuted in 2003, compared with 159 in 1999. The DOJ receives about 12,000 annual complaints of possible civil rights violations.[26]

TRAC reported that federal prosecutors around the country have for many years been reluctant to file charges against enforcement officials, even when recommended by the FBI. Prosecutors took action in only about 2 percent of all civil rights complaints against government officials, including police officers and prison guards. Many officials said the cause for the extremely low level of prosecutions had to do with the social standing of many of the officials involved, such as police officers, and the "unsympathetic" standing of many of the people whose civil rights were violated.[27]

The trend was especially pronounced in the Houston area, where TRAC discovered the rate of these civil rights violations and police abuses to be especially high, and where the U.S. Attorney's office declined to prosecute about 99 percent of these complaints. In the rare instances when violators were prosecuted, the conviction rate was about two-thirds.[28]

2.4.3 Investigations Under the Patriot Act

A series of internal FBI e-mails uncovered in 2006 revealed frustrations within the bureau about what they perceived as reluctance at the administrative level to grant approval of controversial investigative measures made possible under the USA Patriot Act.[29] The e-mails were contained in a report by the EPIC and were obtained from the FBI through the FOIA.

In one e-mail, an unnamed FBI agent criticized the Office of Intelligence Policy and Review (OIPR) at the Justice Department for not approving FBI requests to use a controversial section of the law that grants the bureau authority to acquire business materials such as library, Internet, and bank records in investigations. (OIPR is responsible for reviewing all terrorist warrants.) In the e-mail the agent wrote, "[w]hile radical militant librarians kick us around, true terrorists benefit from OIPR's failure to let us use the tools given to us . . . This should be an OIPR priority!!!"[30] Another e-mail message celebrates the approval of a search request, saying "We got our first business record order signed today!...It only took two and a half years."[31]

EPIC's FOIA lawsuit prompted a federal court to order the FBI to turn over 1,500 pages of material to the group. An earlier EPIC investigation into FBI documents showed a number of FBI procedural violations in surveillance and investigative matters, sometimes breaking federal law. In some cases, agents prolonged surveillance activities without receiving the required approval from supervisors.

In response to EPIC's report, the American Library Association debuted a "Radical Militant Librarians" button at its annual convention.[32] The organization's criticism of the controversial Section 215 in the Patriot Act stems largely from the ability of government agents to access reading lists and reference materials used by suspects under investigation. In addition, a gag order prohibits librarians from telling patrons when material about them has been requested.

3. Challenges

The subjects covered in this chapter are among the most difficult to tackle using freedom of information laws, as they often involve other countries and issues of national security. As such, it is likely that individuals seeking information about these issues will face a claimed exemption, whether it be for claims of national security, individual privacy, or something else. Accordingly, individuals seeking information about issues concerning human rights and/or civil liberties issues are well advised to be persistent and creative in their quest for information.

While the issues explored in this chapter are among the most controversial and the most difficult about which to gather information, they are also some of the most pressing topics to examine. As a result, numerous groups and associations continue to seek information about these issues using the FOIA. Accordingly, in addition to seeking information on your own behalf, you can consult the Web sites and other resources of these organizations to see if they have already obtained information about your particular topic of interest and/or are in the process of attempting to do so. A number of Web sites of organizations that are active in this are identified in Appendix D.

4. Conclusion

The use of the FOIA and other information access laws to obtain information about human rights-related issues is plagued by many problems, but as the examples presented in this chapter show, it also holds considerable promise. Without the FOIA, it is unlikely that we would have been able to learn about many of the significant revelations discussed in this chapter.

Furthermore, this chapter only illustrates a few examples of the numerous revelations made through the use of the FOIA and other information freedom laws.

As the nation is led by a new administration, there is much hope and anticipation that there will be less of a culture of secrecy. Nonetheless, even with an Obama administration that is far more open and transparent than its predecessor, the utility and function of freedom of information laws will not diminish. One can hope, however, that those seeking information under these laws will have far greater success in doing so.

The next chapter examines in further detail how the right to know has been under siege over the course of the past few years. With hope and confidence that the Obama administration will continue to be open and transparent, Chapter Eight explores why a departure away from open government policies would be so dangerous to our democracy.

Notes

1. The National Security Archive, George Washington University, available at http://www.gwu.edu/%7Ensarchiv/ (last visited November 24, 2008).
2. "Mohammad Mosaddeq and the 1953 Coup in Iran," The National Security Archive, June 22, 2004, available at http://www.gwu.edu/~nsarchiv/NSAEBB/NSAEBB126/index.htm (last visited November 24, 2008).
3. "The Kissinger Telcons," The National Security Archive, May 26, 2004, available at http://www.gwu.edu/~nsarchiv/NSAEBB/NSAEBB123/index.htm (last visited November 24, 2008).
4. Scott Shane, "Vietnam War Intelligence 'Deliberately Skewed,' Secret Study Says," *The New York Times*, December 2, 2005, available at http://www.nytimes.com/2005/12/02/politics/02tonkin.html (last visited November 22, 2008).
5. Physicians for Human Rights, "PHR Files Suit Against Defense Department in FOIA Dispute Over Documents Concerning Dasht-e-Leili Mass Grave in Afghanistan," February 19, 2008, available at http://physiciansforhumanrights.org/library/news-2008-02-19.html (last visited November 22, 2008).
6. Miles Moffeit, "GI Sex Cases from Iraq Often Stall," *The Denver Post*, April 12, 2004, at A1.
7. *American Civil Liberties Union, et al. v. Department of Defense, et al.*, Civil Action No. 04-4151 (S.D.N.Y. 2005).
8. "The Detainee Abuse and Accountability Project, By the Numbers," Human Rights Watch, April 25, 2006, available at http://www.hrw.org/en/reports/2006/04/25/numbers (last visited November 22, 2008).
9. Voice of America, "US Army Officer Expected to Be Charged in Connection with Prisoner Abuse," April 26, 2006, available at http://www.voanews.com/english/archive/2006-04/US-Army-Officer-Expected-to-Be-Charged-in-Connection-with-Prisoner-Abuse.cfm?CFID=67785843&CFTOKEN=52043938 (last visited November 22, 2008).
10. Tom Brazaitis, "Some Fear Stronger FBI Will Return to Old Abuses," *The Plain Dealer* (Cleveland), July 7, 2002, at A1.

11. *Jones v. F.B.I.*, 41 F.3d 238, 240 (6th Cir.,1994).

12. *Id.* at 241.

13. *See Id.*, noting that in response to Jones's request, "The FBI eventually located 2,936 responsive documents comprising 10,485 pages, primarily within four central FBI files and various corresponding Cleveland and Cincinnati field office files. The agency released 485 pages in their entirety; released 9,157 pages with 240 portions redacted; and withheld 845 pages in their entirety."

14. *Id.* at 242.

15. *Id.*

16. *Id.*

17. Richard B. Schmitt, "A Flawed Terrorist Yardstick," *Los Angeles Times*, December 21, 2003, available at http://articles.latimes.com/2003/dec/21/nation/na-pittsburgh21 (last visited November 24, 2008).

18. Dan Eggen and Julie Tate, "U.S. Campaign Produces Few Convictions on Terrorism Charges," *The Washington Post*, June 12, 2005, available at http://www.washingtonpost.com/wp-dyn/content/article/2005/06/11/AR2005061100381.html (last visited November 24, 2008).

19. The Center on Law and Security, "Terrorist Trial Report Cards," February 2005–September 2008, available at http://www.lawandsecurity.org/pub_newsletter.cfm?id=3 (last visited November 24, 2008).

20. Jerry Markon, "The Terrorism Case That Wasn't—And Still Is," *The Washington Post*, June 12, 2005, available at http://www.washingtonpost.com/wp-dyn/content/article/2005/06/11/AR2005061100379.html (last visited November 24, 2008).

21. Richard A. Serrano, "Seeing Murder in a Face," *Los Angeles Times*, March 9, 2004, available at http://articles.latimes.com/2004/mar/09/nation/na-prisoner9 (last visited November 24, 2008).

22. "Prison Agency, FBI Faulted in '95 Inmate Suicide Case," *The Washington Post*, December 8, 1999.

23. The American Civil Liberties Union, "Patriot FOIA," August 10, 2004, available at http://www.aclu.org/patriotfoia (last visited November 24, 2008) [hereinafter "Patriot FOIA"].

24. Amy Goldstein, "Patriot Act Provision Invoked, Memo Says," *The Washington Post*, June 18, 2004, available at http://www.washingtonpost.com/wp-dyn/articles/A50524-2004Jun17.html (last visited November 24, 2008).

25. Patriot FOIA, *supra* note 23.

26. "Enforcement of Civil Rights Law Declined Since '99, Study Finds," *Associated Press*, November 22, 2004, available at http://www.nytimes.com/2004/11/22/national/22civil.html (last visited November 24, 2008).

27. The Transactional Records Access Clearinghouse at Syracuse University, "Civil Rights Enforcement by Bush Administration Lags," November 11, 2004, available at http://trac.syr.edu/tracreports/civright/106/ (last visited November 24, 2008).

28. John Frank, "City Rarely Prosecutes Civil Rights Complaints," *The Houston Chronicle*, December 1, 2004.

29. Eric Lichtblau, "At F.B.I., Frustration Over Limits on an Antiterror Law," *The New York Times*, December 11, 2005, available at http://www.nytimes.com/2005/12/11/national/nationalspecial3/11patriot.html (last visited November 24, 2008).

30. *Id.*

31. *Id.*

32. Amy Dorsett, "Librarians Would Shelve Patriot Act," *San Antonio Express-News,* January 25, 2007, available at http://www.mysanantonio.com/news/ MYSA012506_01A_militant_librarians_12d1873c_html8249.html (last visited November 24, 2008).

Chapter Eight

The Freedom of Information Act Under Siege

The liberties of a people never were, nor ever will be, secure, when the transactions of their rulers may be concealed from them.

—Patrick Henry

1. Overview

This chapter shows how the terrorist attacks of September 11, 2001, and the resulting war on terror have impacted open government and information freedom initiatives. It analyzes recent trends in information access in the United States and provides examples of how it has become more difficult for journalists, activists, and other individuals to obtain information from the government post-9/11. In doing so, it also shows why the trends away from openness and towards secrecy are so dangerous to our society and to our democracy at large.

2. Increasing Secrecy

2.1 Overview

The public's right to know has been scaled back significantly under the Bush administration. Years of general progression towards more open government have been reversed under the eight years of President George W. Bush. Perhaps even more significant than the drift towards secrecy has been the manner in which it has been carried out. While the public's right to know has diminished under the Bush administration, most of this pullback has been conducted out of public view and without public debate. We have been making the transition from a society in which the public has the right to know to one in which information is controlled tightly and is made available on a need-to-know basis only.

While all recent indications suggest that the Obama administration will be far more open, it is worthwhile and important to explore the path we have been taking over the past several years.

2.2 Removal of Information Post 9/11

Following the 9/11 attacks, the Bush administration ordered enormous amounts of data removed from the Web sites of government agencies. "For better or worse ... the easy availability of information about myriad government activities is one facet of American society that may have been forever changed by September 11," wrote a *San Diego Union-Tribune* reporter three months after the attacks.[1] The removed online information included a U.S. Geological Survey report on sources of public drinking water; information from the Energy Department on nuclear weapons programs and transporting radioactive materials; Environmental Protection Agency and Department of Health and Human Services reports on chemical plant security and safety; and information relating to the Federal Aviation Administration's enforcement programs. In addition, the removal of this information was completed by individual agencies without specific policy direction.[2]

The removal of information from Web sites was also performed without the maintenance or completion of an accurate record of which information was removed or restricted. Critics noted that the redacted information could have been downloaded prior to its removal, and much of it continued to be available on the Internet on private Web sites. Additionally, families and communities expressed concern over their ability to obtain critical data regarding pipeline maps (showing where pipelines exist and whether they have been inspected), airport safety data, and environmental data that they regard as critical in assessing the safety of their communities and forming emergency contingency plans.[3]

2.3 Increasing Classification of Information

Over the course of the past few years, there has also been the startling move towards an increasing classification of information. For example, according to OpenTheGovernment.org's annual Secrecy Report Card, the number of decisions made to classify information as "top secret," "secret," or "confidential" in 2007 was 233,639, an increase of 1,644 decisions since 2006. More importantly, the number of classification decisions during the Bush administration in general was up quite a bit from the mid-1990s. The jump from 105,163 original classification decisions in 1996 to 233,639 classifications in 2007 represents a more than doubling of classifications over an 11-year period.

Even more dramatic is the fall in the number of overall pages being declassified by federal agencies. In 2007, 37,249,390 pages were declassified, which was up from a low of 28,413,690 in 2004. When compared again with the 1990s, however, the Bush administration clearly had a predilection against classification. For example, in each year between 1996 and 1999, there were more than 125 million pages declassified. In 1997, the number of pages even breached the 200 million mark. At the same time, the number of government employees authorized to classify information rose in 2007 to 4,182, an increase of 2 percent from 2006. However, this metric has been relatively steady since 1993, regardless of which administration is running the government.[4]

In addition to these officially "classified" information designations, there has also been an increasing trend towards restricting access to what officials call "sensitive but unclassified information."[5] A March 2002 memo by White House Chief of Staff Andrew H. Card, Jr., which included guidance from the Department of Justice (DOJ) and the Information Security Oversight Office (ISOO) on "safeguarding information," encouraged agencies to think twice before disclosing information to the public. The DOJ/Card memo instructed agencies to review specific procedures for disclosure of "sensitive but unclassified" information, but left the definition of such information unclear: "The need to protect such sensitive information from inappropriate disclosure should be carefully considered, on a case-by-case basis, together with the benefits that result from the open and efficient exchange of scientific, technical, and like information."[6]

Shortly following the DOJ/Card memo's release, the White House Office of Management and Budget (OMB) was charged with developing guidance for agencies on "sensitive but unclassified" information at the request of the Department of Homeland Security (DHS). Under the OMB's guidelines, government agencies now designate information with a complex series of labels, including "For Official Use Only," "Protected Critical Infrastructure Information," "Limited Distribution Information," and "Sensitive Information."[7]

In September 2002, the Environmental Protection Agency (EPA) released its "Strategic Plan for Homeland Security," which said that it would "review records management procedures to ensure conformance to the DOJ/Card memo direction" and would develop "criteria and guidance on protection of sensitive information."[8]

2.4 Changing the Presumption of Disclosure

During the 1990s, there was a marked trend towards openness in government. During this time of our Information Age, state and federal government agencies, like commercial entities, took advantage of the Internet and related technologies to make information widely available at a relatively low cost. Indeed, between 1996 and 1999, more than 800 federal Web sites were established.[9]

Also during this time period, President Bill Clinton's administration launched a campaign to make a wide range of information available to the public. To advance this campaign, on October 4, 1993, Clinton circulated a memorandum expressing the administration's commitment to information freedom, and the FOIA specifically. The memo read, in part: "Each agency has a responsibility to distribute information on its own initiative, and to enhance public access through the use of electronic information systems. Taking these steps will ensure compliance with both the letter and spirit of the Act."[10] Thus, even before the 1996 enactment of the Electronic Freedom of Information Act Amendments (EFOIA), Clinton was instructing federal agencies to make government information available online.

In a concurrent memo, Attorney General Janet Reno informed federal agencies that they were to adopt a presumption of disclosure regarding the FOIA. "The [DOJ] will no longer defend an agency's withholding of information merely because there is a 'substantial legal basis' for doing so," Reno wrote. "Rather, in determining whether or not to defend a nondisclosure decision, we will apply a presumption of disclosure."

Accordingly, under this presumption, federal agencies were required to disclose information unless it was absolutely necessary not to do so, and Reno made clear that the use of the FOIA's exemptions was to be a last resort, not a tool to evade, delay, or reject FOIA requests on technicalities. "These exemptions are best applied with specific reference to such harm, and only after consideration of the reasonably expected consequences of disclosure in any particular case," she wrote. "Where an item of information might *technically or arguably* fall within an exception, it ought not to be withheld from a FOIA requester unless it *need* be" (emphasis added). Reno claimed that the policy "serve[d] the public interest by achieving the Act's primary objective —maximum responsible disclosure of government information—while preserving essential confidentiality."[11]

This trend towards open government continued, and in 1995 Clinton filed Executive Order 12958[12] revoking the classification scheme that had been established during the Reagan Administration[13] for a policy that was far more transparent. But the government's increasing openness took an about-face in 2001.

On September 14, 2001, three days after the 9/11 attacks, President George W. Bush declared a national emergency,[14] thereby assuming the executive powers granted under the National Emergency Act.[15] Bush then undertook a number of actions intended to respond to the terrorist threat. His administration's philosophy towards open government during that era could be understood by considering his comments made less than three months after the attacks. "We're an open society. But we're at war," Bush told a new group of U.S. Attorneys. "Foreign terrorists and agents must never again be allowed to use our freedoms against us."[16]

Before Bush made those comments, the government's stance on the FOIA had already formally shifted, as evidenced in an October 12, 2001, memo from Attorney General John Ashcroft. The memo instructed agencies, in essence, to withhold information whenever possible. Given the major changes ushered in by the Ashcroft memo, it bears quotation at length. It read in part:

> It is only through a well-informed citizenry that the leaders of our nation remain accountable to the governed and the American people can be assured that neither fraud nor government waste is concealed.
>
> The Department of Justice and this Administration are equally committed to protecting other fundamental values that are held by our society. Among them are safeguarding our national security, enhancing the effectiveness of our law enforcement agencies, protecting sensitive business information and, not least, preserving personal privacy.
>
> Our citizens have a strong interest as well in a government that is fully functional and efficient. Congress and the courts have long recognized that certain legal privileges ensure candid and complete agency deliberations without fear that they will be made public. Other privileges ensure that lawyers' deliberations and communications are kept private. No leader can operate effectively without confidential advice and counsel. Exemption 5 of the FOIA, 5 U.S.C. § 552(b) (5), incorporates these privileges and the sound policies underlying them.
>
> I encourage your agency to carefully consider the protection of all such values and interests when making disclosure determinations under the FOIA. Any discretionary decision by your agency to disclose information protected under the FOIA should be made only after full and deliberate consideration of the institutional, commercial, and personal privacy interests that could be implicated by disclosure of the information.
>
> In making these decisions, you should consult with the Department of Justice's Office of Information and Privacy when significant FOIA issues arise, as well as with our Civil Division on FOIA litigation matters. When you carefully consider FOIA requests and decide to withhold records, in whole or in part, you can be assured that the Department of Justice will defend your decisions unless they lack a sound legal basis or present an unwarranted risk of adverse impact on the ability of other agencies to protect other important records.[17]

The Ashcroft memo, combined with the DOJ/Card memo discussed earlier, represented a fundamental reversal of past policy, which stressed disclosure where possible. For example, Card, writing in broad strokes, encouraged agencies to withhold "any information that could be misused."[18] In the additional guidance provided to agencies by a document attached to Card's memo (and prepared at his request), each agency was granted the discretion to determine what information should be "controlled" as "sensitive but unclassified," even if it did not otherwise meet the standards for classification or reclassification:

> [D]epartments and agencies maintain and control sensitive information related to America's homeland security that might not meet one or more of the standards for classification set forth in Part 1 of Executive Order 12958. The need to protect such sensitive information from inappropriate disclosure should be carefully considered, on a case-by-case basis, together with the benefits that result from the open and efficient exchange of scientific, technical, and like information. All departments and agencies should ensure that in taking necessary and appropriate actions to safeguard sensitive but unclassified information related to America's homeland security, they process any Freedom of Information Act request for records containing such information in accordance with the Attorney General's FOIA Memorandum of October 12, 2001, by giving full and careful consideration to all applicable FOIA exemptions[19] (emphasis added).

Some agencies have taken advantage of the ability to mark information as "sensitive but unclassified" by creating multiple categories of pseudo-classifications that flag material that should be carefully considered before release. As one of many examples, the Centers for Disease Control and Prevention created 27 new categories of sensitive but unclassified information.[20]

Quite significantly, just a day after taking the oath of office, President Obama brought an end to the Bush policy and shifted the presumption back towards one of disclosure. This is a very promising sign regarding the level of openness we are likely to see from this administration.

2.5 Growing Delays in Responding to FOIA Requests

In August 2002, the General Accounting Office (GAO), the investigative arm of Congress that was later renamed the Government Accountability Office, found that while the number of FOIA requests to government agencies were "leveling off, backlogs of pending requests governmentwide [were] substantial and growing." The GAO noted that this indicated agencies were "falling behind in processing requests."[21] A number of other studies since then have revealed similar results.

In September 2005, the Society of Environmental Journalists (SEJ) released a study that concluded the FOIA, which was already plagued by delay and government bureaucracy, "had been further compromised" by 9/11. "Our members have even noticed the government embarking on new attempts to hobble the Freedom of Information Act," the SEJ researchers wrote, "using quibbles about search fees to delay the release of documents and invoking the already-cumbersome FOIA process to dodge simple queries from reporters."[22]

In July 2008, a study came out that called into question claims made by the DOJ the previous month that federal departments and agencies had made "remarkable improvements" in responding to FOIA requests. The now-shuttered Coalition of Journalists for Open Government found that while agencies did reduce their backlogs, the improvement was due more to a decline in requests than a quicker processing of requests. The Coalition's report, titled "An Opportunity Lost," also found that many agencies were actually regressing in many areas, including the amount of time requesters had to wait for an answer.[23]

2.6 Restrictions on the Ability of the News Media to Gather Information

The attacks of 9/11 and the resulting "war on terror" had a dramatic impact on the ability of the news media to gather information, whether through the FOIA or otherwise. Congress passed the USA Patriot Act[24] in late October 2001, which, according to the Free Expression Network, presented serious implications for the freedom of the press. "The drive for government secrecy . . . is part of a much larger effort to insulate government decision-making from the press and public scrutiny," the group wrote in a report released six months after the Patriot Act's passage. "Administration officials have openly limited the ability of the press to cover the war and prevailed on the news media to censor statements by Osama bin Laden and other information," the report read, "and the Defense Department disbanded a planned Office of Strategic Information only after a government employee revealed publicly the intent to use the office to disseminate false information to the American people, and America's allies as well as its enemies."[25]

At Guantanamo Bay, Cuba, restrictions on the press are particularly evident. In September 2002, the *Associated Press* reported that media restrictions at Camp Delta at Guantanamo Bay, where nearly 600 suspected terrorists were then being detained, had become increasingly severe. The military had media escorts, who monitored the press's interviews with military personnel and accompanied journalists "to most places on the base, including bathrooms and vending machines."[26]

In June 2006, officials at Guantanamo shocked human rights groups, members of the legal community, and the media world by temporarily blocking press access altogether. The Pentagon denied all press requests in the wake of three detainee suicides the previous weekend, arguing that it had to concentrate fully on the investigation of the suicides and the aftermath at the base. The ban, which was eventually lifted, was implemented immediately before several journalists were scheduled to depart for Guantanamo; reporters already at the prison, from *The Los Angeles Times*, *The Miami Herald*, and *The Charlotte Observer* were expelled. The blackout came as the prison was facing particularly harsh criticism, not only for the suicides but for a recent conflict that had injured six detainees and for a hunger strike that prison officials mediated by force-feeding. "Now is the time when the media is most needed," said an attorney who has filed legal challenges on behalf of about 40 detainees. "The fact that right now, the most important time in the history of Guantanamo, they are being banned is un-American."[27]

2.7 Limiting Access to Presidential Records

Actions by the Bush Administration have also had the effect of limiting access to presidential records. In November 2001, immediately before nearly 68,000 pages of documents from the Reagan administration were slated for public release, President Bush signed an Executive Order that effectively denied the public's right to access presidential documents. The order gave both sitting and former presidents veto power over any public release of presidential materials and stated that an incumbent president could withhold a former president's papers—even if the former president wanted to make them public. It also required that members of the public show "at least a 'demonstrated, specific need' " for documents before they are considered for release. Additionally, the order stipulated that the sitting president and the former president could review requests for information with no time restriction.[28]

Bush, under the advisement of White House advisor Alberto Gonzalez, had delayed the scheduled release of Reagan documents for nearly half a year before signing the executive order. Included in the documents were confidential communications between Reagan and his advisors, including Bush's father George H. W. Bush, Reagan's vice president, as well as administration officials who served in both Bush administrations.

The Reagan documents were to be the first presidential documents released under the 1978 Presidential Records Act, implemented following Nixon's presidency and the Watergate scandal. The Presidential Records Act stipulates that the public may use the FOIA to seek presidential records 12 years after a president leaves office. Bush's executive order "reverses the very premise of the Presidential Records Act," the executive director of the National Coordinating Committee for the Promotion of History told the *Washington Post*.[29]

Public reaction to the order was extremely negative. An editorial in Cleveland's *Plain Dealer* argued that "Bush either has made a serious misjudgment about the extent of his authority or has deliberately set out to obstruct disclosure of events involving his father and/or some of his key advisers,"[30] while the *New York Times* editorialized that the order "raises the threat of a new era of needless secrecy regarding presidential papers."[31]

2.8 Asserting Executive Privilege

In December 2001, President Bush asserted his first use of executive privilege by withholding documents from the House Government Reform

Committee related to a decades-old Boston mob case and a campaign finance investigation dating to the Clinton administration. It was a powerful shift in practice and a blow to the Congress, which had routinely obtained such information under previous administrations.

Bush's order came following a subpoena by the committee for records from open investigations on Boston mob cases from the 1960s, as well as for records dealing with former Attorney General Janet Reno's decision not to appoint a Special Counsel to investigate possible campaign finance misdeeds by then-Vice President Al Gore. In a memo to Attorney General John Ashcroft instructing him not to release the documents, President Bush wrote that the disclosure would "inhibit the candor necessary" to the President and would be "contrary to the national interest."[32]

Similarly, Bush's lawyers argued in U.S. District Court in August 2002 to extend executive privilege by withholding information in regards to presidential pardons. Responding to a lawsuit brought by the nonprofit group Judicial Watch, the White House filed a 100-plus page report arguing for restricted access to records of the 177 pardons and communications that former president Bill Clinton approved or considered on his last day as president, including the controversial pardons granted to Clinton's brother Roger Clinton and the fugitive Marc Rich.

The FOIA includes a "presidential communications privilege" that exempts certain communications between a president and his advisers within the White House from standard disclosure regulation. In their memorandum to the court, the Bush administration argued: "To exclude these documents from the scope of the privilege merely because they were initially generated at the Justice Department rather than the White House would arbitrarily and unconstitutionally limit the president in his choice of key advisers regarding the exercise of his clemency power, which is entrusted to him directly under the Constitution without limit."[33]

2.9 Secret Deportation Hearings

In late September 2001, a memo issued by Chief Immigration Judge Michael J. Creppy effectively closed all immigration hearings designated by the government to be of "special interest." The memo included provisions deeming that "no visitors, no family and no press" were to be allowed in hearings; that judges would require special security clearances to hear cases; and that all personnel involved in the hearings be instructed "not to discuss the case with anyone."[34] This memo resulted in uncertainty and confusion among family members and the media as to when and if certain hearings were being held.

In 2002, the DOJ reported having designated more than 600 detainees for these special closed hearings. In an affidavit submitted by Dale L. Watson, the FBI's executive assistant director for counterterrorism and counterintelligence, the DOJ argued that opening hearings to the public and press would allow terrorists to find holes in the country's immigration system; reveal government methods in terrorism investigations; encourage terrorist organizations to destroy certain evidence; and alert these organizations to those of their members already detained.[35] Most civil liberties and press freedom advocacy groups opposed the measure. "In this country, under our constitutional system, individuals should not be locked up based on secret hearings without any individualized showing that secrecy is essential," Lee Gelernt of the American Civil Liberties Union told the *Washington Post*.[36]

The courts have ruled inconsistently regarding the legality of the policy. In August 2002, a U.S. Court of Appeals for the 6th Circuit in Cincinnati ruled the provision illegal in the case of a detained Lebanese activist suspected of terrorism. In their ruling, the three-judge panel argued against secrecy, saying, "Democracies die behind closed doors." Two months later, a U.S. Court of Appeals for the 3rd Circuit in Philadelphia ruled 2-1 for the measure, agreeing with the government by citing the policy's necessity in fighting terrorism.[37]

2.10 The Secret Acts of the Vice President's Energy Policy Task Force

Prior to 9/11 and the subsequent obstructions to information access, the Bush administration had already received sharp criticism for refusing to disclose—to Congress or the public—information on Vice President Dick Cheney's energy policy task force. Both Cheney and the president have long-standing ties to the oil industry, and the secrecy surrounding the National Energy Policy Development Group, as the task force was called, raises important questions about access to top-level decision-makers and potential conflicts of interest.[38]

For the first time, the GAO, which is an arm of Congress, sued the executive branch to obtain the names of the private-sector advisers and staffers who attended meetings of Cheney's task force. They also sought to obtain information regarding how much money was spent. The lawsuit and much of the suspicion surrounding Cheney's group came as a result of the energy plan they proposed, which called for more drilling, more nuclear power plants, the opening of the Arctic National Wildlife Refuge to oil companies, and relatively few mentions of conservation or lifestyle shifts. Cheney dismissed the GAO's initial demand for the information by citing confidentiality and executive privilege.[39]

In 2001, the advocacy groups Judicial Watch and the Sierra Club filed suit to obtain the same information from Cheney's task force. In particular, the groups were looking to obtain several thousand task force e-mails and 12 boxes of documents.[40] In February 2003, the GAO dropped its suit, saying it would not appeal a December 2002 federal court decision that ruled the office could not force Cheney to turn over the information. The Judicial Watch/Sierra Club suit fizzled out after a U.S. District Court ruled in May 2005 that the meetings of the task force were not subject to federal open meetings law.[41]

It should be noted that the Natural Resources Defense Council (NRDC) *did* obtain some documents from the energy task force in 2002 after it sued the Department of Energy for withholding information the NRDC had requested via the FOIA.[42] Later, the *Washington Post* also obtained some documents (not via the FOIA) and published a story in November 2005 showing that officials from Exxon Mobil Corp., Conoco (before its merger with Phillips), Shell Oil Co., and BP America Inc. met with Cheney's aides to work on energy policy.[43] However, these partial victories should not obscure the fact that the administration's fight against disclosure in this case was fierce and multi-pronged.

3. Impact

Taken together, the actions and policies described in this chapter have helped to create a culture of secrecy in which mistrust and suspicion of government actions can grow. It is exactly the kind of environment of which our founding fathers and other theorists and experts on democratic government have warned. The trends towards secrecy described in this chapter impact the ability of journalists to gather information about a wide range of issues and activities about which the public has a right to know.

4. Conclusion

Our country and—in fact, the world—has undergone a number of significant changes during the administration of President George W. Bush. One important change is that the government became far more secretive during those eight years, making it much more difficult for society to gather information about what the government is up to through the FOIA and other mechanisms. The high level of secrecy that has permeated the Bush administration has helped to feed suspicion and distrust among the citizenry, all of which has a negative impact on effective democratic government.

With the Obama Administration now firmly in place and all signs suggesting that we will have a far more open government, it is certainly reasonable to be hopeful about the future of our right to know. However, it is not the time to sit back and assume that all problems regarding information access have been resolved.

Notes

1. Toby Eckert, "Federal Agencies Pull Data From Web Sites After Sept. 11," *San Diego Union-Tribune*, December 9, 2001.

2. Paul M. Schoenhard, "Disclosure of Government Information Online: A New Approach from an Existing Framework," *Harvard Journal of Law and Technology*, Volume 15, Number 2, Spring 2002, available at http://jolt.law.harvard.edu/articles/pdf/v15/15HarvJLTech497.pdf (last visited November 28, 2008).

3. Eckert, *supra* note 1.

4. Patrice McDermott and Amy Fuller, *Secrecy Report Card 2008*, OpenTheGovernment.org, September 2008, available at http://www.openthe government.org/otg/SecrecyReportCard08.pdf (last visited November 28, 2008).

5. Lyndsey Layton, "Group Seeks Web-Savvy, More Open Government," *The Washington Post*, November 12, 2008, available at http://www.washingtonpost.com/wp-dyn/content/story/2008/11/12/ST2008111200606.html (last visited November 27, 2008).

6. Andrew H. Card, Jr., "Memorandum for Heads of Executive Departments and Agencies: Action to Safeguard Information Regarding Weapons of Mass Destruction and Other Sensitive Documents Related to Homeland Security," March 19, 2002, available at the Department of Justice's FOIA Post http://www.usdoj.gov/oip/foiapost/2002foiapost10.htm (last visited November 28, 2008).

7. Government Accountability Office, "Information Sharing: The Federal Government Needs to Establish Policies and Processes for Sharing Terrorism-Related and Sensitive but Unclassified Information," March 17, 2006, available at http://www.gao.gov/new.items/d06385.pdf (last visited November 27, 2008).

8. Environmental Protection Agency, "Strategic Plan for Homeland Security," September 2002, available at http://www.epa.gov/epahome/downloads/epa_homeland_security_strategic_plan.pdf (last visited November 27, 2008).

9. Lisa Corbin,*Cyberocracy*, Government Executive, August 30, 1999, available at http://www.govexec.com/story_page.cfm?filepath=/tech/articles/0196s1.htm (last visited November 28, 2008).

10. President William J. Clinton, "Memorandum for Heads of Departments and Agencies: The Freedom of Information Act," October 4, 1993, available via the Federation of Scientists, at http://www.fas.org/sgp/clinton/reno.html (last visited November 28, 2008).

11. Attorney General Janet Reno, "Memorandum for Heads of Departments and Agencies: The Freedom of Information Act," October 4, 1993, available via the Federation of Scientists, at http://www.fas.org/sgp/clinton/reno.html (last visited November 28, 2008).

12. Exec. Order No. 12958, 60 Fed. Reg. 19,825 (April 17, 1995).

13. Exec. Order No. 12356, 47 Fed. Reg. 14,874 (April 6, 1982) (revoked by Exec. Order No. 12,958, 60 Fed. Reg. 19,825 (April 17, 1995).

14. Proclamation No. 7463, 66 Fed. Reg. 48,199 (September 14, 2001).

15. National Emergency Act, 50 U.S.C 1601 et. seq. (2002).

16. The White House Office of the Press Secretary, "President Says U.S. Attorneys on Front Line in War," November 29, 2001, available at http://www.whitehouse.gov/news/releases/2001/11/20011129-12.html (last visited November 28, 2008).

17. Attorney General John Ashcroft, Attorney General, "Memorandum for Heads of All Federal Departments and Agencies: The Freedom of Information Act," October 12, 2001, available at http://www.doi.gov/foia/foia.pdf (last visited November 28, 2008).

18. Card, *supra* note 6.

19. Laura L. S. Kimberly (Information Security Oversight Office), Richard L. Huff, and Daniel J. Metcalfe (Department of Justice), "Memorandum for Departments and Agencies: Safeguarding Information Regarding Weapons of Mass Destruction and Other Sensitive Records Related to Homeland Security," March 19, 2002, available at http://www.usdoj.gov/oip/foiapost/2002foiapost10.htm#guidance (last visited November 28, 2008).

20. Centers for Disease Control and Prevention, "Sensitive But Unclassified Information," July 22, 2005, available at http://www.fas.org/sgp/othergov/cdc-sbu.pdf (last visited November 28, 2008).

21. General Accounting Office, "Information Management: Update on the Implementation of the 1996 Electronic Freedom of Information Act Amendments, Implementation Status, August 30, 2002," available at http://www.gao.gov/new.items/d02493.pdf (last visited November 27, 2008).

22. Society of Environmental Journalists, "A Flawed Tool—Environmental Reporters' Experiences With the Freedom of Information Act," September 12, 2005, available at http://www.sej.org/foia/SEJ_FOIA_Report2005.pdf (last visited November 27, 2008).

23. The Coalition of Journalists for Open Government, "An Opportunity Lost: An In-Depth Analysis of FOIA Performance from 1998 to 2007," July 3, 2008, available at http://www.cjog.net/documents/Part_1_2007_FOIA_Report.pdf (last visited November 27, 2008).

24. The USA Patriot Act, Public Law 107-56 (2001).

25. The Free Expression Network, "The USA Patriot Act Six Months Later: A Statement by Members of the Free Expression Network," April 26, 2002, available at http://www.freeexpression.org/patriotstmt.htm (last visited November 28, 2008).

26. Paisley Dodds, "As Detention Center Expands in Guantanamo, So Do Press Restrictions," *The Associated Press*, September 14, 2002.

27. Ben Fox, "Media Access to Guantanamo Blocked Altogether," *The Associated Press*, available at http://www.usatoday.com/news/world/2006-06-15-guantanamo-media_x.htm (last visited November 27, 2008).

28. George Lardner, Jr., "Bush Clamping Down on Presidential Papers," *The Washington Post*, November 1, 2001.

29. *Id.*

30. "Abusing the Privilege," *Plain Dealer* (Cleveland), November 20, 2001.

31. "Cheating History," *The New York Times*, November 15, 2001, available at: http://query.nytimes.com/gst/fullpage.html?res=9501E6DC163BF936A25752C1A9679C8B63 (last visited November 27, 2008).

32. Karen Gullo, "Bush Invokes Executive Privilege to Keep Justice Department Documents Secret," *The Associated Press*, December 14, 2001.

33. Sandra Sobieraj, "Bush Administration Argues Privacy for Pardons Review Process," *The Associated Press*, August 27, 2002.

34. George Lardner Jr., "Democrats Blast Order on Tribunals," *The Washington Post*, November 29, 2001.

35. Dale L. Watson, affidavit in *Detroit Free Press, et al v. Department of Justice*, available at http://www.cnss.org/watsonaffidavit.pdf (last visited November 27, 2008).

36. Steve Fainaru, "Court Backs Closing of Detainees' Hearings," *The Washington Post*, October 9, 2002.

37. *Id.*

38. "Shedding Light on Cheney," *The Boston Globe*, August 11, 2001.

39. Dana Milbank, "White House Girds for Protracted Fight; GAO Lawsuit Seeks Energy Information," *The Washington Post*, February 22, 2002.

40. Layton, *supra* note 5.

41. Judicial Watch, "Appeals Court Permits Energy Task Force Records to Remain Secret," May 10, 2005, available at http://www.judicialwatch.org/5442.shtml (last visited November 27, 2008).

42. Pete Yost, "Judge Says He Assumes Bush Administration Is 'Stalling' in Cheney Task Force Document Production Case," *The Associated Press*, February 28, 2002.

43. Dana Milbank and Justin Blum, "Document Says Oil Chiefs Met With Cheney Task Force," *The Washington Post*, November 16, 2005, available at http://www.washingtonpost.com/wp-dyn/content/article/2005/11/15/AR2005111501842_pf.html (last visited November 27, 2008).

Chapter Nine

Best Practices

Secrecy is for losers ... It is time to dismantle government secrecy, this most persuasive of Cold War-era regulations. It is time to begin building the supports for the era of openness that is already upon us.
—Senator Patrick Moynihan, Secrecy: The American Experience, 1998

1. Introduction

This book has aimed to demonstrate the critical role that information freedom has to play in all free nations, including our own democracy. The examples of significant revelations that were made using freedom of information laws highlight their utmost importance. Drawing upon the case examples discussed in previous chapters, this chapter presents important lessons that can be learned from the current administration of these laws and puts forward best practices for those attempting to secure information via the FOIA and related laws.

2. Best Practices

The examples presented in the previous chapters show clearly that the FOIA can be an extremely important tool in the quest for information about a wide range of very important issues. However, it is also clear that no system of information freedom is flawless, even in the United States. As highlighted in the last chapter, the proper and effective administration of the FOIA has been harmed by the secrecy of the prior administration. However, even without taking into consideration the Bush administration's propensity for secrecy, the implementation of the FOIA has been plagued by various problems, including delays, missing information, overreliance on exemptions, and other issues. The following section identifies both general and specific tips that can be employed by people seeking to obtain information through freedom of information laws.

2.1 Use the Internet

In order to combat the penchant for secrecy that was established throughout the past several years under the Bush administration, U.S. citizens have been forced to unearth new sources for information that they were once able to read in their daily newspapers or by other readily accessible means. Although the government became more restrictive and the ability to use the FOIA to gather information became more difficult under the Bush administration, the Internet, along with a number of dedicated individuals and public interest associations, is helping to ensure that certain material is easier to come by. Open government Web sites provide a wide variety of information and may be a good place to commence one's research. These sources represent the creation of alternate channels for public access to government information. While they do not solve the secrecy problem, they can help the public be more informed about official secrecy, and about means to fight it.

Appendix D presents a summary of select open government organization sites, along with contact information and a description as well as examples of notable information that is available on each site. While the chart is not an all-inclusive listing of such sites, it does provide details about several useful resources. While individuals and organizations seeking information should absolutely still consider filing FOIA requests, these publicly available Web sites can serve as very useful resources—especially when one is struggling to determine the proper starting point in the search for information.

In addition, as highlighted in Chapter 2, the EFOIA requires agencies to establish and make available electronic reading rooms. While it is true that since 9/11 certain agencies have been making cuts to what is being made available, these reading rooms, and the Web sites of government agencies in general, continue to be very important resources. The sites house a wealth of important information, and if you perform well-thought-out and thorough searches, you might be surprised at what you can find.

2.2 Use the FOIA and File Requests for Information

While this book has emphasized that the administration of the FOIA has become more restrictive and the ability of individuals and organizations to obtain information has become more limited, this does not mean that one should not attempt to use the FOIA and related laws. Despite some of the obstacles and problems that people have experienced, journalists and private citizens alike have still been able to obtain very valuable information via the FOIA—even during the restrictive years of the Bush administration.

Even when the FOIA system is not operating as effectively and efficiently as is desirable, the legislation can still be an essential tool for obtaining information held by the government. While the government's response to FOIA requests can be subject to delays and the overreliance on statutory exceptions, generally the government does respond (eventually) to requests. For example, the Health Research Group of Ralph Nader's advocacy group Public Citizen filed 300 requests with the FDA in one year and obtained 90 percent of them.[1] Do not allow the obstacles described in this book to dissuade you from making requests for information under the existing freedom of information laws.

2.3 Journalists Have Special Rights

As demonstrated throughout this book, the FOIA is a very important information-gathering tool for all individuals, irrespective of profession. Nonetheless, journalists have special rights under the FOIA. If you are a journalist, do not hesitate to exercise the special powers that you have. For example, journalists do not have to pay for search time under the FOIA. In addition, members of the media are able to get their requests addressed in advance of others if they can demonstrate an "urgency to inform the public" on government activity. With the definition of "journalist" expanding to include less traditional forms of journalism, more individuals may be able to avail themselves of the special rights afforded to journalists.

2.4 Develop a System for Making Requests

As this book has attempted to demonstrate, there is a vast amount of information out there that may be sought and obtained through the FOIA. If you plan on making multiple requests for information, it is best to develop a system in order to process your requests more quickly and easily. One way to do this is through the development of form templates that you can use again and again. A sample template request letter is included in Appendix B-1. It is advisable to develop your own form letter that can be available for repeated use.

There are other forms and templates that you can use as well. It may be useful to craft different working definitions of what you may request from various agencies depending on your particular need. For example, you could have a definition to be used when commencing research or when trying to get a lot of information about a particular topic. In such a definition, you would try to cover the subject broadly by, for example, requesting "all releasable records concerning [x] since [date]." Conversely, you could also have a definition that is more focused, for use when requesting a specific type of record. In such cases, you should also review the agency's own regulations and craft your request accordingly, so as to improve the likelihood that you will receive precisely what you wish. When conducting this kind of request, you may also wish to attach a copy of the type of record you want and ask for all other records of its type or all other records concerning the same subject.

You should also compile a list of the points of contact that you tend to use on a regular basis. Appendix C includes a detailed listing of agencies and their contact information. Consider compiling a list of those agencies you contact most often. Keep track of Internet resources that are useful to you and your research. In addition, when you encounter an agency staffer who was particularly helpful, make sure to add that person to your database so that you may contact him or her again in the future with additional requests.

2.5 Work with Agency Staff

You will often find that you can achieve greater success by working co-operatively with agency staff members. You should consider making it part of your standard practice to communicate with several individuals within an agency to determine what records you need and how best to obtain those records. It will likely take some time to determine who is best to contact for particular information, and this may change, depending upon the request and the particular agency at issue. Sometimes, it will be useful to speak with regulators, inspectors, and/or other enforcement staff. These individuals can often be very helpful, both for initial requests and as a point of contact on an ongoing basis. In addition to asking any specific questions about desired records, you can use these resources to ask general questions about the agencies' policies and procedures.

2.6 Speed Up the Process

Time may be a very important factor for many researchers attempting to use the FOIA—especially when a request concerns critical issues, such as matters concerning health, safety, environmental protections, human rights, and where time is of the essence. If time is of the essence, it is essential to expedite the process and make filing FOIA requests—and obtaining the requisite information—a speedier process. There are small, procedural steps that you can take to improve the likelihood that your request will be addressed more quickly. For example, when possible, consider using fax or e-mail instead of mail to make your request. You may also wish to consider sending your request to a smaller, less busy local or regional office instead of a particular agency's headquarters.

There are also things you can do when structuring your search to speed up the process. For example, when you have a sense of what you are looking for, narrow your request. Requesting specific documents may help to ensure that you receive a quicker response than you would if you requested all documents about a particular topic within a particular date range.

You should also communicate with agency staff to ensure that they are aware of the urgency of the particular request. When filing the request, explain why it is urgent and then be persistent in following up. Set a deadline for receiving the information and then call the applicable agency a day or two after making the request to check in. You should also do whatever possible to make it easier for the agency to respond promptly. For example, you could ask for access to review a set of materials instead of copies of a particular record. Where appropriate, you may also try to ask for a summary instead of an entire file.

2.7 Dealing with Exemptions

It is undeniable that the exemptions to the FOIA can be troubling and can present an obstacle to one's research. When making requests under the FOIA, it is likely that sooner or later you will be told that one or more records cannot be released due to an exemption. When encountering claimed exemptions, it will be helpful to recall that all segregable nonexempt portions must be released even if other parts of the record are deleted. In other words, if part of a record is exempt from disclosure, the agency must redact or remove that part of the record, and release the remainder. Accordingly, when all you can get is the redacted record, go ahead and get it, so you will at least have something to start with. You never know what information even the redacted record could reveal and where, in turn, that could take you.

You should also do what you can to work with the exemptions. While there are a relatively small number of exemptions, they are drafted so broadly that they can cover a vast amount of FOIA requests. The exemptions have been cited as the rationale for refusing a great number of disclosures. Consider a case involving the National Zoo in Washington, D.C. In 2002, after the death of Ryma, a giraffe well-regarded by many visitors, a writer from the *Washington Post* contacted the National Zoo to request animal medical records and necropsy and pathology reports.[2] In an e-mail reply back to the journalist, the zoo's director stated that it would provide detailed summaries generated by the individuals who had prepared the animal records but would not release the animal records themselves because doing so would violate the animal's privacy rights.

While many animal-protection advocates would likely be pleased to learn that animals have health privacy rights, or any privacy rights for that matter, most would find outright laughable the notion that a zoo could withhold an animal's medical records on that basis. Freedom of access advocates were suspicious of the rationale behind the denial and speculated that it was intended to keep the information quiet for one reason or another, not to protect animal privacy.

In this case, the possibility of legal recourse was very limited because the U.S. Court of Appeals in 1998 ruled that the Smithsonian Institution, the organization in charge of the National Zoo, is not considered a government agency for purposes of the FOIA.

The case involving the Smithsonian suggests that one should not be surprised by the refusal of any FOIA request on the grounds that an exemption applies. After all, if the government was able to claim that an animal's privacy rights constitutes a valid FOIA exemption and grounds for a refusal to disclose information, there is reason to believe that other unusual grounds for exemptions can—and will—be cited. Accordingly, one must resist the tendency to get too tied up in the exemptions. It is important to work with what you can get and not to spend too much time on the potential application of the exemptions. Even if the government refuses to turn over records with the argument that an exemption applies, you can think about the flip side—that is, what is *not* exempt.

In addition, there are certain tactics that can be utilized to get around the exemptions. The suggested tactics will vary, based upon the facts at issue and the particular exemptions claimed. Consider first, for example, the claim of the privacy exemption. As the zoo case indicates, privacy is an oft-cited justification for denying the disclosure of information. The FOIA allows an agency to weigh the public interest in disclosure against the privacy of the people named. The Supreme Court has held the only acceptable public interest was the extent to which disclosure would shed light on government operations or activities.[3] So as stated above, be sure to cast your purpose as shedding light on government operations or activities.

The internal-agency memoranda exemption is another popular exemption, which can be countered with a request to "redact and release." If you expect to encounter this exemption, let the agency know in your initial letter making the request. You may note in your request that: "Factual parts of pre-decisional documents are not exempt and must be released." The agency must make a case of "foreseeable harm" to trigger the exemption, and even in that case the agency can make a discretionary disclosure of internal agency memoranda.

When making FOIA requests, you may also expect to encounter the law enforcement exemption, which applies to open investigative files in ongoing or potential enforcement proceedings. Clearly, this will make it difficult to argue with the keepers of the secret file, but you can work with what they do have to give. For example, when a case has gone to trial, has resulted in civil penalties, or has not been sustained—in other words, when the case file is indisputably closed—then ask for the investigative file.

The trade secrets exemption, another one that is cited rather frequently, applies to information given to the government by individuals or private businesses that, if disclosed, would cause substantial harm to that person or business or impair the government's ability to obtain that information in the future. However, the exemption does not apply to documents the government prepares based primarily on information it gathers from outside sources. In addition, it does not apply to information that has been publicly disseminated. Accordingly, be sure to look and see who wrote the record and whether it is referenced in any public setting.

If you will be making requests for information under the FOIA, it is likely that sooner or later you will receive a response from the government asserting that the information cannot be shared due to an exemption. Nothing can be done to prevent the government from making this claim, so you should make an effort to be best prepared to respond to claimed exemptions.

3. The Government's Role

As mentioned throughout this book, there is a lot of anticipation about the possible effects that the Obama administration may have on the administration of the FOIA in the United States. While everything suggests that the Obama presidency will be far more open and transparent than its successor, it is also without a doubt that the Obama administration faces challenges in balancing the needs of open government with other needs such as national security. In November 2008, the Sunshine in Government Initiative, a coalition of media groups devoted to government accessibility, released a series of recommendations for President-elect Barack Obama regarding transparency and integrity in the government.[4] It noted the "broad expansion of government secrecy" seen through the years of the Bush administration, stressing the immediacy of the issue and the need for concrete solutions.

The report laid out four specific recommendations. The first was to restore the FOIA's presumption of disclosure by establishing policy requiring federal agencies to disclose information unless it contains information posing a "foreseeable harm" to an interest exempted by the FOIA. The Coalition argues that President George W. Bush and Attorney General John Ashcroft instituted a policy of secrecy early in the Bush administration by encouraging agencies to look critically at disclosure requests and withhold information deemed as having a "sound legal basis" for denial.

The second recommendation was to establish a governmentwide ombudsman within the National Archives to help citizens access government information and act as an independent source for freedom of information guidance. This office would streamline requests and simplify an often-confusing process—one the report points out had become extremely backlogged under the Bush administration. Additionally, the office would allow for easier online access to information.

The Coalition also advises Obama to limit federal agencies from proposing new statutory exemptions to the FOIA under Exemption 3. These sorts of exemptions allow agencies to specifically withhold information as it is requested, according to the report, and are never formally reviewed to determine their necessity. The group recommends only proposing Exemption 3 statutes when standing FOIA exemptions protecting national security and personal privacy interests are not adequate.

Finally, the group recommends that Obama and members of his administration speak on the record whenever making public statements regarding viewpoints or news events. This runs counter to historic precedent, in which many administration officials often speak to journalists only under "not for attribution" conditions.

4. Conclusion

The benefits of information freedom are clear and numerous. The public is only able to truly participate in the democratic process when it has all necessary information about government activities and policies.

Freedom of information is a fundamental right of all human beings. The freedom to access information held by governments allows communities, groups, and individuals to better protect their rights. The freedom of information protects against dangerous conditions, abuses, mismanagement, corruption, and crime.

While much can, and has been, said about the importance of the freedom of information to individuals, the freedom is also very beneficial to governments themselves. Openness and transparency in government can improve the trust and confidence of citizens, thereby contributing to more effective government and a more content society.

This book has highlighted a diverse selection of revelations uncovered by the FOIA and other information access laws. Many of these revelations were groundbreaking. Some helped to connect history, while others helped to protect health and safety. Some brought government waste and corruption to light, thereby causing it to cease and helping to bring perpetrators to justice. Still others helped to protect animal welfare and other important aspects of our natural environment.

At the same time, this book has shown that much remains to be done to achieve a truly transparent government. The data and examples highlighted in this book show that the Bush administration had a particular propensity for secrecy. This has impacted our society in a number of ways and has had a particularly harsh impact on the freedom of information. As compared with the Bush administration, the Obama administration promises to be far more transparent and open. Here's hoping that this greater openness will enable our society to undo some of the damage that has been done to our freedom of information and get us back on track to being the society that President Woodrow Wilson hoped for almost 100 years ago, with a government that is "all outside and no inside."[5]

Notes

1. Freedom of Information Act: Hearings Before the Subcomm. on the Constitution of the Senate Comm. On the Judiciary, 97th Cong., 1st Sess. 604, 390 (1981).

2. James V. Grimaldi, "National Zoo Cites Privacy Concerns in Its Refusal to Release Animal Medical Records," *The Washington Post*, May 6, 2002, at E12.

3. *Bibles v. Or. Natural Desert Ass'n*, 519 U.S. 355, 356 (1997).

4. Media Coalition Recommendations for Action by the Obama Administration to Strengthen Transparency and Integrity in Government, available at: www .sunshineingovernment.org/transition/sgi_obama_recs.pdf.

5. Woodrow Wilson, *The New Freedom: A Call for the Emancipation of the Generous Energies of a People* (Library Reprints, 1913).

Appendix A

The Freedom of Information Act, 5 U.S.C. § 552

[As Amended By Public Law No. 110-175, 121 Stat. 2524]

§ 552. Public information; agency rules, opinions, orders, records, and proceedings

1. Each agency shall make available to the public information as follows:

(a) Each agency shall separately state and currently publish in the Federal Register for the guidance of the public—

(i) descriptions of its central and field organization and the established places at which, the employees (and in the case of a uniformed service, the members) from whom, and the methods whereby, the public may obtain information, make submittals or requests, or obtain decisions;

(ii) statements of the general course and method by which its functions are channeled and determined, including the nature and requirements of all formal and informal procedures available;

(iii) rules of procedure, descriptions of forms available or the places at which forms may be obtained, and instructions as to the scope and contents of all papers, reports, or examinations;

(iv) substantive rules of general applicability adopted as authorized by law, and statements of general policy or interpretations of general applicability formulated and adopted by the agency; and

(v) each amendment, revision, or repeal of the foregoing.

Except to the extent that a person has actual and timely notice of the terms thereof, a person may not in any manner be required to resort to, or be adversely affected by, a matter required to be published in the Federal Register and not so published. For the purpose of this paragraph, matter reasonably available to the class of persons affected thereby is deemed published in the Federal Register when incorporated by reference therein with the approval of the Director of the Federal Register.

(b)   Each agency, in accordance with published rules, shall make available for public inspection and copying—

(i)   final opinions, including concurring and dissenting opinions, as well as orders, made in the adjudication of cases;

(ii)   those statements of policy and interpretations which have been adopted by the agency and are not published in the Federal Register;

(iii)   administrative staff manuals and instructions to staff that affect a member of the public;

(iv)   copies of all records, regardless of form or format, which have been released to any person under paragraph (3) and which, because of the nature of their subject matter, the agency determines have become or are likely to become the subject of subsequent requests for substantially the same records; and

(v)   a general index of the records referred to under subparagraph (D);

unless the materials are promptly published and copies offered for sale. For records created on or after November 1, 1996, within one year after such date, each agency shall make such records available, including by computer telecommunications or, if computer telecommunications means have not been established by the agency, by other electronic means. To the extent required to prevent a clearly unwarranted invasion of personal privacy, an agency may delete identifying details when it makes available or publishes an opinion, statement of policy, interpretation, staff manual, instruction, or copies of records referred to in subparagraph (D). However, in each case the justification for the deletion shall be explained fully in writing, and the extent of such deletion shall be indicated on the portion of the record which is made available or published, unless including that indication would harm an interest protected by the exemption in subsection (b) under which the deletion is made. If technically feasible, the extent of the deletion shall be indicated at the place in the record where the deletion was made. Each agency shall also maintain and make available for public inspection and copying current indexes providing identifying information for the public as to any matter issued, adopted, or promulgated after July 4, 1967, and required by this paragraph to be made available or published. Each agency shall promptly publish, quarterly or more frequently, and distribute (by sale or otherwise) copies of each index or supplements thereto unless it determines by order published in the Federal Register that the publication would be unnecessary and impracticable, in which case the agency shall nonetheless provide copies of an index on request at a cost not to exceed the direct cost of duplication. Each agency shall make the index referred to in subparagraph (E) available by computer telecommunications by December 31, 1999. A final order, opinion, statement of policy, interpretation, or staff manual or instruction that affects a member of the public may be relied on, used, or cited as precedent by an agency against a party other than an agency only if—

(A)   it has been indexed and either made available or published as provided by this paragraph; or

(B)   (ii) the party has actual and timely notice of the terms thereof.

(c)   (i) Except with respect to the records made available under paragraphs (1) and (2) of this subsection, and except as provided in subparagraph (E), each agency, upon any request for records which (i) reasonably describes such records and (ii) is made in accordance with published rules stating the time, place, fees (if any), and procedures to be followed, shall make the records promptly available to any person.

(ii)   In making any record available to a person under this paragraph, an agency shall provide the record in any form or format requested by the person if the record is readily reproducible by the agency in that form or format. Each agency shall make reasonable efforts to maintain its records in forms or formats that are reproducible for purposes of this section.

(iii)   In responding under this paragraph to a request for records, an agency shall make reasonable efforts to search for the records in electronic form or format, except when such efforts would significantly interfere with the operation of the agency's automated information system.

(iv)   For purposes of this paragraph, the term "search" means to review, manually or by automated means, agency records for the purpose of locating those records which are responsive to a request.

(v)   An agency, or part of an agency, that is an element of the intelligence community (as that term is defined in section 3(4) of the National Security Act of 1947 (50 U.S.C. 401a(4))) shall not make any record available under this paragraph to—

(A)   any government entity, other than a State, territory, commonwealth, or district of the United States, or any subdivision thereof; or

(B)   a representative of a government entity described in clause (i).

(d)   (i) (A) In order to carry out the provisions of this section, each agency shall promulgate regulations, pursuant to notice and receipt of public comment, specifying the schedule of fees applicable to the processing of requests under this section and establishing procedures and guidelines for determining when such fees should be waived or reduced. Such schedule shall conform to the guidelines which shall be promulgated, pursuant to notice and receipt of public comment, by the Director of the Office of Management and Budget and which shall provide for a uniform schedule of fees for all agencies.

(B)   Such agency regulations shall provide that—

(1)   fees shall be limited to reasonable standard charges for document search, duplication, and review, when records are requested for commercial use;

(2)   fees shall be limited to reasonable standard charges for document duplication when records are not sought for commercial use and the request is made by an educational or noncommercial scientific institution, whose purpose is scholarly or scientific research; or a representative of the news media; and

(3)   for any request not described in (I) or (II), fees shall be limited to reasonable standard charges for document search and duplication.

In this clause, the term 'a representative of the news media' means any person or entity that gathers information of potential interest to a segment of the public, uses its editorial skills to turn the raw materials into a distinct work, and distributes that work to an audience. In this clause, the term 'news' means information that is about current events or that would be of current interest to the public. Examples of news-media entities are television or radio stations broadcasting to the public at large and publishers of periodicals (but only if such entities qualify as disseminators of 'news') who make their products available for purchase by or subscription by or free distribution to the general public. These examples are not all-inclusive. Moreover, as methods of news delivery evolve (for example, the adoption of the electronic dissemination of newspapers through telecommunications services), such alternative media shall be considered to be news-media entities. A freelance journalist shall be regarded as working for a news-media entity if the journalist can demonstrate a solid basis for expecting publication through that entity, whether or not the journalist is actually employed by the entity. A publication contract would present a solid basis for such an expectation; the Government may also consider the past publication record of the requester in making such a determination.

(C)   Documents shall be furnished without any charge or at a charge reduced below the fees established under clause (ii) if disclosure of the information is in the public interest because it is likely to contribute significantly to public understanding of the operations or activities of the government and is not primarily in the commercial interest of the requester.

(D)   Fee schedules shall provide for the recovery of only the direct costs of search, duplication, or review. Review costs shall include only the direct costs incurred during the initial examination of a document for the purposes of determining whether the documents must be disclosed under this section and for the purposes of withholding any portions exempt from disclosure under this section. Review costs may not include any costs incurred in resolving issues of law or policy that may be raised in the course of processing a request under this section. No fee may be charged by any agency under this section—

(1)   if the costs of routine collection and processing of

the fee are likely to equal or exceed the amount of the fee; or

(2)   for any request described in clause (ii)(II) or (III)

of this subparagraph for the first two hours of search time or for the first one hundred pages of duplication.

(E)   No agency may require advance payment of any fee

unless the requester has previously failed to pay fees in a timely fashion, or the agency has determined that the fee will exceed $250.

(F)   Nothing in this subparagraph shall supersede fees

chargeable under a statute specifically providing for setting the level of fees for particular types of records.

(G)   In any action by a requester regarding the waiver of fees

under this section, the court shall determine the matter de novo: *Provided*, that the court's review of the matter shall be limited to the record before the agency.

(H)   An agency shall not assess search fees (or in the case of

a requester described under clause (ii)(II), duplication fees) under this subparagraph if the agency fails to comply with any time limit under paragraph (6), if no unusual or exceptional circumstances (as those terms are defined for purposes of paragraphs (6)(B) and (C), respectively) apply to the processing of the request. [**Effective one year from date of enactment**]

(ii)   On complaint, the district court of the United States in the

district in which the complainant resides, or has his principal place of business, or in which the agency records are situated, or in the District of Columbia, has jurisdiction to enjoin the agency from withholding agency records and to order the production of any agency records improperly withheld from the complainant. In such a case the court shall determine the matter de novo, and may examine the contents of such agency records in camera to determine whether such records or any part thereof shall be withheld under any of the exemptions set forth in subsection (b) of this section, and the burden is on the agency to sustain its action. In addition to any other matters to which a court accords substantial weight, a court shall accord substantial weight to an affidavit of an agency concerning the agency's determination as to technical feasibility under paragraph (2)(C) and subsection (b) and reproducibility under paragraph (3)(B).

(iii) Notwithstanding any other provision of law, the defendant shall serve an answer or otherwise plead to any complaint made under this subsection within thirty days after service upon the defendant of the pleading in which such complaint is made, unless the court otherwise directs for good cause is shown.

(iv) [**Repealed. Pub. L. 98-620, title IV, Sec. 402(2), Nov. 8, 1984, 98 Stat. 3357.**]

(v) (A) The court may assess against the United States reasonable attorney fees and other litigation costs reasonably incurred in any case under this section in which the complainant has substantially prevailed.

(B) For purposes of this subparagraph, a complainant has substantially prevailed if the complainant has obtained relief through either—

(1) a judicial order, or an enforceable written agreement or consent decree; or

(2) a voluntary or unilateral change in position by the agency, if the complainant's claim is not insubstantial.

(vi) (A) Whenever the court orders the production of any agency records improperly withheld from the complainant and assesses against the United States reasonable attorney fees and other litigation costs, and the court additionally issues a written finding that the circumstances surrounding the withholding raise questions whether agency personnel acted arbitrarily or capriciously with respect to the withholding, the Special Counsel shall promptly initiate a proceeding to determine whether disciplinary action is warranted against the officer or employee who was primarily responsible for the withholding. The Special Counsel, after investigation and consideration of the evidence submitted, shall submit his findings and recommendations to the administrative authority of the agency concerned and shall send copies of the findings and recommendations to the officer or employee or his representative. The administrative authority shall take the corrective action that the Special Counsel recommends.

(B) The Attorney General shall—

(1) notify the Special Counsel of each civil action described under the first sentence of clause (i); and

(2) annually submit a report to Congress on the number of such civil actions in the preceding year.

(C) The Special Counsel shall annually submit a report to Congress on the actions taken by the Special Counsel under clause (i).

(vii) In the event of noncompliance with the order of the court, the district court may punish for contempt the responsible employee, and in the case of a uniformed service, the responsible member.

(e)   Each agency having more than one member shall maintain and make available for public inspection a record of the final votes of each member in every agency proceeding.

(f)   (i) Each agency, upon any request for records made under paragraph (1), (2), or (3) of this subsection, shall—

(A)   determine within 20 days (excepting Saturdays, Sundays, and legal public holidays) after the receipt of any such request whether to comply with such request and shall immediately notify the person making such request of such determination and the reasons therefor, and of the right of such person to appeal to the head of the agency any adverse determination; and

(B)   make a determination with respect to any appeal within twenty days (excepting Saturdays, Sundays, and legal public holidays) after the receipt of such appeal. If on appeal the denial of the request for records is in whole or in part upheld, the agency shall notify the person making such request of the provisions for judicial review of that determination under paragraph (4) of this subsection.

The 20-day period under clause (i) shall commence on the date on which the request is first received by the appropriate component of the agency, but in any event not later than ten days after the request is first received by any component of the agency that is designated in the agency's regulations under this section to receive requests under this section. The 20-day period shall not be tolled by the agency except—

(1)   that the agency may make one request to the requester for information and toll the 20-day period while it is awaiting such information that it has reasonably requested from the requester under this section; or

(2)   if necessary to clarify with the requester issues regarding fee assessment. In either case, the agency's receipt of the requester's response to the agency's request for information or clarification ends the tolling period.

[Effective one year from date of enactment]

(ii)   (A) In unusual circumstances as specified in this subparagraph, the time limits prescribed in either clause (i) or clause (ii) of subparagraph (A) may be extended by written notice to the person making such request setting forth the unusual circumstances for such extension and the date on which a determination is expected to be dispatched. No such notice shall specify a date that would result in an extension for more than ten working days, except as provided in clause (ii) of this subparagraph.

(B)   With respect to a request for which a written notice under clause (i) extends the time limits prescribed under clause (i) of subparagraph (A), the agency shall notify the person making the request if the request cannot be processed within the time limit specified in that clause and shall provide the person an opportunity to limit the scope of the request so that it may be processed within that time limit or an opportunity to arrange with the agency an alternative time frame for processing the request or a modified request. To aid the requester, each agency shall make available its FOIA Public Liaison, who shall assist in the resolution of any disputes between the requester and the agency. [**Effective one year from date of enactment**]. Refusal by the person to reasonably modify the request or arrange such an alternative time frame shall be considered as a factor in determining whether exceptional circumstances exist for purposes of subparagraph (C).

(C)   As used in this subparagraph, "unusual circumstances" means, but only to the extent reasonably necessary to the proper processing of the particular requests—

(1)   the need to search for and collect the requested records from field facilities or other establishments that are separate from the office processing the request;

(2)   the need to search for, collect, and appropriately examine a voluminous amount of separate and distinct records which are demanded in a single request; or

(3)   the need for consultation, which shall be conducted with all practicable speed, with another agency having a substantial interest in the determination of the request or among two or more components of the agency having substantial subject-matter interest therein.

(D)   Each agency may promulgate regulations, pursuant to notice and receipt of public comment, providing for the aggregation of certain requests by the same requestor, or by a group of requestors acting in concert, if the agency reasonably believes that such requests actually constitute a single request, which would otherwise satisfy the unusual circumstances specified in this subparagraph, and the requests involve clearly related matters. Multiple requests involving unrelated matters shall not be aggregated.

(iii) (A) Any person making a request to any agency for records under paragraph (1), (2), or (3) of this subsection shall be deemed to have exhausted his administrative remedies with respect to such request if the agency fails to comply with the applicable time limit provisions of this paragraph. If the Government can show exceptional circumstances exist and that the agency is exercising due diligence in responding to the request, the court may retain jurisdiction and allow the agency additional time to complete its review of the records. Upon any determination by an agency to comply with a request for records, the records shall be made promptly available to such person making such request. Any notification of denial of any request for records under this subsection shall set forth the names and titles or positions of each person responsible for the denial of such request.

(B)   For purposes of this subparagraph, the term "exceptional circumstances" does not include a delay that results from a predictable agency workload of requests under this section, unless the agency demonstrates reasonable progress in reducing its backlog of pending requests.

(C)   (iii) Refusal by a person to reasonably modify the scope of a request or arrange an alternative time frame for processing a request (or a modified request) under clause (ii) after being given an opportunity to do so by the agency to whom the person made the request shall be considered as a factor in determining whether exceptional circumstances exist for purposes of this subparagraph.

(iv)   (A) Each agency may promulgate regulations, pursuant to notice and receipt of public comment, providing for multitrack processing of requests for records based on the amount of work or time (or both) involved in processing requests.

(B)   Regulations under this subparagraph may provide a person making a request that does not qualify for the fastest multitrack processing an opportunity to limit the scope of the request in order to qualify for faster processing.

(C)   This subparagraph shall not be considered to affect the requirement under subparagraph (C) to exercise due diligence.

(v)   (A) Each agency shall promulgate regulations, pursuant to notice and receipt of public comment, providing for expedited processing of requests for records—

(1)   in cases in which the person requesting the records demonstrates a compelling need; and

(2)   in other cases determined by the agency.

(B)   Notwithstanding clause (i), regulations under this subparagraph must ensure—

(1)   that a determination of whether to provide expedited processing shall be made, and notice of the determination shall be provided to the person making the request, within 10 days after the date of the request; and

(2)   expeditious consideration of administrative appeals of such determinations of whether to provide expedited processing.

(C)   An agency shall process as soon as practicable any request for records to which the agency has granted expedited processing under this subparagraph. Agency action to deny or affirm denial of a request for expedited processing pursuant to this subparagraph, and failure by an agency to respond in a timely manner to such a request shall be subject to judicial review under paragraph (4), except that the judicial review shall be based on the record before the agency at the time of the determination.

(D)   A district court of the United States shall not have jurisdiction to review an agency denial of expedited processing of a request for records after the agency has provided a complete response to the request.

(E)   For purposes of this subparagraph, the term "compelling need" means—

(1)   that a failure to obtain requested records on an expedited basis under this paragraph could reasonably be expected to pose an imminent threat to the life or physical safety of an individual; or

(2)   with respect to a request made by a person primarily engaged in disseminating information, urgency to inform the public concerning actual or alleged Federal Government activity.

(F)   A demonstration of a compelling need by a person making a request for expedited processing shall be made by a statement certified by such person to be true and correct to the best of such person's knowledge and belief.

(vi)   In denying a request for records, in whole or in part, an agency shall make a reasonable effort to estimate the volume of any requested matter the provision of which is denied, and shall provide any such estimate to the person making the request, unless providing such estimate would harm an interest protected by the exemption in subsection (b) pursuant to which the denial is made.

(g)   Each agency shall—

(i)   establish a system to assign an individualized tracking number for each request received that will take longer than ten days to process and provide to each person making a request the tracking number assigned to the request; and

(ii)   establish a telephone line or Internet service that provides information about the status of a request to the person making the request using the assigned tracking number, including—

(A)   the date on which the agency originally received the request; and

(B)   an estimated date on which the agency will complete action on the request.

[Effective one year from date of enactment]
2.   This section does not apply to matters that are—

(a)   (A) specifically authorized under criteria established by an Executive order to be kept secret in the interest of national defense or foreign policy and (B) are in fact properly classified pursuant to such Executive order;

(b)   related solely to the internal personnel rules and practices of an agency;

(c)   specifically exempted from disclosure by statute (other than section 552b of this title), provided that such statute (A) requires that the matters be withheld from the public in such a manner as to leave no discretion on the issue, or (B) establishes particular criteria for withholding or refers to particular types of matters to be withheld;

(d)   trade secrets and commercial or financial information obtained from a person and privileged or confidential;

(e)   inter-agency or intra-agency memorandums or letters which would not be available by law to a party other than an agency in litigation with the agency;

(f)   personnel and medical files and similar files the disclosure of which would constitute a clearly unwarranted invasion of personal privacy;

(g)   records or information compiled for law enforcement purposes, but only to the extent that the production of such law enforcement records or information (A) could reasonably be expected to interfere with enforcement proceedings, (B) would deprive a person of a right to a fair trial or an impartial adjudication, (C) could reasonably be expected to constitute an unwarranted invasion of personal privacy, (D) could reasonably be expected to disclose the identity of a confidential source, including a State, local, or foreign agency or authority or any private institution which furnished information on a confidential basis, and, in the case of a record or information compiled by a criminal law enforcement authority in the course of a criminal investigation or by an agency conducting a lawful national security intelligence investigation, information furnished by a confidential source, (E) would disclose techniques and procedures for law enforcement investigations or prosecutions, or would disclose guidelines for law enforcement investigations or prosecutions if such disclosure could reasonably be expected to risk circumvention of the law, or (F) could reasonably be expected to endanger the life or physical safety of any individual;

(h)   contained in or related to examination, operating, or condition reports prepared by, on behalf of, or for the use of an agency responsible for the regulation or supervision of financial institutions; or

(i)   geological and geophysical information and data, including maps, concerning wells.

Any reasonably segregable portion of a record shall be provided to any person requesting such record after deletion of the portions which are exempt under this subsection. The amount of information deleted, and the exemption under which the deletion is made, shall be indicated on the released portion of the record, unless including that indication would harm an interest protected by the exemption in this subsection under which the deletion is made. If technically feasible, the amount of the information deleted, and the exemption under which the deletion is made, shall be indicated at the place in the record where such deletion is made.

3. (a) Whenever a request is made which involves access to records described in subsection (b)(7)(A) and—

      (i) the investigation or proceeding involves a possible violation of criminal law; and

      (ii) there is reason to believe that (i) the subject of the investigation or proceeding is not aware of its pendency, and (ii) disclosure of the existence of the records could reasonably be expected to interfere with enforcement proceedings, the agency may, during only such time as that circumstance continues, treat the records as not subject to the requirements of this section.

    (b) Whenever informant records maintained by a criminal law enforcement agency under an informant's name or personal identifier are requested by a third party according to the informant's name or personal identifier, the agency may treat the records as not subject to the requirements of this section unless the informant's status as an informant has been officially confirmed.

    (c) Whenever a request is made which involves access to records maintained by the Federal Bureau of Investigation pertaining to foreign intelligence or counterintelligence, or international terrorism, and the existence of the records is classified information as provided in subsection (b)(1), the Bureau may, as long as the existence of the records remains classified information, treat the records as not subject to the requirements of this section.

4. This section does not authorize the withholding of information or limit the availability of records to the public, except as specifically stated in this section. This section is not authority to withhold information from Congress.

5. (a) On or before February 1 of each year, each agency shall submit to the Attorney General of the United States a report which shall cover the preceding fiscal year and which shall include—

      (i) the number of determinations made by the agency not to comply with requests for records made to such agency under subsection (a) and the reasons for each such determination;

      (ii) (A) the number of appeals made by persons under subsection (a)(6), the result of such appeals, and the reason for the action upon each appeal that results in a denial of information; and

        (B) a complete list of all statutes that the agency relies upon to authorize the agency to withhold information under subsection (b)(3), the number of occasions on which each statute was relied upon, a description of whether a court has upheld the decision of the agency to withhold information under each such statute, and a concise description of the scope of any information withheld;

(iii) the number of requests for records pending before the agency as of September 30 of the preceding year, and the median and average number of days that such requests had been pending before the agency as of that date;

(iv) the number of requests for records received by the agency and the number of requests which the agency processed;

(v) the median number of days taken by the agency to process different types of requests, based on the date on which the requests were received by the agency;

(vi) the average number of days for the agency to respond to a request beginning on the date on which the request was received by the agency, the median number of days for the agency to respond to such requests, and the range in number of days for the agency to respond to such requests;

(vii) based on the number of business days that have elapsed since each request was originally received by the agency—

(A) the number of requests for records to which the agency has responded with a determination within a period up to and including 20 days, and in 20-day increments up to and including 200 days;

(B) the number of requests for records to which the agency has responded with a determination within a period greater than 200 days and less than 301 days;

(C) the number of requests for records to which the agency has responded with a determination within a period greater than 300 days and less than 401 days; and

(D) the number of requests for records to which the agency has responded with a determination within a period greater than 400 days;

(viii) the average number of days for the agency to provide the granted information beginning on the date on which the request was originally filed, the median number of days for the agency to provide the granted information, and the range in number of days for the agency to provide the granted information;

(ix) the median and average number of days for the agency to respond to administrative appeals based on the date on which the appeals originally were received by the agency, the highest number of business days taken by the agency to respond to an administrative appeal, and the lowest number of business days taken by the agency to respond to an administrative appeal;

(x)   data on the 10 active requests with the earliest filing dates pending at each agency, including the amount of time that has elapsed since each request was originally received by the agency;

(xi)   data on the 10 active administrative appeals with the earliest filing dates pending before the agency as of September 30 of the preceding year, including the number of business days that have elapsed since the requests were originally received by the agency;

(xii)   the number of expedited review requests that are granted and denied, the average and median number of days for adjudicating expedited review requests, and the number adjudicated within the required 10 days;

(xiii) the number of fee waiver requests that are granted and denied, and the average and median number of days for adjudicating fee waiver determinations;

(xiv) the total amount of fees collected by the agency for processing requests; and

(xv)   the number of full-time staff of the agency devoted to processing requests for records under this section, and the total amount expended by the agency for processing such requests.

(b)   Information in each report submitted under paragraph (1) shall be expressed in terms of each principal component of the agency and for the agency overall.

(c)   Each agency shall make each such report available to the public including by computer telecommunications, or if computer telecommunications means have not been established by the agency, by other electronic means. In addition, each agency shall make the raw statistical data used in its reports available electronically to the public upon request.

(d)   The Attorney General of the United States shall make each report which has been made available by electronic means available at a single electronic access point. The Attorney General of the United States shall notify the Chairman and ranking minority member of the Committee on Government Reform and Oversight of the House of Representatives and the Chairman and ranking minority member of the Committees on Governmental Affairs and the Judiciary of the Senate, no later than April 1 of the year in which each such report is issued, that such reports are available by electronic means.

(e)   The Attorney General of the United States, in consultation with the Director of the Office of Management and Budget, shall develop reporting and performance guidelines in connection with reports required by this subsection by October 1, 1997, and may establish additional requirements for such reports as the Attorney General determines may be useful.

(f)   The Attorney General of the United States shall submit an annual report on or before April 1 of each calendar year which shall include for the prior calendar year a listing of the number of cases arising under this section, the exemption involved in each case, the disposition of such case, and the cost, fees, and penalties assessed under subparagraphs (E), (F), and (G) of subsection (a)(4). Such report shall also include a description of the efforts undertaken by the Department of Justice to encourage agency compliance with this section.

6. For purposes of this section, the term—

(a)   "agency" as defined in section 551(1) of this title includes any executive department, military department, Government corporation, Government controlled corporation, or other establishment in the executive branch of the Government (including the Executive Office of the President), or any independent regulatory agency; and

(b)   "record and any other term used in this section in reference to information includes any information that would be an agency record subject to the requirements of this section when maintained by an agency in any format, including an electronic format.

(c)   'record' and any other term used in this section in reference to information includes—

(i)   any information that would be an agency record subject to the requirements of this section when maintained by an agency in any format, including an electronic format; and

(ii)   any information described under subparagraph (A) that is maintained for an agency by an entity under Government contract, for the purposes of records management.

7. The head of each agency shall prepare and make publicly available upon request, reference material or a guide for requesting records or information from the agency, subject to the exemptions in subsection (b), including—

(a)   an index of all major information systems of the agency;

(b)   a description of major information and record locator systems maintained by the agency; and

(c)   a handbook for obtaining various types and categories of public information from the agency pursuant to chapter 35 of title 44, and under this section.

8. (a) There is established the Office of Government Information Services within the National Archives and Records Administration.

(b)   The Office of Government Information Services shall—

(i)   review policies and procedures of administrative agencies under this section;

(ii) review compliance with this section by administrative agencies; and

(iii) recommend policy changes to Congress and the President to improve the administration of this section.

(c)   The Office of Government Information Services shall offer mediation services to resolve disputes between persons making requests under this section and administrative agencies as a non-exclusive alternative to litigation and, at the discretion of the Office, may issue advisory opinions if mediation has not resolved the dispute.

9. The Government Accountability Office shall conduct audits of administrative agencies on the implementation of this section and issue reports detailing the results of such audits.

10. Each agency shall designate a Chief FOIA Officer who shall be a senior official of such agency (at the Assistant Secretary or equivalent level).

11. The Chief FOIA Officer of each agency shall, subject to the authority of the head of the agency—

(a)   have agency-wide responsibility for efficient and appropriate compliance with this section;

(b)   monitor implementation of this section throughout the agency and keep the head of the agency, the chief legal officer of the agency, and the Attorney General appropriately informed of the agency's performance in implementing this section;

(c)   recommend to the head of the agency such adjustments to agency practices, policies, personnel, and funding as may be necessary to improve its implementation of this section;

(d)   review and report to the Attorney General, through the head of the agency, at such times and in such formats as the Attorney General may direct, on the agency's performance in implementing this section;

(e)   facilitate public understanding of the purposes of the statutory exemptions of this section by including concise descriptions of the exemptions in both the agency's handbook issued under subsection (g), and the agency's annual report on this section, and by providing an overview, where appropriate, of certain general categories of agency records to which those exemptions apply; and

(f)   designate one or more FOIA Public Liaisons.

12. FOIA Public Liaisons shall report to the agency Chief FOIA Officer and shall serve as supervisory officials to whom a requester under this section

can raise concerns about the service the requester has received from the FOIA Requester Center, following an initial response from the FOIA Requester Center Staff. FOIA Public Liaisons shall be responsible for assisting in reducing delays, increasing transparency and understanding of the status of requests, and assisting in the resolution of disputes.

Appendix B-1

Sample FOIA Request Letter

Agency Head [or Freedom of Information Act Officer]
Name of Agency
Address of Agency
City, State, Zip Code

Re: Freedom of Information Act Request

Dear [_____]:

This is a request under the Freedom of Information Act.

I request that a copy of the following documents [or documents containing the following information] be provided to me: [identify the documents for information as specifically as possible].

In order to help to determine my status for purposes of determining the applicability of any fees, you should know that I am (insert a suitable description of the requester and the purpose of the request).

   [Sample requester descriptions:

   a representative of the news media affiliated with the _____ newspaper (magazine, television station, etc), and this request is made as part of news gathering and not for a commercial use.

affiliated with an educational or noncommercial scientific institution, an this request is made for a scholarly or scientific purpose and not for a commercial use.

an individual seeking information for personal use and not for a commercial use.

affiliated with a private corporation and am seeking information for us in the company's business.]

[Optional] I am willing to pay fees for this request up to a maximum of $_____. If you estimate that the fees will exceed this limit, please inform me first.

[Optional] I request a waiver of all fees for this request. Disclosure of the requested information to me is in the public interest because it is likely to contribute significantly to public understanding of the operations or activities of the government and is not primarily in my commercial interest. [Include specific details, including how the requested information will be disseminated by the requester for public benefit.]

[Optional] I request that the information I seek be provided in electronic format, and I would like to receive it on a CD-ROM or via email].

[Optional] I ask that my request receive expedited processing because _____. [Include specific details concerning your "compelling need," such as being someone "primarily engaged in disseminating information" and specifics concerning your "urgency to inform the public concerning actual or alleged Federal Government activity."]

[Optional] I also include a telephone number at which I can be contacted during the hours of _____, if necessary, to discuss any aspect of my request.

Thank you for your consideration of this request.

Sincerely,

Name
Address
City, State, Zip Code
Telephone Number [Optional]
E-mail address [Optional]

Appendix B-2

Sample FOIA Appeal Letter

Agency Head or Appeal Officer
Name of Agency
Address of Agency
City, State, Zip Code

Re: Freedom of Information Act Appeal

Dear [_____]:

This is an appeal under the Freedom of Information Act.

On [date), I requested documents under the Freedom of Information Act. My request was assigned the following identification number: _____. On (date), I received a response to my request in a letter signed by (name of official). I appeal the denial of my request.

[Optional] I enclose a copy of the response letter.

[Optional] The documents that were withheld must be disclosed under the FOIA because (provide details you would want an agency head or appeal officer to consider when deciding your appeal.)

[Optional] I appeal the decision to deny my request for a waiver of fees. I believe that I am entitled to a waiver of fees. Disclosure of the documents I requested is in the public interest because it is likely to contribute significantly to public understanding of the operations or activities of the government and is not primarily in my commercial interest. (Provide details)

[Optional] I appeal the decision to require me to pay review costs for this request. I am not seeking the documents for a commercial use. (Provide details)

[Optional] I appeal the decision to require me to pay search and/or review charges for this request. I am a representative of the news media seeking information as part of news gathering and not for commercial use.

[Optional] I appeal the decision to require me to pay search and/or review charges for this request. I am a representative of an educational institution seeking information for a scholarly purpose.

[Optional] I appeal the decision to require me to accept the information I seek in a paper or hardcopy format. I requested this information, which the agency maintains in an electronic form, in an electronic format, specifically on a CD-ROM or transmitted via email to _____.

[Optional] I also include a telephone number at which I can be contacted during the hours of _____, if necessary, to discuss any aspect of my appeal.

Thank you for your consideration of this appeal.

Sincerely,

Name
Address
City, State, Zip Code
Telephone Number [Optional]
E-mail address [Optional]

Appendix C

Select Agency Addresses

CABINET DEPARTMENTS

AGRICULTURE

United States Department of Agriculture
Contact individual departments, or:
USDA FOIA Officer
Room 209-A, Jamie Whitten Bldg.
1400 Independence Ave., SW
Washington, DC 20250-0103
Tel: (202) 720-8164
Fax: (202) 720-7808
http://www.da.usda.gov/foia.htm

Food Safety and Inspection Service
Freedom of Information Act Officer
USDA, Food Safety and Inspection Service
Room 1140-South Bldg.
1400 Independence Ave., SW
Washington, DC 20250
Tel: (202) 690-3882
Fax: (202) 690-3023
http://www.fsis.usda.gov/FOIA/index.asp

Office of the Inspector General
USDA, Office of Inspector General
Room 441-E Jamie Whitten Bldg. - Legal Staff
1400 Independence Ave., SW
Washington, DC 20250-2308
Tel: (202) 720-5677
Fax: (202) 690-6305
Email: FOIASTAFF@oig.usda.gov
www.usda.gov/oig/foia.htm

COMMERCE

United States Department of Commerce
Contact individual departments, or:
Department of Commerce
Departmental FOIA Officer
Office of Management and Organization
1401 Constitution Ave., NW
Washington, DC 20230
Tel: (202) 482-4115
Fax: (202) 482-3270
Email: EFoia@doc.gov
http://www.osec.doc.gov/omo/FOIA/FOIAWEBSITE.htm

DEFENSE

Department of Defense
Contact individual departments, bases or activities, or:

Office of Freedom of Information
1155 Defense Pentagon
Washington, DC 20301-1155

Air Force
HAF/IMII
1000 Air Force Pentagon
Washington, DC 20330-1000
Fax: (703) 693-2746
e-mail: haf.foia@pentagon.af.mil
www.foia.af.mil

Army
Department of the Army Freedom of
   Information and Privacy Office
7701 Telegraph Road Suite 144
Alexandria, VA 22315-3905
Tel: (703) 806-7820
Fax: (703) 806-7135
Email: FOIA@rmda.belvoir.army.mil
http://www.armyg1.army.mil/foia/
   default.asp

Defense Contract Audit Agency
Headquarters, Defense Contract Audit
   Agency
Attn: CMR, FOIA Service Center
8725 John J. Kingman Road, Suite
   2135
Fort Belvoir, VA 22060-6219
Tel: (703) 767-1002
Fax: (703) 767-1011
e-mail: DCAA-FOIA@dcaa.mil
www.dcaa.mil/foia.htm

**Defense Contract Management
   Agency**
FOIA/Privacy Officer
PO Box 151300
Alexandria, VA 22315-9998
Tel: (703) 428-1951
www.dcma.mil/foia.htm

**Defense Finance and Accounting
   Service**
FOIA/PA Program Manager
Corporate Communications
DFAS-DCC/DE

6760 E. Irvington Place
Denver, CO 80279-8000
Tel: (303) 676-6045
Fax: (303) 676-7710
e-mail: linda.krabbenhoft@dfas.mil
www.dfas.mil/library/foia.htm

**Defense Information Systems
   Agency**
Defense Information Systems Agency
ATTN: Headquarters FOIA Requester
   Service Center
P.O. Box 4502
Arlington, VA 22204-4502
Tel: (703) 607-6515
Fax: (703) 607-4344
http://www.disa.mil/about/legal/
   foia/index.html

Defense Intelligence Agency
FOIA Requester Service Center
Defense Intelligence Agency
ATTN: DAN-1A (FOIA)
200 MacDill Blvd
Washington, DC 20340-5100
Tel: (301) 394-5587
Fax: (301) 394-5356
e-mail: www.foia@dia.mil

Defense Logistics Agency
FOIA Desk Officer
Headquarters, Defense Logistics
   Agency
ATTN: DG/FOIA & Privacy Act
   Team
8725 John J. Kingman Road, Stop
   2533
Fort Belvoir, VA 22060-6221
Tel: 703-767-5247
e-mail: hq-foia@dla.mil

Defense Security Service
Office of FOIA and Privacy, GCF
1340 Braddock Place
Alexandria, VA 22314-1651
Tel: (703) 325-5991
Fax: (703) 325-5341

www.dss.mil/contactus/
about.foia.htm

Defense Threat Reduction Agency
Freedom of Information Act/Privacy
    Act Office
Defense Threat Reduction Agency
8725 John J. Kingman Road
MSC 6201 Fort Belvoir, VA 22060-
    6201
Tel: (703) 767-1792
Fax: (703) 767-3623
e-mail: efoia@dtra.mil

Marine Corps
FOIA Requester Service Center
Headquarters, U.S. Marine Corps
Code ARSF-SVC
2 Navy Annex
Washington, DC 20380-1775
Tel: (703) 695-6192
Fax: (703) 614-6287
e-mail: SMB.HQMC.FOIA@usmc.mil

**National Geospatial-Intelligence
    Agency**
National Geospatial-Intelligence
    Agency
FOIA Requester Service Center
4600 Sangamore Road, D-10, FOIA
Bethesda, Maryland 20816
Tel: 301-227-2268; DSN 287-2268
Fax: 301-227-2035
e-mail: FOIANGA@nga.mil

National Reconnaissance Office
*Requests may be submitted via online
    Webform*
National Reconnaissance Office
Information Access and Release Team
14675 Lee Road
Chantilly, VA 20151-1715
Tel: (703) 227-9326
Fax: (703) 227-9198
e-mail: foia@nro.mil
Webform: http://www.nro.gov/foia/
    RequestInput.aspx

National Security Agency
*Requests may be submitted via online
    Webform*
National Security Agency
Attn: FOIA/PA Office (DJP4)
9800 Savage Road, Suite 6248
Ft. George G. Meade, MD 20755-
    6248
Fax: 443-479-3612
Webform: https://www.nsa.gov/
    forms/foia_request_form.cfm

Navy
Chief of Naval Operations
(DNS-36)
2000 Navy Pentagon
Washington, DC 20350-2000
POC: FOIA Requester Service Center
Tel: (202) 685-6546/6530
Fax: (202) 685-6580
e-mail: foia@ogc.law.navy.mil

Office of the Inspector General
*Requests may be submitted via online
    Webform*
Inspector General, Department of
    Defense
FOIA Requester Service Center/
    Privacy Act Office
400 Army Navy Drive, Room 1034
Arlington, Virginia 22202-4704
Tel: (703) 604-9775
Fax: (703) 602-0294
e-mail: FOIA@dodig.mil
webform: http://www.dodig.osd.mil/
    fo/Foia/foiaReqForm.php

EDUCATION

U.S. Department of Education
*Requests may be submitted via online
    Webform*
U.S. Department of Education
Office of Management
Regulatory Information Management
    Services
400 Maryland Avenue, SW, LBJ
    2W105

Washington, DC 20202-4536
ATTN: FOIA Public Liaison
Fax: (202) 401-0920
Email: EDFOIAManager@ed.gov
Web form: http://www.ed.gov/
   policy/gen/leg/foia/foia
   _request_form_1.html

ENERGY

Department of Energy
*Requests may be submitted via online
   Webform*
FOIA Officer, United States
   Department of Energy
1000 Independence Avenue, SW
Washington, DC 20585
Tel: (202) 586-5955
Webform: http://
   www.management.energy.gov/
   FOIA/foia_request_form.htm

HEALTH AND HUMAN SERVICES

**Department of Health and Human
   Services**
Department of Health and Human
   Services FOIA Office
Freedom of Information Officer
Mary E. Switzer Building, Room 2221
300 C Street, SW
Washington, D.C. 20201
Tel: (202) 690-7453
Fax: (202) 690-8320
www.hhs.gov/foia

**Centers for Medicare and Medicaid
   Services (CMS)**
Centers for Medicare & Medicaid
   Services
Office of Strategic Operations and
   Regulatory Affairs
Freedom of Information Group
Room N2-20-16
7500 Security Boulevard
Baltimore, Maryland 21244-1850
Tel: 410-786-5353
www.cms.hhs.gov/foia/

Food and Drug Administration
Food and Drug Administration
Office of Management Programs
Division of Freedom of Information
   (HFI-35)
5600 Fishers Lane
Rockville, MD 20857
Tel: (301) 827-6567
Fax: (301) 443-1726
http://www.fda.gov/foi/default.htm

National Institutes of Health (NIH)
Freedom of Information Office, NIH
Building 31, Room 5B35
9000 Rockville Pike
Bethesda, MD 20892
fax: (301) 402-4541
http://www.nih.gov/icd/od/foia/
   index.htm

HOMELAND SECURITY

Department of Homeland Security
U.S. Department of Homeland
   Security
Privacy Office
Director, Disclosure & FOIA
245 Murray Drive SW, Building 410
STOP-0550
Washington, DC 20528-0550
Tel: 703-235-0790 or 866-431-0486
Fax: 703-235-0443
E-mail: foia@hq.dhs.gov

**Bureau of Citizenship and
   Immigration Services (BCIS)**
U.S. Citizenship and Immigration
   Services
National Records Center, FOIA/PA
   Office
P.O. Box 648010
Lee's Summit, MO 64064-8010
Tel: (816) 350-5570
Fax (816) 350-5785
Email: uscis.foia@dhs.gov

**Bureau of Customs and Border
   Protection (BCBP)**
U.S. Customs and Border Protection

1300 Pennsylvania Ave., NW,
Attn: Mint Annex Building, FOIA
    Division
Washington, D.C. 20229
Tel: (202) 572-0640
http://www.cbp.gov/xp/cgov/
    admin/fl/foia/

**Federal Emergency Management
    Agency**
FOIA Officer
500 C Street, SW, Room 840
Washington, D.C. 20472
Tel: 202-646-3323
Fax: 202-646-3347
E-mail: fema-foia@dhs.gov

**Federal Law Enforcement Training
    Center**
Federal Law Enforcement Training
    Center
Freedom of Information/Privacy
    Office
Building 681, Suite 187B
Glynco, GA 31524
Tel: (912) 267-3103
Fax: (912) 267-3113
Email: fletc-foia@dhs.gov

**Transportation Security
    Administration**
Transportation Security
    Administration, TSA-20, East
    Tower
FOIA Division
601 South 12th Street
Arlington, VA 22202-4220
Fax: (571) 227-1406
Email: FOIA.TSA@dhs.gov

United States Coast Guard
Commandant (CG-611)
2100 2nd Street, SW
Washington, DC 20593-0001
Attn: FOIA
Tel: 202-475-3522
Fax: 202-475-3927
e-mail: EFOIA@uscg.mil
http://www.uscg.mil/foia/

United States Secret Service
Communications Center (FOI/PA)
245 Murray Lane
Building T-5
Washington, D.C. 20223
Tel: 202-406-6370
Fax: 202-406-5154
Email: FOIA@usss.dhs.gov

HOUSING AND URBAN
    DEVELOPMENT

**U.S. Department of Housing and
    Urban Development**
Make requests to regional offices, or:
Vicky J. Lewis
Office of the Executive Secretariat
U.S. Department of Housing and
    Urban Development
451 7th Street, SW, room 10139
Washington, DC 20410
Tel: 202-708-3054
e-mail: foia_hud@hud.gov
www.hud.gov/offices/ogc/foia/
    index.cfm

INTERIOR

**United States Department of the
    Interior**
Departmental FOIA Officer
MS-7438, MIB
1849 C Street, NW
Washington, DC 20240
Tel: 202/208-5342
fax: (202) 208-6867
e-mail: doifoia@ios.doi.gov
www.doi.gov/foia

Bureau of Indian Affairs
Office of the Chief Information Officer
Office of Information Planning
625 Herndon Parkway
Herndon, VA 20171
Tel: (703) 735-4123
Fax: (703) 735-4108

Bureau of Land Management
Room 725 (WO-560)

1849 C Street, NW
Washington, D.C. 20240
Tel: (202) 452-0314
Fax: (202) 452-5002
Email: wo_foia@blm.gov

Bureau of Reclamation
Bureau of Reclamation FOIA Officer
PO Box 25007
Denver CO 80225-0007
Tel: (303) 445-2048
Fax: (303) 445-6575
E-mail: borfoia@usbr.gov

Fish & Wildlife Service
Division of Information Resources &
    Technology Management (IRTM)
Arlington Square
4401 North Fairfax Drive
Mailstop #380
Arlington, VA 22203
Tel: (703) 358-2504 or (703) 358-
    2257
Fax: (703) 358-2251
E-mail: r9foia@fws.gov

Forest Service
USDA FS, FOIA Service Center
1400 Independence Avenue, SW
Mail Stop: 1143
Washington, DC 20250-1143
Tel: (212) 205-1542
Fax: (202) 260-3245
Email: wo_foia@fs.fed.us
www.fs.fed.us/im/foia

Geological Survey
12201 Sunrise Valley Drive
MS-807, National Center
Room 2C314
Reston, VA 20192
Tel: (703) 648-7158
Fax: (703) 648-6853
Email: foia@usgs.gov

National Park Service
*Requests may be submitted via online
    Webform*

Office of the Chief Information Officer
    (OCIO)
1849 C Street, NW
Mailstop: 1201 Eye Street, 8th Floor
Washington, DC 20240
Tel: (202) 354-1925
Fax: (202) 371-5584
Webform: http://www.nps.gov/pwr/
    foia-contact.htm

**Natural Resources Conservation
    Service**
FOIA Officer
Natural Resources Conservation
    Service
5601 Sunnyside Avenue
Stop 5471
Beltsville, MD 20705-5000
Tel: (301) 504-2286
Fax: (301) 504-2161
www.info.usda.gov/nrcs_foia

JUSTICE

United States Department of Justice
FOIA/PA Mail Referral Unit
Department of Justice
Room 115
LOC Building
Washington, DC 20530-0001
Tel: (301) 583-7354
Fax: (301) 341-0772

Office of the Attorney General
Office of Information and Privacy
Department of Justice
Suite 11050
1425 New York Avenue, N.W.
Washington, DC 20530-0001
Tel: (202) 514-FOIA
www.usdoj.gov/ag/foia.htm

**Office of the Deputy Attorney
    General**
Office of Information and Privacy
Department of Justice
Suite 11050
1425 New York Avenue, N.W.

Washington, DC 20530-0001
Tel: (202) 514-FOIA
www.usdoj.gov/ag/foia.htm

Office of the Associate Attorney General
Office of Information and Privacy
Department of Justice
Suite 11050
1425 New York Avenue, N.W.
Washington, DC 20530-0001
Tel: (202) 514-FOIA
www.usdoj.gov/ag/foia.htm

Antitrust Division
Chief, FOIA/PA Unit
Antitrust Division
Department of Justice
Liberty Square Building
Suite 1000, 450 5th Street, NW
Washington, DC 20530-0001
Tel: (202) 514-2692
www.usdoj.gov/atr/foia.html

Bureau of Alcohol, Tobacco, Firearms and Explosives
Chief, Disclosure Division
Bureau of Alcohol, Tobacco, Firearms, and Explosives
Department of Justice
Suite 1E360
99 New York Avenue, NE
Washington, DC 20226
Tel: (202) 648-8740
www.atf.gov/about/foia/foia.htm

Civil Division
Freedom of Information/Privacy Act Officer
Civil Division
Department of Justice
Room 7304, 20 Massachusetts Avenue, NW
Washington, DC 20530-0001
Tel: (202) 514-3319
www.usdoj.gov/civil/foia/foia.htm

Civil Rights Division
FOIA/PA Branch

Civil Rights Division
Department of Justice
Room 311, NALC Building
Washington, DC 20530
Tel: (202) 514-4209
www.usdoj.gov/crt/foia/crt.htm

Community Relations Service
FOIA/PA Coordinator
Community Relations Service
Department of Justice
Suite 6000, 600 E Street, NW
Washington, DC 20530-0001
Tel: (202) 305-2935
www.usdoj.gov/crs/foia.htm

Criminal Division
Chief, FOIA/PA Unit
Criminal Division
Department of Justice
Suite 1127, Keeney Building
Washington, DC 20530-0001
Tel: (202) 616-0307
www.usdoj.gov/criminal/foia/
crmfoia.html

Drug Enforcement Administration
Freedom of Information Operations Unit
FOI/Records Management Section
Drug Enforcement Administration
Department of Justice
700 Army Navy Drive
Arlington, VA 22202
Tel: (202) 307-7596
www.usdoj.gov/dea/foia/dea.htm

Environment and Natural Resources Division
Law and Policy Section
Environment and Natural Resources Division
Department of Justice
PO Box 4390, Ben Franklin Station
Washington, DC 20044-4390
Tel: (202) 305-0641
www.usdoj.gov/enrd/foia.htm

Executive Office for Immigration Review
Senior Associate General Counsel
Office of the General Counsel
Executive Office for Immigration
    Review
Department of Justice
Suite 2600, 5107 Leesburg Pike
Falls Church, VA 22041
Tel: (703) 605-1297
www.usdoj.gov/eoir/mainfoia.html

Executive Office of United States Attorneys
FOIA/Privacy Unit
Executive Office for United States
    Attorneys
Department of Justice
Room 7300, 600 E Street, NW
Washington, DC 20530-0001
Tel: (202) 616-6757
www.usdoj.gov/usao/reading_room/
    index.html

Executive Office of United States Trustees
FOIA/PA Counsel
Office of the General Counsel
Department of Justice
Executive Office for United States
    Trustees
Suite 8000, 20 Massachusetts Avenue,
    NW
Washington, DC 20530-0001
Tel: (202) 307-1399
www.usdoj.gov/ust/foiahome.htm

Federal Bureau of Investigation
Record/Information Dissemination
    Section
Records Management Division
Federal Bureau of Investigation
Department of Justice
170 Marcel Drive
Winchester, VA 22602-4843
Tel: (540) 868-4591
Fax: (540) 868-4995

Email: foiparequest@ic.fbi.gov
www.foia.fbi.gov

Federal Bureau of Prisons
FOIA/Privacy Act Requests
Federal Bureau of Prisons
Department of Justice
Room 841, HOLC Building
320 First Street, NW
Washington, DC 20534
Tel: (202) 514-6655
www.bop.gov/ogcpg/ogcfoia.html

Foreign Claims Settlement Commission
Attorney Advisor - International
Foreign Claims Settlement
    Commission
Department of Justice
Room 6002, 600 E Street, NW
Washington, DC 20579-0001
Tel: (202) 616-6975
www.usdoj.gov/fcsc/foia.htm

INTERPOL-United States National Central Bureau
FOIA/PA Specialist
Office of General Counsel
INTERPOL-United States National
    Central Bureau
Department of Justice
Washington, DC 20530-0001
Tel: (202) 616-9000
www.usdoj.gov/usncb/foia/foia.html

Justice Management Division
FOIA Contact
Justice Management Division
Department of Justice
Room 1111 RFK, 950 Pennsylvania
    Avenue, NW
Washington, DC 20530-0001
Tel: (202) 514-3101
www.usdoj.gov/jmd/foia.htm

National Drug Intelligence Center
FOIA Coordinator
National Drug Intelligence Center

Department of Justice
319 Washington Street
Johnstown, PA 15901-1622
Tel: (814) 532-4601
www.usdoj.gov/ndic/foia.htm

**Office of Community Oriented
   Policing Services**
FOIA Officer, Legal Division
Office of Community Oriented
   Policing Services
Department of Justice
12th Floor, 1100 Vermont Avenue
Washington, DC 20530-0001
Tel: (202) 514-3750
fax: (202) 514-3456
e-mail: cops.foia@usdoj.gov
www.cops.usdoj.gov/Default.asp?
   Item=40

Office of Dispute Resolution
FOIA Officer
Office of Dispute Resolution
Department of Justice
Room 5736, 950 Pennsylvania
   Avenue, NW
Washington, DC 20530-0001
Tel: (202) 616-9471

**Office of the Federal Detention
   Trustee**
Attention: FOIA Staff
Office of the Federal Detention
   Trustee
Department of Justice
Suite 910
4601 N. Fairfax Drive
Arlington, VA 22203
Tel: (202) 353-4601
www.usdoj.gov/ofdt/foia.htm

Office of Information and Privacy
Attention: FOIA Staff
Office of Information and Privacy
Department of Justice
Suite 11050
1425 New York Avenue, NW
Washington, DC 20530-0001

Tel: (202) 514-FOIA
www.usdoj.gov/04foia/
   readingrooms/oip.htm

Office of the Inspector General
Attention: FOIA Staff
Office of the Inspector General
Department of Justice
Room 4726
950 Pennsylvania Avenue, NW
Washington, DC 20530-0001
Tel: (202) 616-0646
Fax: (202) 616-9152
www.usdoj.gov/oig/igefoia1.htm

**Office of Intergovernmental and
   Public Liaison**
Attention: FOIA Staff
Office of Information and Privacy
Department of Justice
Suite 11050
1425 New York Avenue, NW
Washington, DC 20530-0001
Tel: (202) 514-FOIA
www.usdoj.gov/oipl/oipl_foia.htm

Office of Justice Programs
Attention: FOIA Staff
Office of Justice Programs
Department of Justice
Room 5400, 810 7th Street, N.W.
Washington, DC 20531
Tel: (202) 616-3267
Fax: (202) 307-1419
e-mail: FOIAOJP@ojp.usdoj.gov
www.ojp.usdoj.gov/about/foia/
   foia.htm

Office of Legal Policy
Attention: FOIA Staff
Office of Information and Privacy
Department of Justice
Suite 11050
1425 New York Avenue, N.W.
Washington, DC 20530-0001
Tel: (202) 514-FOIA
www.usdoj.gov/olp/foia.htm

Office of Legislative Affairs
Attention: FOIA Staff
Office of Information and Privacy
Department of Justice
Suite 11050
1425 New York Avenue, N.W.
Washington, DC 20530-0001
Tel: (202) 514-FOIA
www.usdoj.gov/ola/foia.htm

Office of the Pardon Attorney
FOIA Officer
Office of the Pardon Attorney
Department of Justice
Suite 11000
1425 New York Avenue, NW
Washington, DC 20530-0001
Tel: (202) 616-6070
www.usdoj.gov/pardon/pardon_
   foia.htm

Office of Professional Responsibility
Special Counsel for Freedom of
   Information and Privacy Acts
Office of Professional Responsibility
Department of Justice
950 Pennsylvania Avenue, NW
Suite 3529
Washington, DC 20530
Tel: (202) 514-3365
www.usdoj.gov/opr/foia.htm

Office of Public Affairs
Attention: FOIA Staff
Office of Information and Privacy
Department of Justice
Suite 11050
1425 New York Avenue, N.W.
Washington, DC 20530-0001
Tel: (202) 514-FOIA
www.usdoj.gov/opa/readingroom/
   pub_aff.htm

Office of the Solicitor General
Office of the Solicitor General
Department of Justice
Room 6640, 950 Pennsylvania
   Avenue, NW

Washington, DC 20530-0001
Tel: (202) 514-2203
www.usdoj.gov/osg/foia.htm

**Professional Responsibility Advisory
   Office**
Information Management Specialist
Professional Responsibility Advisory
   Office
Department of Justice
Suite 12000, 1425 Pennsylvania
   Avenue, NW
Washington, DC 20530
Tel: (202) 514-0458
www.usdoj.gov/prao/foia.htm

Tax Division
Division Counsel for FOIA and PA
   Matters
Tax Division
Department of Justice
Post Office Box 227
Ben Franklin Station
Washington, DC 20044
Tel: (202) 307-6320
www.usdoj.gov/tax/readingroom/
   foia/foia1.htm

United States Marshals Service
FOIA/PA Officer
Office of General Counsel
United States Marshals Service
Department of Justice
CS-3, 12th Floor
Washington, DC 20530-1000
Tel: (202) 307-9054
www.usdoj.gov/marshals/foia.html

United States Parole Commission
FOIA Officer
United States Parole Commission
Department of Justice
Suite 420, 5550 Friendship Boulevard
Chevy Chase, Maryland 20815
Tel: (301) 492-5959 (ext 237)
www.usdoj.gov/uspc/foia.htm
LABOR

United States Department of Labor
Division of Legislation and Legal
  Counsel
Office of the Solicitor
Room N-2428, 200 Constitution
  Avenue, NW
Washington, DC 20210
Attention: FOIA Request
Tel: (202) 693-5500
Fax: (202) 693-5538
Email: foiarequest@dol.gov
www.dol.gov/dol/foia/main.htm

STATE

Department of State
Office of Information Programs and
  Services
A/ISS/IPS/RL
U.S. Department of State
Washington, DC 20522-8100
Tel: (202) 261-8300
Fax: 202-261-8579
www.foia.state.gov

TRANSPORTATION

Department of Transportation
Departmental FOIA Office (C-12)
400 Seventh Street, SW, Room 5432
Washington, DC 20590,
Attention: FOIA Request
Tel: (202) 366-4542
Fax: (202) 366-8536
www.dot.gov/foia/index.html

**Federal Aviation Administration
  (FAA)**
*Requests may be submitted via online
  Webform*
National Freedom of Information Act
  Staff, ARC-40
Federal Aviation Administration
800 Independence Avenue, SW
Washington, DC 20591
Tel: (202) 267-9165
Fax: (202) 493-5032

Webform: http://www.faa.gov/foia/
  email_foia/index.cfm?region=hq
http://www.faa.gov/foia/

Federal Highway Administration
Federal Highway Administration
Attn: FOIA Officer
1200 New Jersey Ave., SE
Washington, DC 20590
Fax: (202) 366-1938
E-mail: foia.officer@fhwa.dot.gov
www.fhwa.dot.gov/foia/index.htm

Federal Railroad Administration
Freedom of Information Act
  Coordinator
Office of Chief Counsel
Federal Railroad Administration
1200 New Jersey Avenue, Stop 10
Washington, DC 20590
Tel: (202) 493-6039
Fax: (202) 493-6068
http://www.fra.dot.gov/us/foia

Federal Transit Administration
FOIA Requester Service Center
Federal Transit Administration
1200 New Jersey Avenue, SE
4th Floor East Building
Washington, DC 20590
Tel: (202) 366-4043
Fax: (202) 366-7164
Email: fta.foia@dot.gov
http://www.fta.dot.gov/about/
  about_FTA_186.html

**National Highway Traffic Safety
  Administration**
NHTSA
Executive Secretariat
1200 New Jersey Avenue, SE
West Building, 41-304
Washington, D.C. 20590
Tel: (202) 366-1834
Fax: (202) 493-2929
Email: Webmaster@nhtsa.dot.gov
www.nhtsa.dot.gov/nhtsa/whatsup/
  foia

TREASURY

**United States Department of the
Treasury**
Contact individual bureaus, or:
FOIA/PA Request
Disclosure Services
Department of the Treasury
Washington, DC 20220
Tel: (202) 622-0930
Fax: (202) 622-3895
www.ustreas.gov/foia

DEPARTMENT OF VETERANS
AFFAIRS

Department of Veterans Affairs
Contact individual bureaus, or:
Department of Veterans Affairs
Chief FOIA Officer - 583 VACO
810 Vermont Avenue, NW
Washington, DC 20420
Tel: (202) 461-7450
Fax: (202) 273-5981
www.va.gov/foia

EXECUTIVE OFFICE OF THE
PRESIDENT
www.whitehouse.gov/government/
eop-foia.html

The Executive Office of the President
(EOP) entities subject to the FOIA
are:

- Council on Environmental Quality
- Office of Management and Budget
- Office of National Drug Control
  Policy
- Office of Science and Technology
  Policy
- United States Trade Representative

The EOP entities exempt from the
provisions of the FOIA are:

- White House Office
- Office of the Vice President
- Council of Economic Advisers
- National Security Council
- Office of Policy Development
- President's Foreign Intelligence
  Advisory Board

Council on Environmental Quality
Freedom of Information Officer
Council on Environmental Quality
722 Jackson Place, NW
Washington, DC 20503
Tel: (202) 395-5750
Fax: (202) 456-0753
Email: efoia@ceq.eop.gov
www.whitehouse.gov/ceq/foia

**Office of Management and Budget
(OMB)**
FOIA Officer
Office of Management and Budget
725 17th Street, NW, Room 9026
Washington, DC 20503
Tel: (202) 395-FOIA
Fax: (202) 395-3504
http://www.whitehouse.gov/omb/
foia/

**Office of National Drug Control
Policy**
Office of Legal Counsel
Attn: General Counsel
Office of National Drug Control
Policy
750 17th Street, NW
Washington, DC 20503
Tel: (202) 395-6622
Fax: (202) 395-5543
www.whitehousedrugpolicy.gov/
about/foia

**Office of Science and Technology
Policy**
Office of Science and Technology
Policy

Attn: FOIA Officer
725 17th Street, Room 5228
Washington, DC 20502
Tel: (202) 456-6002
Fax: (202) 456-6022
Email: ostpfoia@ostp.eop.gov

**Office of the United States Trade
    Representative**
FOIA Officer
Office of the U.S. Trade
    Representative
600 17th Street, NW
Washington, DC 20508
Tel: (202) 395-3419
Fax: (202) 395-9458
http://www.ustr.gov/Legal/
    Reading_Room/FOIA/
    Section_Index

INDEPENDENT FEDERAL
AGENCIES

Broadcasting Board of Governors
FOIA/PA Officer
BBG, FOIA/PA Unit, Room 3349
330 Independence Avenue, SW
Washington, DC 20237
Tel: (202) 203-4550
Fax: (202) 203-4585
www.bbg.gov/foia

Central Intelligence Agency
requests can be faxed
Information and Privacy Coordinator
Central Intelligence Agency
Washington, DC 20505
(703) 613-1287
fax: (703) 613-3007
www.foia.cia.gov

**Chemical Safety and Hazard
    Investigation Board**
CSB FOIA Officer
Chemical Safety and Hazard
    Investigation Board
2175 K Street, NW, Suite C-100
Washington, DC 20037-1809

Tel: (202) 261-7619
Fax: (202) 261-7650
Email: info@csb.gov
www.usdoj.gov/cgi-bin/outside.cgi?
    www.csb.gov/legal_affairs/
    index.cfm?ID=2

Commission on Civil Rights
Solicitor
U.S. Commission on Civil Rights
624 Ninth Street, NW
Suite 621
Washington, DC 20425
Tel: (202) 376-7796
Fax: (202) 376-1163
Email: emonroig@usccr.gov
www.usccr.gov/foia/foiandx

**Commodity Futures Trading
    Commission**
Assistant Secretary of the Commission
    for FOIA Matters
Commodity Futures Trading
    Commission
Three Lafayette Centre, 1155 21st
    Street, NW
Washington, DC 20581
Tel: (202) 418-5105
Fax: (202) 418-5124
www.cftc.gov/cftc/cftcfoia

**Consumer Product Safety
    Commission**
FOIA Officer
Consumer Product Safety Commission
4330 East West Highway, Suite 502
Bethesda, MD 20814-4408
Tel: (301) 504-7923
Fax: (301) 504-0127
Email: cpsc-os@cpsc.gov
www.cpsc.gov/library/foia/foia.html

**Corporation for National and
    Community Service**
Corporation for National and
    Community Service
Office of the General Counsel

Attn: Freedom of Information Act
  Officer
1201 New York Avenue, N.W., Room
  10606
Washington D.C., 20525
(202) 606-6671
Fax: (202) 606-3467
Email: aholland@cns.gov
http://www.nationalservice.gov/
  home/foia/index

**Court Services and Offender
  Supervision Agency for the
  District of Columbia**
*Requests may be submitted via online
  Webform*
Court Services & Offender Supervision
  Agency
Attn: FOIA Officer
633 Indiana Avenue, NW
Room 1254
Washington, DC 20004-2902
Tel: (202) 220-5355
Fax: (202) 220-5350
Webform: http://www.csosa.gov/
  foia/requestform
www.csosa.gov/foia_index.html

Defense Nuclear Facilities Board
Information/FOIA Officer
Defense Nuclear Facilities Safety Board
625 Indiana Avenue NW, Suite 700
Washington, DC 20004
Tel: (202) 694-7000 or (800) 788-
  4016
Fax: (202) 208-6518
Email: mailbox@dnfsb.gov
www.dnfsb.gov/foia/index.html

**Environmental Protection Agency
  (EPA)**
*Requests may be submitted via online
  Webform*
National Freedom of Information
  Officer
U.S. Environmental Protection Agency
1200 Pennsylvania Avenue, NW
  (2822T)

Washington, DC 20460
Tel: (202) 566-1667
Fax: (202) 566-2147
Email: hq.foia@epa.gov
web form: www.epa.gov/foia/
  requestform.html
www.epa.gov/foia

**Equal Employment Opportunity
  Commission**
Contact regional offices, or:
Assistant Legal Counsel/FOIA
EEOC
1801 L Street, NW, 6th Floor
Washington, DC 20507
Tel: (202) 663-4640
Fax: (202) 663-4639
Email: foia@eeoc.gov
www.eeoc.gov/foia/index.html

**Export Import Bank of the United
  States**
Freedom of Information and Privacy
  Office
Export Import Bank of the United
  States
811 Vermont Avenue, NW
Washington, DC 20571
Tel: (202) 565-3241
Fax: (202) 565-3294
Email: foia@exim.gov
www.exim.gov/about/disclosure/
  foia.html

Farm Credit Administration
*Requests may be submitted via online
  Webform*
Freedom of Information Officer
Farm Credit Administration
1501 Farm Credit Drive
McLean, VA 22102-5090
Tel: (703) 883-4022
Fax: (703) 790-0052
Email: foiaofficer@fca.gov

Webform: www.fca.gov/ogc/
  foiarequ.nsf/FOIARequest/?
  OpenForm

http://www.fca.gov/home/freedom
_info.html

Farm Credit Insurance Corporation
Freedom of Information Officer
Farm Credit System Insurance
  Corporation
1501 Farm Credit Drive
McLean, VA 22102-5090
Tel: (703) 883-4022
Fax: (703) 950-0052
Email: foiaofficer@fca.gov
www.fcsic.gov/foia.html

Federal Communications Commission (FCC)
Requests may be submitted via online Webform
Attention: FOIA Officer
Federal Communications Commission
445 12th Street, SW, Room 1-A836
Washington, DC 20554
Tel: (202) 418-0440 or (202) 418-0212
Fax: (202) 418-2826 or (202) 418-0521
Email: FOIA@fcc.gov
web form: www.fcc.gov/foia/
  #reqform
www.fcc.gov/foia/

Federal Deposit Insurance Corporation
Requests may be submitted via online Webform
FDIC
Legal Division
FOIA/PA Group
550 17th Street, NW
Washington, DC 20429
Tel: (202) 736-0526
Fax: (202) 898-6910
Email: efoia@fdic.gov
Webform: www2.fdic.gov
  /EFOIAREQUEST
http://www.fdic.gov/about/
  freedom/index.html

Federal Election Commission
Federal Election Commission
Attn: FOIA Requester Service Center
Room 408
999 E Street, NW
Washington, DC 20463
Tel: (202) 694-1220 or (800) 424-9530
Fax: (202) 219-1043
Email: FOIA@fec.gov
http://www.fec.gov/press/foia.shtml

Federal Energy Regulatory Commission
Freedom of Information Act Request
FOIA Officer
Federal Energy Regulatory
  Commission
888 First Street, NE, Room 11H-1
Washington, DC 20426
Tel: (202) 502-8004
Fax: (202) 208-2106
e-mail: foia-ceii@ferc.gov
www.ferc.gov/legal/ceii-foia/foia.asp

Federal Housing Finance Board
requests can be faxed or e-mailed
FOIA Officer
Federal Housing Finance Board
1625 Eye Street NW
Washington, DC 20006
Tel: (202) 408-2511
Fax: (202) 408-2580
Email: FOIA@fhfb.gov

Federal Labor Relations Authority
Contact regional offices, or:
Office of the General Counsel - Second
  Floor
c/o OGC FOIA Officer
1400 K Street, NW
Washington, D.C. 20424-0001
Tel: (202) 218-7910
Fax: (202) 482-6636

e-mail: solmail@flra.gov
www.flra.gov/gc/gc_foia.html

Federal Maritime Commission
Secretary
Federal Maritime Commission
800 North Capitol Street, NW
Washington, DC 20573
Tel: (202) 523-5725
Fax: (202) 523-0014 (Subject: FOIA
  Request)
Email: secretary@fmc.gov
http://www.fmc.gov/reading/
  FreedomofInformationAct.asp

**Federal Mediation and Conciliation
  Service**
FOIA Program
FMCS
2100 K Street, NW
Washington, DC 20427
Tel: (202) 606-5444
Fax: (202) 606-5345
e-mail: foia@fmcs.gov
www.fmcs.gov/internet/
  itemDetailNoNav.asp?
  categoryID=90&itemID=16303

**Federal Mine Safety and Review
  Commission**
Chief FOIA Officer
Federal Mine Safety and Health
  Review Commission
601 New Jersey Avenue, NW
Washington, DC 20001-2021
Tel: (202) 434-9905
Fax: (202) 434-9944
Email: fmshrc@fmshrc.gov
www.fmshrc.gov/foia/foia.html

Federal Reserve
*Requests may be submitted via online
  Webform*
Freedom of Information Office
Board of Governors of the Federal
  Reserve System
20th Street and Constitution Avenue,
  NW
Washington, DC 20551
Tel: (202) 452-3684 or (202) 452-
  2407; TDD (202) 263-4869

Fax: (202) 872-7565
Webform: www.federalreserve.gov/
  generalinfo/foia/EFOIA/
  EFOIAForm.cfm
www.federalreserve.gov/generalinfo/
  Foia

**Federal Retirement Thrift
  Investment Board**
FOIA Officer
Federal Retirement Thrift Investment
  Board
1250 H Street, NW, 2nd Floor
Washington, DC 20005-3952
Tel: (202) 942-1670
Fax: (202) 942-1676
www.frtib.gov/FOIA/index.html

Federal Trade Commission (FTA)
*Requests may be submitted via online
  Webform*
Freedom of Information Act Request
Office of General Counsel
Federal Trade Commission
600 Pennsylvania Avenue, NW
Washington, DC 20580
Tel: (202) 326-2013
Fax: (202) 326-2477
Email: foia@ftc.gov
web form: https://www.ftc.gov/ftc/
  foia.htm
www.ftc.gov/foia

General Services Administration
*Requests may be submitted via online
  Webform*
General Services Administration
FOIA Requester Service Center
  (ACMA)
1800 F Street, NW, Room 6001
Washington, DC 20405
Tel: (202) 501-2262
Fax: (202) 501-2727
Email: gsa.foia@gsa.gov
web form: www.gsa.gov/Portal/gsa/
  ep/contentView.do?
  contentType=GSA
  _BASIC&contentId=15462

Institute of Museum and Library Services
Freedom of Information Act Officer
Institute of Museum and Library Services
1100 Pennsylvania Avenue, NW, Suite 510
Washington, DC 20506
Tel:(202) 606-8536 or (202) 219-3696
Fax: (202) 653-4625
Email: foia@imls.gov
http://www.imls.gov/about/foia.shtm

Inter-American Foundation
Office of the General Council
Inter-American Foundation
901 N. Stuart St., 10th Floor
Arlington, VA 22203
Tel: (703) 306-4301
Email: foia@iaf.gov
http://www.iaf.gov/privacy_security/privacy_statement_en.asp?pr_id=22

Legal Services Corporation
FOIA Request
Office of Legal Affairs
Legal Services Corporation
3333 K Street, NW, 3rd Floor
Washington, DC 20007-3522
Tel: (202) 295-1500
Fax: (202) 337-6519
Email: FOIA@lsc.gov
http://www.lsc.gov/foia2/

Library of Congress Copyright Office
by mail only
FOIA Requester Service Center
Copyright Office
GC/I&R
P.O. Box 70400
Washington, DC 20024
Tel: (202) 707-0600 or (202) 707-6800
Fax: (202) 707-6859
www.copyright.gov/foia

Merit Systems Protection Board
FOIA/PA Officer
Office of the Clerk
Merit Systems Protection Board
1615 M Street, NW
Washington, DC 20419-0001
Tel: (202) 653-7200, ext. 1162
Fax: (202) 653-7130
Email: FOIAHQ@mspb.gov
http://www.mspb.gov/sites/mspb/pages/FOIA.aspx

National Aeronautics and Space Administration (NASA)
Requests may be submitted via online Webform
FOIA Officer
NASA Headquarters
300 E Street, SW
Room 9R35
Washington, DC 20546
Tel: (202) 358-2265 or (202) 358-0845
Fax: (202) 358-4331
Email: foia@hq.nasa.gov
Webform: www.hq.nasa.gov/office/pao/FOIA/request.html
www.hq.nasa.gov/office/pao/FOIA/

National Archives and Records Administration
FOIA Officer
National Archives and Records Administration
NGC-Room 3110
8601 Adelphi Road
College Park, MD 20740
Tel: (301) 837-FOIA (3642)
Fax: (301) 837-0293
Email: foia@nara.gov
http://www.archives.gov/foia/index.html

National Credit Union Administration
Attn: FOIA Officer, Office of General Counsel
National Credit Union Administration

1775 Duke Street
Alexandria, VA 22314-3428
Tel: (703) 518-6540 or (703) 518-6563
Fax: (703) 518-6569
Email: FOIA@ncua.gov
http://www.ncua.gov/FOIA/
foia.html

National Endowment for the Arts
FOIA Requests
Office of General Counsel
National Endowment for the Arts
1100 Pennsylvania Avenue, NW,
Room 518
Washington, DC 20506
Tel: (202) 682-5418
Fax: (202) 682-5572
Email: arts_fioa@nea.gov
www.arts.gov/about/FOIA/
index.html

National Endowment for the Humanities
Requests may be submitted via online Webform
Freedom of Information Act Officer
Office of the General Counsel
National Endowment for the
Humanities
1100 Pennsylvania Avenue, NW,
Room 529
Washington, DC 20506
Tel: (202) 606-8322
Fax: (202) 606-8600
Email: gencounsel@neh.gov or foia@
neh.gov
Webform: www.neh.gov/whoweare/
foia/request.asp
www.neh.gov/whoweare/
foiamain.html

National Indian Gaming Commission
FOIA Officer
National Indian Gaming Commission
1441 L Street, NW, Suite 9100
Washington, DC 20005

Tel: (202) 632-7003
Fax: (202) 632-7066
http://www.nigc.gov/Freedom
ofInformationAct/tabid/535/
Default.aspx

National Labor Relations Board
Requests may be submitted via online Webform
FOIA Officer
National Labor Relations Board
1099 14th Street, N.W., Room 10600
Washington, D.C. 20570
Tel: (202) 273-3825
Fax: (202) 273-4275
Webform: http://www.nlrb.gov
/FOIA/e_FOIA_Requests.aspx
http://www.nlrb.gov/FOIA/

National Mediation Board
FOIA Officer
National Mediation Board
1301 K Street, NW, Suite 250 East
Washington, DC 20005-7011
Tel: (202) 692-5040
Fax: (202) 692-5085
www.nmb.gov/publicinfo/
inquiry.html

National Railroad Passenger Corporation (AMTRAK)
National Railroad Passenger
Corporation
Freedom of Information Office
60 Massachusetts Avenue, NE
Washington, DC 20002
Tel: (202) 906-2728
Fax: (202) 906-3741
Email: foiarequests@amtrak.com
http://www.amtrak.com/servlet/
ContentServer?pagename=Amtrak/
FOIA

National Science Foundation
National Science Foundation
FOIA Officer (Rm 1265)
4201 Wilson Blvd
Arlington, VA 22230

Tel: (703) 292-8060
Fax: (703) 292-9041
Email: foia@nsf.gov
http://www.nsf.gov/policies/foia.jsp

National Transportation Safety Board
Requests may be submitted via online Webform
National Transportation Safety Board
Attention: FOIA Requester Service Center, CIO-40
490 L'Enfant Plaza, SW
Washington, DC 20594-2000
Tel: (202) 314-6551 or (202) 314-6540 or (800) 877-6799
Fax: (202) 314-6132
web form: www.ntsb.gov/pubmail/pubmail.asp
www.ntsb.gov/info/foia.htm

Nuclear Regulatory Commission
Requests may be submitted via online Webform
FOIA/PA Officer
U.S. Nuclear Regulatory Commission
Mailstop: T-5F11
Washington, DC 20555-0001
Tel: (301) 415-5130
Fax: (301) 415-5130
Email: FOIA.resource@nrc.gov
Webform: www.nrc.gov/reading-rm/foia/foia-submittal-form.html
www.nrc.gov/reading-rm/foia/foia-privacy.html

Occupational Safety and Health Review Commission
Occupational Safety and Health Review Commission
Freedom of Information Act (FOIA) Disclosure Officer
1120 20th Street, NW, Room 941
Washington, DC 20036-3457
Tel: (202) 606-5700
Fax: (202) 606-5417
http://www.oshrc.gov/foia/foia.html

Office of Federal Housing Enterprise Oversight
FOIA Officer
Office of Federal Housing Enterprise Oversight
1700 G Street, NW, 4th Floor
Washington, DC 20552
Tel: (202) 414-6425
Fax: (202) 414-8917
Email: foia.office@ofheo.gov
http://www.ofheo.gov/PublicInformation.aspx?Nav=93

Office of Government Ethics
OGE FOIA Officer
Office of Government Ethics
Suite 500, 1201 New York Avenue, NW
Washington, DC 20005-3917
Tel: (202) 482-9245
Fax: (202) 482-9237
Email: usoge@oge.gov
http://www.usoge.gov/about/foia.aspx

Office of Personnel Management
U.S. Office of Personnel Management
FOIA Requester Service Center
1900 E Street, NW
Room 5415
Washington, DC 20415-7900
Tel: (202) 606-2150
Fax: (202) 418-3251
Email: foia@opm.gov
www.opm.gov/efoia/index.asp

Office of Special Counsel
FOIA Officer
U.S. Office of Special Counsel
1730 M St., N.W. (Suite 218)
Washington, DC 20036-4505
Tel: (202) 254-3716
Fax: (202) 653-5151
www.osc.gov/foia.htm

Overseas Private Investment Corporation
FOIA Director

Overseas Private Investment
  Corporation
1100 New York Avenue, NW
Washington, DC 20527
Tel: (202) 336-8418
Fax: (202) 408-0297
Email: FOIA@opic.gov
http://www.opic.gov/pubs/foia/

Peace Corps
Peace Corps
FOIA Officer
Office of Management
1111 20th Street, NW
Washington, DC 20526
Tel: (202) 692-1236
Fax: (202) 692-1385
Email: foia@peacecorps.gov
www.peacecorps.gov/index.cfm?shell=
  pchq.policies.FOIA

Pension Benefit Guaranty
  Corporation
Disclosure Officer
Pension Benefit Guaranty Corporation
1200 K Street, NW, Suite 11101
Washington, DC 20005
Tel: (202) 326-4040
Fax: (202) 326-4042
http://www.pbgc.gov/about/
  foia.html

Postal Rate Commission
*Requests may be submitted via online
  Webform*
Chief Administrative Officer and
  Secretary
Postal Regulatory Commission
901 New York Avenue, NW, Suite 200
Washington, DC 20268-0001
Tel: (202) 789-6840
Fax: (202) 789-6886
Email: PRC-Admin@prc.gov
web form: http://www.prc.gov/prc-
  pages/misc/foia/onlineform.aspx
http://www.prc.gov/prc-pages/misc/
  foia/default.aspx

Railroad Retirement Board
Chief FOIA Officer (General Counsel)
Railroad Retirement Board
844 North Rush Street
Chicago, Illinois 60611-2092
Tel: (312) 751-4948
Fax: (312) 751-7102
http://www.rrb.gov/blaw/foia/
  foia.asp

Securities and Exchange
  Commission (SEC)
Attn: FOIA Officer
100 F Street NE
Mail Stop 5100
Washington, DC 20549
Tel: (202) 551-8300
Fax: (202) 772-9337
Email: foiapa@sec.gov
www.sec.gov/foia.shtml

Selective Service System
Selective Service System
National Headquarters
FOIA Officer
Arlington, VA 22209-2425
Tel: (703) 605-4012
Fax: (703) 605-4006
www.sss.gov/freedomhome.htm

Small Business Administration
FOI/PA Office/Requester Service
  Center
Small Business Administration
409 3rd Street, SW
Washington, DC 20416
Tel: (202) 401-8203
Fax: (202) 205-7059
Email: foia@sba.gov
www.sba.gov/foia

Social Security Administration
Social Security Administration
Office of Public Disclosure
3-A-6 Operations Building
6401 Security Boulevard
Baltimore, Maryland 21235

Tel: (410) 966-6645 or (410) 965-5662
Fax: (410) 966-4304
Email: foia.pa.officers@ssa.gov
www.ssa.gov/foia

Surface Transportation Board
FOIA/Privacy Act Officer
Surface Transportation Board
395 E Street, SW
Washington, DC 20423-0001
Tel: (202) 245-0269
Fax: (202) 245-0460
Email: FOIA.Privacy@stb.dot.gov
http://www.stb.dot.gov/stb/foia.html

Tennessee Valley Authority
TVA FOIA Officer
400 West Summit Hill Drive, WT 7D
Knoxville, TN 37902-1499
Tel: (865) 632-6945
Fax: (865) 632-6901
Email: foia@tva.gov
www.tva.gov/foia/

United States Agency for International Development (USAID)
FOIA Team Leader
Information & Records Division
Office of Administrative Services
United States Agency for International Development
Room 2.07C, RRB
Washington, D.C. 20523-2701
Tel: (202) 712-1217
Fax: (202) 216-3070
Email: foia@usaid.gov
www.usaid.gov/about/foia/index.html

United States International Trade Commission
Secretary
United States International Trade Commission
500 E Street, SW, Room 112A
Washington, DC 20436

Tel: (202) 205-2000
Fax: (202) 205-2104
Email: FOIA.SE.SE@usitc.gov
http://www.usitc.gov/secretary/foia/index.htm

United States Postal Service
Freedom of Information/Privacy Acts Officer
U.S. Postal Service
475 L'Enfant Plaza, SW, Rm 5821
Washington, DC 20260
Tel: (202) 268-2608
Fax: (202) 268-5353
Email: foia@uspsoig.gov
www.usps.com/foia

United States Trade and Development Agency
FOIA Requester Service Center
U.S. Trade and Development Agency
1000 Wilson Boulevard, Suite 1600
Arlington, VA 22209-3901
Tel: (703) 875-4357
Fax: (703) 875-4009
http://www.ustda.gov/pubs/foia/

FBI Addresses & phone numbers nationwide
FBI Albany
200 McCarty Avenue
Albany, New York 12209
albany.fbi.gov/
(518) 465-7551

FBI Albuquerque
4200 Luecking Park Ave. NE
Albuquerque, New Mexico 87107
albuquerque.fbi.gov
(505) 889-1300

FBI Atlanta
Suite 400
2635 Century Parkway, Northeast
Atlanta, Georgia 30345-3112
atlanta.fbi.gov
(404) 679-9000

FBI Anchorage
101 East Sixth Avenue
Anchorage, Alaska 99501-2524
anchorage.fbi.gov
(907) 276-4441

FBI Baltimore
2600 Lord Baltimore
Baltimore, Maryland 21244
baltimore.fbi.gov
(410) 265-8080

FBI Boston
Suite 600
One Center Plaza
Boston, Massachusetts 02108
boston.fbi.gov
(617) 742-5533

FBI Birmingham
1000 18th Street North
Birmingham, Alabama 35203
birmingham.fbi.gov
(205) 326-6166

FBI Buffalo
One FBI Plaza
Buffalo, New York 14202-2698
buffalo.fbi.gov
(716) 856-7800

FBI Charlotte
Suite 900, Wachovia Building
400 South Tyron Street
Charlotte, North Carolina 28285-
   0001
charlotte.fbi.gov
(704) 377-9200

FBI Cleveland
Federal Office Building
1501 Lakeside Avenue
Cleveland, Ohio 44114
cleveland.fbi.gov
(216) 522-1400

FBI Chicago
2111 West Roosevelt Road

Chicago, IL 60608-1128
chicago.fbi.gov
(312) 421-6700

FBI Columbia
151 Westpark Blvd
Columbia, South Carolina 29210-
   3857
columbia.fbi.gov
(803) 551-4200

FBI Cincinnati
Room 9000
550 Main Street
Cincinnati, Ohio 45202-8501
cincinnati.fbi.gov
(513) 421-4310

FBI Dallas
One Justice Way
Dallas, Texas 75220
dallas.fbi.gov
(972) 559-5000

FBI Detroit
26th. Floor, P. V. McNamara FOB
477 Michigan Avenue
Detroit, Michigan 48226
detroit.fbi.gov
(313) 965-2323

FBI Denver
Federal Office Building, Room 1823
1961 Stout Street, 18th. Floor
Denver, Colorado 80294-1823
denver.fbi.gov
(303) 629-7171

FBI El Paso
660 S. Mesa Hills Drive
El Paso, Texas 79912-5533
elpaso.fbi.gov
(915) 832-5000

FBI Honolulu
Room 4-230, Kalanianaole FOB
300 Ala Moana Boulevard
Honolulu, Hawaii 96850-0053

honolulu.fbi.gov
(808) 566-4300

FBI Houston
2500 East TC Jester
Houston, Texas 77008-1300
houston.fbi.gov
(713) 693-5000

FBI Indianapolis
Room 679, FOB
575 North Pennsylvania Street
Indianapolis, Indiana 46204-1585
indianapolis.fbi.gov
(317) 639-3301

FBI Jackson
Room 1553, FOB
100 West Capitol Street
Jackson, Mississippi 39269-1601
jackson.fbi.gov
(601) 948-5000

FBI Jacksonville
Suite 200
7820 Arlington Expressway
Jacksonville, Florida 32211-7499
jacksonville.fbi.gov
(904) 721-1211

FBI Kansas City
1300 Summit
Kansas City, Missouri 64105-1362
kansascity.fbi.gov
(816) 512-8200

FBI Knoxville
Suite 600, John J. Duncan FOB
710 Locust Street
Knoxville, Tennessee 37902-2537
knoxville.fbi.gov
(865) 544-0751

FBI Las Vegas
John Lawrence Bailey Building
1787 West Lake Mead Boulevard
Las Vegas, Nevada 89106-2135
lasvegas.fbi.gov
(702) 385-1281

FBI Los Angeles
Suite 1700, FOB
11000 Wilshire Boulevard
Los Angeles, California 90024-3672
losangeles.fbi.gov
(310) 477-6565

FBI Little Rock
#24 Shackleford West Boulevard
Little Rock, Arkansas 72211-3755
littlerock.fbi.gov
(501) 221-9100

FBI Louisville
Room 500
600 Martin Luther King Jr. Place
Louisville, Kentucky 40202-2231
louisville.fbi.gov
(502) 583-3941

FBI Memphis
Suite 3000, Eagle Crest Bldg.
225 North Humphreys Blvd.
Memphis, Tennessee 38120-2107
memphis.fbi.gov
(901) 747-4300

FBI Minneapolis
Suite 1100
111 Washington Avenue, South
Minneapolis, Minnesota 55401-2176
minneapolis.fbi.gov
(612) 376-3200

FBI North Miami Beach
16320 Northwest Second Avenue
North Miami Beach, Florida 33169-
   6508
miami.fbi.gov
(305) 944-9101

FBI Mobile
200 N. Royal Street
Mobile, Alabama 36602
mobile.fbi.gov
(251) 438-3674

FBI Milwaukee
Suite 600
330 East Kilbourn Avenue
Milwaukee, Wisconsin 53202-6627
milwaukee.fbi.gov
(414) 276-4684

FBI Newark
11 Centre Place
Newark, New Jersey 07102-9889
newark.fbi.gov
(973) 792-3000

FBI New York
26 Federal Plaza, 23rd. Floor
New York, New York 10278-0004
newyork.fbi.gov
(212) 384-1000

FBI New Haven
600 State Street
New Haven, Connecticut 06511-6505
newhaven.fbi.gov
(203) 777-6311

FBI Norfolk
150 Corporate Boulevard
Norfolk, Virginia 23502-4999
norfolk.fbi.gov
(757) 455-0100

FBI New Orleans
2901 Leon C. Simon Dr.
New Orleans, Louisiana 70126
neworleans.fbi.gov
(504) 816-3000

FBI Oklahoma City
3301 West Memorial Drive
Oklahoma City, Oklahoma 73134
oklahomacity.fbi.gov
(405) 290-7770

FBI Omaha
10755 Burt Street
Omaha, Nebraska 68114-2000
omaha.fbi.gov
(402) 493-8688

FBI Philadelphia
8th. Floor
William J. Green Jr. FOB
600 Arch Street
Philadelphia, Pennsylvania 19106
philadelphia.fbi.gov
(215) 418-4000

FBI Pittsburgh
3311 East Carson St.
Pittsburgh, PA 15203
pittsburgh.fbi.gov
(412) 432-4000

FBI Phoenix
Suite 400
201 East Indianola Avenue
Phoenix, Arizona 85012-2080
phoenix.fbi.gov
(602) 279-5511

FBI Portland
Suite 400, Crown Plaza Building
1500 Southwest 1st Avenue
Portland, Oregon 97201-5828
portland.fbi.gov
(503) 224-4181

FBI Richmond
1970 E. Parham Road
Richmond, Virginia 23228
richmond.fbi.gov
(804) 261-1044

FBI Sacramento
4500 Orange Grove Avenue
Sacramento, California 95841-4205
sacramento.fbi.gov
(916) 481-9110

FBI San Francisco
450 Golden Gate Avenue, 13th. Floor
San Francisco, California 94102-9523
sanfrancisco.fbi.gov
(415) 553-7400

FBI St. Louis
2222 Market Street

St. Louis, Missouri 63103-2516
stlouis.fbi.gov
(314) 231-4324

FBI San Juan
Room 526, U.S. Federal Bldg.
150 Carlos Chardon Avenue
Hato Rey
San Juan, Puerto Rico 00918-1716
sanjuan.fbi.gov
(787) 754-6000

FBI Salt Lake City
Suite 1200, 257 Towers Bldg.
257 East, 200 South
Salt Lake City, Utah 84111-2048
saltlakecity.fbi.gov
(801) 579-1400

FBI Seattle
1110 Third Avenue
Seattle, Washington 98101-2904
seattle.fbi.gov
(206) 622-0460

FBI San Antonio
Suite 200
U.S. Post Office Courthouse Bldg.
615 East Houston Street

San Antonio, Texas 78205-9998
sanantonio.fbi.gov
(210) 225-6741
FBI Springfield
900 East Linton Avenue
Springfield, Illinois 62703
springfield.fbi.gov
(217) 522-9675

FBI San Diego
Federal Office Building
9797 Aero Drive
San Diego, California 92123-1800
sandiego.fbi.gov
(858) 565-1255

FBI Tampa
5525 West Gray Street
Tampa, Florida 33609
tampa.fbi.gov
(813) 253-1000

FBI Washington
Washington Metropolitan Field Office
601 4th Street, N.W.
Washington, D.C. 20535-0002
washingtondc.fbi.gov
(202) 278-2000

Appendix D

FOIA Request Processing by Agency

Agency (2007)	Pending End FY06	Received	Processed	Pending End FY07	Backlog as a percentage of yearly processing	Median number of days to process simple and complex requests during fiscal year 2007 and median number of days that requests pending at the end of year have been awaiting response	For more information please refer to the agency's Web site at:
CIA	896	2,911	3,031	776	25.6%	Simple Requests: 8 Complex Requests: 56 Median number of days that requests pending at the end of year have been awaiting response: FOIA 257; Privacy Act 80	www.foia.cia.gov/ annual_report.asp
CPSC	84	4,598	4,402	280	6.4%	Simple Requests: 10 Complex Requests: 40 Median number of days that requests pending at the end of year have been awaiting response: 48	http://www.cpsc .gov/cpscpub/pubs/ reprots/foia07.pdf
DOC (for 2006)	Pending Ending FY06 278	2,018	1,987	Pending Ending FY06 309	15.6%	Simple Requests: 12 Complex Requests: 45 Median number of days that requests pending at the end of year have been awaiting response	http://www .osec.doc.gov/omo/ FOIA/06rpt.htm
DOD	18,288	86,299	78,392	26,195	33.4%	Simple Requests: 11.5 Complex Requests: 45.5 Median number of days that requests pending at the end of year have been awaiting response: 111	http://www.dod.mil/ pubs/foi/FY2007 report.pdf

Agency (2007)	Pending End FY06	Received	Processed	Pending End FY07	Backlog as a percentage of yearly processing	Median number of days to process simple and complex requests during fiscal year 2007 and median number of days that requests pending at the end of year have been awaiting response	For more information please refer to the agency's Web site at:
DOT	2,041	9,695	9,542	2,194	23%		http://www.dot.gov/foia/reports/2007annualreport.htm#v
DOI	1,422	4,891	5,437	876	16.1%		http://www.doi.gov/foia/report.html
Educ.	541	1,792	1,670	663	39.7%	Simple Requests: 35 Complex Requests: 66 Median number of days that requests pending at the end of year have been awaiting response: 78	http://www.ed.gov/about/reports/annual/foia/foiafy07.pdf
EEOC	1,693	14,602	14,879	1,416	9.5%	Simple Requests: 18 Complex Requests: N/A Median number of days that requests pending at the end of year have been awaiting response: 9	http://www.eeoc.gov/foia/annrep2007.html
Energy	910	3,434	3,698	646	17.5%		http://management.energy.gov/ocuments/annual_reports.htm

Appendix D: FOIA Request Processing by Agency (continued)

Agency (2007)	Pending End FY06	Received	Processed	Pending End FY07	Backlog as a percentage of yearly processing	Median number of days to process simple and complex requests during fiscal year 2007 and median number of days that requests pending at the end of year have been awaiting response	For more information please refer to the agency's Web site at:
EPA	1,973	11,820	12,066	1,727	14.3%		www.epa.gov/foia/docs/2007report.pdf
FDA	19,328	12,320	14,190	17,458	123%	Simple Requests Complex Requests (where multiple tracks used): 146 Where single tracks used): 653 Single Trace Requests: 86 Median number of days that requests pending at the end of year have been awaiting response: 311	http://www.fda.gov/foi/annual2007.html
FRB	9	813	817	5	.61%	Simple Requests: 1 Complex Requests: 14 Median number of days that requests pending at the end of year have been awaiting response: 3	http://www.federalreserve.gov/generalinfo/foia/anrpt_2007.htm

Agency (2007)	Pending End FY06	Received	Processed	Pending End FY07	Backlog as a percentage of yearly processing	Median number of days to process simple and complex requests during fiscal year 2007 and median number of days that requests pending at the end of year have been awaiting response	For more information please refer to the agency's Web site at:
FTC	19	1,038	1,055	2	.19%	Simple Requests: 4 Complex Requests: 19 Median number of days that requests pending at the end of year have been awaiting response: 6	http://www.ftc.gov/foia/2007r-fo.pdf
GSA	79	1,354	1,347	86	6.4%	Simple Requests: N/A Complex Requests: 25 Median number of days that requests pending at the end of year have been awaiting response: 43	http://www.gsa.gov/portal/Gsa/ep/contentView.do?contenttype=GSA_DOCUMENT=114068&noc=2
Homeland	110,542	108,416	135,297	83,661	61.8%		www.dhs.gov/xlibrary/assets/foia/privacy_rpt_foia_2007.pdf
HHS	28,728	289,721	290,315	28,134	9.7%		http://www.hhs.gov/foia/reports/07anlrpt.html

Appendix D: FOIA Request Processing by Agency (continued)

Agency (2007)	Pending End FY06	Received	Processed	Pending End FY07	Backlog as a percentage of yearly processing	Median number of days to process simple and complex requests during fiscal year 2007 and median number of days that requests pending at the end of year have been awaiting response	For more information please refer to the agency's Web site at:
Justice	9,278	52,260	53,889	7,649	14.2%		http://www.usdoj.gov/oip/annual_report/2007/07contents.htm
HUD	4,941	3,484	7,661	764	10%		http://www.hud.gov/offices/adm/foia/foia2007annualreport.doc
Labor	906	27,944	27,581	1,269	4.6%		http://www.dol.gov/sol/foia/2008anrpt.htm
NARA	5,378	12,185	12,386	5,177	41.8%	Simple Requests: 9 Complex Requests: 1,603 Median number of days that requests pending at the end of year have been awaiting response: Simple=894 Complex=2,063	http://www.archives.gov/foia/reports/index.html

Agency (2007)	Pending End FY06	Received	Processed	Pending End FY07	Backlog as a percentage of yearly processing	Median number of days to process simple and complex requests during fiscal year 2007 and median number of days that requests pending at the end of year have been awaiting response	For more information please refer to the agency's Web site at:
NASA	241	1,416	1,326	331	25%	Simple Requests: 21 Complex Requests: 38 Median number of days that requests pending at the end of year have been awaiting response: 87	http://www.hq.nasa .gov/office/pao/ FOIA/FY_2007_ report.pdf
NLRB	116	4,320	4,278	158	3.7%	Median number of days to process requests (tracks not used): 6 Median number of days that requests pending at the end of year have been awaiting response: 15	http://www.nlrb.gov/ FOIA/Annual_FOIA_ Reports.aspx
OPM	925	14,459	14,398	986	6.8%	Median number of days to process requests (tracks not used): 15 Median number of days that requests pending at the end of year have been awaiting response: 41	http://www.opm.gov/ efoia/pdf/ FOIA_FY2007.reports
Peace Corps	57	5,950	5,962	45	.75%	Simple Requests: 5 Complex Requests: N/A Median number of days that requests pending at the end of year have been awaiting response: 7	http://www .peaccecorps.gov/ multimedia/pdf/ policies/foia2007.pdf

Appendix D: FOIA Request Processing by Agency (continued)

Agency (2007)	Pending End FY06	Received	Processed	Pending End FY07	Backlog as a percentage of yearly processing	Median number of days to process simple and complex requests during fiscal year 2007 and median number of days that requests pending at the end of year have been awaiting response	For more information please refer to the agency's Web site at:
SBA	46	3,333	3,348	31	.93%	Median number of days to process requests (tracks not used): 7 Median number of days that requests pending at the end of year have been awaiting response: 12 FOIA_ANNUAL_REPORTS_INDEX.html	http://www.sba.gov/aboutsba/foiaprograms/foia/
SEC	10,403	9,070	12,564	6,909	55%	Simple Requests: 67 Complex Requests: 705 Median number of days that simple requests pending at the end of year have been awaiting response: 365 Median number of days that complex requests pending at the end of year have been awaiting response: 671	http://www.sec.gov/foia/arfoia07.htm

Agency (2007)	Pending End FY06	Received	Processed	Pending End FY07	Backlog as a percentage of yearly processing	Median number of days to process simple and complex requests during fiscal year 2007 and median number of days that requests pending at the end of year have been awaiting response	For more information please refer to the agency's Web site at:
SSA	1,156	18,995,845	18,995,719	1,282	.0067%		'http://www.ssa.gov/foia/html/2007%2055A's%20Annual%20FOIA%20Report.doc
State	3,799	5,078	4,792	4,085	85.2%	Simple Requests: 67 Complex Requests: 212 Median number of days that requests pending at the end of year have been awaiting response: 226	http://www.state.gov/m/a/ips/
Treas.	3,924	27,927	28,785	3,066	10.7%		http://www.ustreas.gov/foia/reports/fy07-ag.pdf
USDA	1,834	31,500	31,651	1,683	5.3%		http://www.usda.gov/da/foia_reading_room.htm
USPS	111	1,608	1,579	140	8.9%	Simple Requests: 12 Median number of days that requests pending at the end of year have been awaiting response: 14	http://www.usps.com/foia/annualreports/welcome.htm
VA	38,664	2,008,589	2,011,887	35,366	118%		http://www.foia.gogov/

Appendix E

Select Open Government Organizations

Open Government Organization	Description	Notable Information
Federation of American Scientists Project on Government Secrecy www.fas.org/sgp	Through research, advocacy and public education, the FAS Project on Government Secrecy works to challenge excessive government secrecy and to promote public oversight.	Includes information on the group's work to obtain national intelligence budgets through the FOIA.
George Washington University's National Security Archive www.gwu.edu/%7Ensarchiv	Maintains the largest non-governmental collection of declassified government documents and other valuable resources.	Telephone conversations of former U.S. Secretary of State Henry Kissinger, berating high-level subordinates for their efforts in 1976 to restrain human rights abuses by military dictators in Chile and Argentina.
OpenTheGovernment.org www.openthegovernment.org	A new coalition of 33 organizations dedicated to combating unwarranted government secrecy and promoting freedom of information.	An evaluation by The Reporters Committee for Freedom of the Press on "the likely impact of Attorney General nominee Alberto Gonzales on press freedoms and the public's right to know," based on Reporters Committee research of Gonzales' performance as a judge on the Texas Supreme Court from January 1999 to December 2000 and as White House counsel since January 2001.

Open Government Organization	Description	Notable Information
National Freedom of Information Coalition www.nfoic.org	Promotes freedom of information particularly at the state level.	Each year the National Freedom of Information Coalition (NFOIC) offers approximately $220,000 in pass-through grants to state coalitions. These grants foster the creation and growth of state FOI coalitions, and further public access to government records and meetings.
Sunshine in Government Initiative www.sunshineingovernment.org	A coalition of media groups committed to promoting policies that ensure the government is accessible, accountable and open.	Research on the organization's Web site includes documents showing the U.S. government turned down hundreds of millions of dollars in aid following Hurricane Katrina, as well as news of funding shortages hampering cleanups at "Superfund" hazardous waste sites.
Coalition of Journalists for Open Government www.cjog.net	The stated goal of the organization is to provide timely information on freedom of information issues and on what journalism organizations are doing to foster greater transparency in government.	The coalition's Web site reports "the Department of Homeland Security is requiring all of its 180,000 employees and others outside the federal government to sign binding non-disclosure agreements covering unclassified information. Breaking the agreement could mean loss of job, stiff fines and imprisonment."

Appendix D: Select Open Government Organizations (continued)

Open Government Organization	Description	Notable Information
Government Attic www.governmentattic.org	Offers miscellaneous records on a variety of topics.	Web site maintains comprehensive Department of Defense and Department of Justice FOIA logs in PDF format from 2000 onward.
James Madison Project www.jamesmadisonproject.org	The organization pursues public education and litigation in the interest of open government.	Web site offers stories and documents showing higher reaction rates to Anthrax vaccines among government employees than originally reported by the Food and Drug Administration.
The Memory Hole www.thememoryhole.org	The organization collects and publishes elusive records and documents that have been withdrawn from the public domain.	Web site holds a wealth of hard-to-find information including corporate memos, government files, police reports and photographs. Includes the FBI's complete file on Martin Luther King, Jr.
Cryptome www.cryptome.org	Offers a rich collection of new official and unofficial documents on security policy.	DVDs for sale on their Web site contain all documents from their site plus 23,000 (updated) pages of counter-intelligence dossiers declassified by the U.S. Army Information and Security Command, dating from 1945 to 1985.

Open Government Organization	Description	Notable Information
BushSecrecy.org www.bushsecrecy.org	Provides resources and analysis of Bush Administration secrecy policies from Public Citizen.	Contains analysis and documentation regarding a 2001 presidential order limiting access provided in the Presidential Papers Act.
The Reporters Committee for Freedom of the Press www.rcfp.org	Provides news and assistance on freedom of information matters.	Answers questions and provides guidance via a national hotline (1-800-336-4243).
OMB Watch www.ombwatch.org	Provides resources, news and analysis on the "right to know."	Web site contains comprehensive information from the Emergency Planning and Community Right-to-Know Act (EPCRA), the EPA's collection of data on releases and transfers of certain toxic chemicals from industrial facilities for public disclosure.
Nautilus Institute: Global Disclosure Project www.nautilus.org/foia	Specializes in nuclear weapons policy and strategy.	Web site includes a number of hard-to-find reports about U.S. nuclear and military strategy in Korea and Japan from the 1960s to the present.
GlobalSecurity.org www.globalsecurity.org	Provides resources on all aspects of national security policy	Web site includes comprehensive reporting and analysis of U.S. casualties in Iraq, as well as a section devoted to government satellite imagery.

Appendix D: Select Open Government Organizations (continued)

Open Government Organization	Description	Notable Information
Guide to Declassified Documents and Archival Materials for U.S. Foreign Policy and World Politics by David N. Gibbs, University of Arizona www.gened.arizona.edu/dgibbs/declassified.htm		Provides links to a number of national security documents on the Internet, as well as other FOIA resources.
The Resource Shelf www.resourceshelf.com	Provides news on all aspects of government information policy and links to valuable source documents.	A daily newsletter contains tips for research and updates on government information policy.
Project on Government Oversight www.pogo.org	Performs independent investigations to promote openness and government accountability.	Web site contains the group's Federal Contractor Misconduct Database, which compiles misconduct information for the government's top 50 private contractors.
Electronic Privacy Information Center www.epic.org	Offers many important declassified documents and insights on cryptography policy, privacy and more.	Web site contains links to a number of internet privacy documents, including a wealth of recent documents on the FBI's Carnivore Internet Surveillance System.
Center for Democracy and Technology www.cdt.org	Addresses access to government information along with its main focus on civil liberties.	Maintains an updated "10 Most Wanted Government Documents" list and advocates for open government legislation.

Open Government Organization	Description	Notable Information
Freedominfo.org www.freedominfo.org	Offers news and resources for freedom of information advocates around the world.	Web site provides up-to-date information about obtaining government information in countries in Europe, Asia and Latin America, as well as advocacy for countries without freedom of information laws.
Public Citizen's Freedom of Information Clearinghouse www.citizen.org/litigation/free_info	Includes abundant resources on the Freedom of Information Act.	Web site contains a large database of government FOIA contact information and provides support for filing a request.
Access Reports www.accessreports.com	Provides news and expert analysis on freedom of information policy from Harry Hammitt.	Contains a comprehensive listing of access and privacy statutes.

Selected References

Articles

Tina Adler, *Marine Science: Surf's Yuck*, Environ Health Perspectives August 2004; 112(11): A614.

Arthur Allen, "The Not-So-Crackpot Autism Theory," *The New York Times*, November 10, 2002, available at http://query.nytimes.com/gst/fullpage.html?res=9B03EFD7153EF933A25752C1A9649C8B63 (last visited November 5, 2008).

Felicity Barringer, "Polar Bear Is Made a Protected Species," *The New York Times*, May 15, 2008, http://www.nytimes.com/2008/05/15/us/15polar.html?fta=y (last visited November 11, 2008).

Felicity Barringer, "White House Refused to Open Pollutants E-Mail," *The New York Times*, June 25, 2008, available at http://www.nytimes.com/2008/06/25/washington/25epa.html?_r=1&adxnnl=1&oref=slogin&adxnnlx=1216983823-z6z/aCL/aiwzML4yaNbLXA (last visited November 4, 2008).

Kenneth R. Bazinet, "Veep Tried to Aid Firm: Prez Raps Probes of Enron," (New York) *Daily News*, January 18, 2002, available at http://www.nydailynews.com/archives/news/2002/01/18/2002-01-18_veep_tried_to_aid_firm_prez_.html (last visited November 17, 2008).

Justin Blum, "Drug, Food Risks Stay Secret as Inquiries to U.S. FDA Pile Up," Bloomberg.com, June 19, 2008, available at: http://www.bloomberg.com/apps/news?pid=20601103&sid=a91FU255oQBM&refer=news (last visited November 1, 2008).

Tom Brazaitis, "Some Fear Stronger FBI Will Return to Old Abuses," *The Plain Dealer* (Cleveland), July 7, 2002, at A1.

Timothy J. Burger, "Veep Tried to Aid Firm: Key Role in India Debt Row," (New York) *Daily News*, January 18, 2002, available at http://www.nydailynews.com/archives/news/2002/01/18/2002-01-18_veep_tried_to_aid_firm_key_r.html (last visited November 17, 2008).

Joel Brinkley, "U.S. Versus Microsoft: The Reaction," *The New York Times*, November 7, 1999, available at http://query.nytimes.com/gst/fullpage.html? res=9F06E5DC143AF934A35752C1A96F958260 (last visited November 17, 2008).

Marian Burros, "Second Thoughts on Mercury in Fish," *The New York Times*, March 13, 2002, available at http://query.nytimes.com/gst/fullpage.html? res=9E07E7DC1539F930A25750C0A9649C8B63 (last visited November 5, 2008).

Tracey Colton Green, "Providing for the Common Defense Versus Providing for the General Welfare: The Conflicts Between National Security and National Environmental Policy," *Southeastern Environmental Law Journal* 137 (1997).

Archibald Cox, "Executive Privilege," 122 *University of Pennsylvania Law Review* 1383 (1974).

James Cox, "Study: Bush Donors Rake in Contracts," *USA Today*, October 30, 2003, available at http://www.usatoday.com/money/companies/2003-10-30-contracts_x.htm (last visited November 17, 2008).

Margaret Cronin Fisk, "Suit Targets Mercury-Laced Vaccinations," *The Recorder* (American Lawyer Media), March 26, 2002.

Lee Davidson, "Sailors Exposed to Deadly Agents," *The Deseret News*, May 24, 2002.

Amy Dorsett, "Librarians Would Shelve Patriot Act," *San Antonio Express-News*, January 25, 2007, available at http://www.mysanantonio.com/news/ MYSA012506_01A_militant_librarians_12d1873c_html8249.html (last visited November 24, 2008).

Jim Drinkard and Mark Memmott, "HHS Says It Paid Columnist for Help," *USA Today*, January 27, 2005, available at http://www.usatoday.com/news/ washington/2005-01-27-hhs_x.htm (last visited November 13, 2008).

Jim Efstathiou Jr., "Obama to Declare Carbon Dioxide Dangerous Pollutant," *Bloomberg News*, October 16, 2008, available at http://www.bloomberg.com/ apps/news?pid=newsarchive&sid=alHWVvGnkcd4 (last visited November 8, 2008).

Dan Eggen and Julie Tate, "U.S. Campaign Produces Few Convictions on Terrorism Charges," *The Washington Post*, June 12, 2005, available at http://www .washingtonpost.com/wp-dyn/content/article/2005/06/11/AR20050611003 81.html (last visited November 24, 2008).

Juliet Eilperin, "Judge Rebukes EPA on Rat Poison Reversal," *The Washington Post*, August 9, 2005, available at http://www.washingtonpost.com/wp-dyn/content/ article/2005/08/08/AR2005080801225.html (last visited November 22, 2008).

Juliet Eilperin, "Rat-Poison Makers Stall Safety Rules; EPA Had Drafted Regulations To Protect Children, Animals," *The Washington Post*, April 15, 2004, at A03.

Dixie Farley, "Dangers of Lead Still Linger," *FDA Consumer*, January/February 1998, available at http://www.fda.gov/FDAC/features/1998/198_lead.html (last visited November 1, 2008).

John Frank, "City Rarely Prosecutes Civil Rights Complaints," *The Houston Chronicle*, December 1, 2004.

Sydney P. Freedberg and Connie Humburg, "Wandering Weapons: America's Lax Arsenal," *St. Petersburg Times*, May 11, 2003, available at http://www

.sptimes.com/2003/05/11/Worldandnation/Wandering_weapons__Am.shtml (last visited October 13, 2008).

Chris Fusco, "Number of Missing DCFS Wards Doubles," *Chicago Sun-Times*, April 29, 2003.

Gilbert M. Gaul, "Emergency Funds Spent To Replace Beach Sand," *The Washington Post*, May 30, 2004, available at http://www.washingtonpost.com/wp-dyn/articles/A1111-2004May29.html (last visited August 5, 2008).

Gilbert Gaul, "Inefficient Spending Plagues Medicare," *The Washington Post*, July 24, 2005.

Lance Gay, "Store Chicken Filled with 'Defects," *Scripps Howard News Service* via the *Chicago Sun-Times*, March 2, 2001.

Amy Goldstein, "Patriot Act Provision Invoked, Memo Says," *The Washington Post*, June 18, 2004, available at http://www.washingtonpost.com/wp-dyn/articles/A50524-2004Jun17.html (last visited November 24, 2008).

Tee L. Guidotti, Thomas Calhoun, John O. Davies-Cole, Maurice E. Knuckles, Lynette Stokes, Chevelle Glymph, Garret Lum, Marina S. Moses, David F. Goldsmith, and Lisa Ragain, "Elevated Lead in Drinking Water in Washington, D.C., 2003–2004: The Public Health Response," *Environmental Health Perspectives*, May 2007, available at http://www.ehponline.org/members/2007/8722/8722.html (last visited November 1, 2008).

James Heaney, "The Half-Billion-Dollar Bust," *Buffalo News*, November 14, 2004, at A01.

Timothy R. Henderson, "September 11th: How It Has Changed a Community's Right to Know," *The Maryland Bar Journal*, July/August 2002.

Douglas Jiehl, "C.I.A. Defers to Congress, Agreeing to Disclose Nazi Records," *The New York Times*, February 7, 2005.

Marc Kaufman, "Many FDA Scientists Had Drug Concerns, 2002 Study Shows," *The Washington Post*, December 16, 2004, available at http://www.washingtonpost.com/wp-dyn/articles/A3135-2004Dec15.html (last visited November 6, 2008).

Sally Kestin and Megan O'Matz, "FEMA Disaster Aid Operations Tightened After Frances," *Sun-Sentinel*, August 6, 2005, available at http://www.sun-sentinel.com/news/local/southflorida/sfl-fema06aug06,0,4025655.story (last visited November 13, 2008).

Tom Kizzia, "E-mail Reveals State Dispute Over Polar Bear Listing," *Anchorage Daily News*, May 25, 2008, available at: http://www.adn.com/polarbears/story/416432.html (last visited November 3, 2008).

Howard Kurtz, "Writer Backing Bush Plan Had Gotten Federal Contract," *The Washington Post*, January 26, 2005, available at http://www.washingtonpost.com/wp-dyn/articles/A36545-2005Jan25.html (last visited November 13, 2008).

Lyndsey Layton, "Lawmakers Agree to Ban Toxins in Children's Items," *The Washington Post*, July 29, 2008, available at http://www.washingtonpost.com/wp-dyn/content/article/2008/07/28/AR2008072802586.html (last visited November 22, 2008).

Christopher Lee, "USDA Paid Freelance Writer $7,500 for Articles," *The Washington Post*, May 11, 2005, available at http://www.washingtonpost.com/wp-dyn/content/article/2005/05/10/AR2005051001593.html (last visited August 30, 2008).

Carol D. Leonnig and David Nakamura, "D.C. Knew of Lead Problems in 2002; Timing of E-Mails Contradicts Claims," *The Washington Post*, March 29, 2004.

Eric Lichtblau, "At F.B.I., Frustration Over Limits on an Antiterror Law," *The New York Times*, December 11, 2005, available at http://www.nytimes.com/2005/12/11/national/nationalspecial3/11patriot.html (last visited November 24, 2008).

Christian Lowe, "Marine Corps Issued Flawed Armor," *Marine Corps Times*, May 9, 2005

Randy Ludlow, "Legislators Move More Records Off Table," *Columbus Dispatch*, January 31, 2008, available at http://blog.dispatch.com/know/2008/01/lawmakers_moving_more_records.shtml (last visited November 16, 2008).

Randy Ludlow, "Foster Parent Records Were Public, Court Rules," *Columbus Dispatch*, April 17, 2008, available at http://blog.dispatch.com/know/2008/04/foster_parent_records_were_public_court_rules.shtml#more (last visited November 16, 2008).

Beverley Lumpkin, "Corps of Engineers Lists 122 Levees at Risk from Coast to Coast," *Associated Press*, February 2, 2007.

Jerry Markon, "The Terrorism Case That Wasn't—And Still Is," *The Washington Post*, June 12, 2005, available at http://www.washingtonpost.com/wp-dyn/content/article/2005/06/11/AR2005061100379.html (last visited November 24, 2008).

Andrew McIntosh, "Special Report: Some Rescuers Pose Threat," *The Sacramento Bee*, January 28, 2007, available at: http://www.sacbee.com/797/story/114035.html (last visited November 6, 2008).

Jenifer B. McKim, "County Fights Release of Details," *Orange County Register*, September 15, 2006, available at http://www.ocregister.com/ocregister/news/article_1274522.php (last visited November 16, 2008).

Jenifer B. McKim, "Lost Lives," *Orange County Register*, September 15, 2006, available at http://www.ocregister.com/ocregister/news/article_1274888.php (last visited November 16, 2008).

Donald G. McNeil, Jr., "Where the Cows Come Home," *The New York Times*, January 2, 2004, available at http://query.nytimes.com/gst/fullpage.html?sec=health&res=9C03E3DB1631F931A35752C0A9629C8B63&n=Top%2FNews%2FScience%2FTopics%2FLivestock (last visited November 6, 2008).

Stephanie Mencimer, "Why Mercury Tuna Is Still Legal," *Mother Jones*, September/October 2008, available at http://www.motherjones.com/news/feature/2008/09/exit-strategy-tuna-surprise.html (last visited November 5, 2008).

Martha Mendoza, "Birth Control Patch Appears Riskier Than Pill," *The Associated Press* via the *Los Angeles Times*, July 17, 2005, available at http://articles.latimes.com/2005/jul/17/news/adna-patch17 (last visited November 5, 2008).

Alan C. Miller and Kevin Sack, "The Vertical Vision/Part I: The Widow Maker," *The Los Angeles Times*, December 15, 2002.

Alan C. Miller and Kevin Sack, "Congressional Hearings Will Focus on Marine Harrier Jet," *Los Angeles Times*, January 8, 2003, available at http://www.latimes.com/news/nationworld/nation/la-na-harrier8jan08,0,5634215.story (last visited November 22, 2008).

Alan C. Miller and Kevin Sack, "Accident-Prone Harrier Jet Faces Further Investigation," *Los Angeles Times*, January 21, 2003, available at http://www.latimes.com/

news/nationworld/nation/la-na-harrier21jan21,0,3075887.story (last visited November 22, 2008).

Alan C. Miller and Kevin Sack, "North Carolina Crash Is Second in a Month for Marine Harrier Jet," *Los Angeles Times*, July 16, 2005, available at http://www.latimes.com/news/nationworld/nation/la-na-harrier8jan08,0,5634215.story (last visited November 22, 2008).

Miles Moffeit, "GI Sex Cases from Iraq Often Stall," *The Denver Post*, April 12, 2004, at A1.

Maryann Mott, "Wild Horses Sold by U.S. Agency Sent to Slaughter," *National Geographic News*, May 5, 2005, available at http://news.nationalgeographic.com/news/2005/05/0505_050505_wildhorses.html (last visited October 3, 2008).

Anne C. Mulkern, "Experts Say USDA Officials Underestimate Mad-Cow Risk," *The Denver Post*, February 13, 2004.

Evelyn Nieves, "A Roundup of Wild Horses Stirs Up a Fight in the West," *The New York Times*, February 25, 2002, available at http://query.nytimes.com/gst/fullpage.html?res=9806E7D91F3EF936A15751C0A9649C8B63 (last visited November 4, 2008).

Barack Obama, "Letter to the Editor," *Las Vegas Review-Journal*, May 20, 2007, available at http://www.lvrj.com/opinion/7598337.html (last visited November 8, 2008).

Sarah Palin, "Bearing Up," *The New York Times*, January 5, 2008, available at http://www.nytimes.com/2008/01/05/opinion/05palin.html?_r=2&oref=slogin&oref=slogin (last visited October 29, 2008).

M. B. Pell and Jim Morris, " 'Safe' Pesticides Now First in Poisonings," The Center for Public Integrity, July 30, 2008, available at http://www.publicintegrity.org/investigations/pesticides/pages/introduction (last visited November 4, 2008).

Melody Peterson and Christopher Drew, "The Slaughterhouse Gamble," *The New York Times*, October 10, 2003, available at http://query.nytimes.com/gst/fullpage.html?res=9502E1DC143FF933A25753C1A9659C8B63 (last visited November 5, 2008).

Physicians for Human Rights, "PHR Files Suit Against Defense Department in FOIA Dispute Over Documents Concerning Dasht-e-Leili Mass Grave in Afghanistan," February 19, 2008, available at http://physiciansforhumanrights.org/library/news-2008-02-19.html (last visited November 22, 2008).

Eric Pianin, "Widespread Water Violations Decried," *The Washington Post*, August 7, 2002.

Stephen Power and Ian Talley, "Administration Releases EPA Report, Then Repudiates It," *The Wall Street Journal*, July 12, 2008, available at http://online.wsj.com/article/SB121578600530545953.html (last visited November 4, 2008).

Dana Priest, "False Evidence Cited in Overturning Arms Dealer's Case," *The Washington Post*, October 30, 2003.

Erik Reece, "Moving Mountains," *Grist*, February 16, 2006, available at http://www.grist.org/news/maindish/2006/02/16/reece/ (last visited October 30, 2008).

Patty Reinert, "NASA Can't Find Millions in Property," *The Houston Chronicle*, February 27, 2004.

Andrew C. Revkin, "Climate Expert Says NASA Tried to Silence Him," *The New York Times*, January 26, 2006, available at http://www.nytimes.com/2006/01/29/science/earth/29climate.html (last visited November 8, 2006).

Nicolas Riccardi, "FBI Keeps Watch on Activists," *Los Angeles Times*, March 27, 2006, available at http://articles.latimes.com/2006/mar/27/nation/na-fbi27 (last visited November 15, 2008).

Keith Rogers, "Documents Say 60 Nuclear Chain Reactions Possible," *Las Vegas Review-Journal*, November 26, 2003.

Manuel Roif-Franzia and Catharine Skipp, "Tainted Water in the Land of Semper Fi," *The Washington Post*, January 28, 2004, available at http://www.washingtonpost.com/ac2/wp-dyn?pagename=article&node=&contentId=A54143-2004Jan27&notFound=true (last visited November 6, 2008).

Seth Rosenfeld, "Reagan, Hoover and the Red Scare," *San Francisco Chronicle*, June 9, 2002, available at http://www.sfgate.com/cgi-bin/article.cgi?f=/chronicle/archive/2002/06/09/MNCFINTRO.DTL (last visited November 15, 2008).

Seth Rosenfeld, "Feinstein Demands Answers from FBI," *San Francisco Chronicle*, June 23, 2002, available at http://www.sfgate.com/cgi-bin/article.cgi?file=/c/a/2002/06/23/MN135007.DTL (last visited November 15, 2008).

Seth Rosenfeld, "FBI Chief Admits '60s Spying on UC 'Wrong,'" *San Francisco Chronicle*, February 16, 2003, available at http://www.sfgate.com/cgi-bin/article.cgi?f=/c/a/2003/02/16/MN162401.DTL (last visited November 15, 2008).

Derek Sands, "DOI Sued for Sanctioning Chance Harm to Polar Bears in Chukchi Sea Drilling," *Inside Energy with Federal Lands*, July 14, 2008.

Christopher H. Schmitt and Edward T. Pound, "Keeping Secrets," *US News & World Report*, December 22, 2003, available at http://www.usnews.com/usnews/news/articles/secrecy/22secrecy.htm (last visited November 4, 2008).

Richard B. Schmitt, "A Flawed Terrorist Yardstick," *Los Angeles Times*, December 21, 2003, available at http://articles.latimes.com/2003/dec/21/nation/na-pittsburgh21 (last visited November 24, 2008).

Elana Schor, "Cheney Accused of Suppressing Testimony on Climate Change's Risks," *The Guardian*, July 8, 2008, available at http://www.guardian.co.uk/world/2008/jul/08/dickcheney.usa (lasted visited November 4, 2008).

Richard A. Serrano, "Seeing Murder in a Face," *Los Angeles Times*, March 9, 2004, available at http://articles.latimes.com/2004/mar/09/nation/na-prisoner9 (last visited November 24, 2008).

Dave Shaffer, "Salmonella Rates High at State Plants," *Star Tribune*, April 14, 2006.

Scott Shane, "Vietnam War Intelligence 'Deliberately Skewed,' Secret Study Says," *The New York Times*, December 2, 2005, available at http://www.nytimes.com/2005/12/02/politics/02tonkin.html (last visited November 22, 2008).

Elizabeth Shogren, "Federal Coal-Mining Policy Comes Under Fire," *Los Angeles Times*, January 7, 2004, available at http://articles.latimes.com/2004/jan/07/nation/na-mining7 (last visited November 12, 2008).

Manori J. Silva, Dana B. Barr, John A. Reidy, Nicole A. Malek, Carolyn C. Hodge, Samuel P. Caudill, John W. Brock, Larry L. Needham, and Antonia M. Calafat, "Urinary Levels of Seven Phthalate Metabolites in the U.S. Population from the National Health and Nutrition Examination Survey (NHANES) 1999–2000," *Environmental Health Perspectives*, March 2004, available at http://

www.ehponline.org/members/2003/6723/6723.html (last visited November 5, 2008).

Mathew Silverman, "National Security and the First Amendment: A Judicial Role in Maximizing Public Access to Information," 78 *Indiana Law Journal* 1101 (2003).

Kevin Spear and Jim Leusner, "Critical Flaws in Shuttles Loom as Potential Disaster," *Orlando Sentinel*, August 17, 2003, available at http://www.globalsecurity.org/org/news/2003/030817-shuttle-flaws01.htm (last visited November 22, 2008).

D. Stöfen, "The Health Dangers of Lead in Drinking Water," *Social and Preventive Medicine*, January 1971.

Gary Stoller, "Doomed Plane's Gaming System Exposes Holes in FAA Oversight," *USA Today*, February 16, 2003, available at http://www.usatoday.com/money/biztravel/2003-02-16-swissair-investigation_x.htm (last visited November 22, 2008).

Greg Toppo, "Education Dept. Paid Commentator to Promote Law," *USA Today*, January 7, 2005, available at http://www.usatoday.com/news/washington/2005-01-06-williams-whitehouse_x.htm (last visited August 31, 2008).

David Voreacos, "J&J Paid $68 Million to Settle Birth-Control Cases," *Bloomberg News*, October 10, 2008, available at http://www.bloomberg.com/apps/news?pid=20601109&sid=amZT0X84_8zU&refer=home (last visited November 6, 2008).

David Voreacos and Patricia Hurtado, "J&J Pays $1.25 Million to Settle Suit Over Death of 14-Year-Old," *Bloomberg News*, October 24, 2007, available at http://www.bloomberg.com/apps/news?pid=newsarchive&sid=aTTqmPEzxr9U (last visited November 6, 2008).

Patricia M. Wald, "The Freedom of Information Act: A Short Case Study in the Perils and Paybacks of Legislating Democratic Values," 33 *Emory Law Journal* 649 (1984).

Holly Watt, "ATF Lost Guns, Computers," *The Washington Post*, September 18, 2008, available at http://www.washingtonpost.com/wp-dyn/content/article/2008/09/17/AR2008091703662.html (last visited November 15, 2008).

Leticia Yáñez, et al., "Overview of Human Health and Chemical Mixtures: Problems Facing Developing Countries," *Environmental Health Perspectives*, December 2002, available at http://www.ehponline.org/members/2002/suppl-6/901-909yanez/ehp110s6p901.pdf (last visited November 11, 2008).

Books

Harold L. Cross, *The People's Right to Know: Legal Access to Public Records and Proceedings* (1953).

Hammitt et al., *Litigation Under the Federal Open Government Laws* (2008).

Dominique Lapierre and Javier Moro, *Five Past Midnight in Bhopal* (Warner Books, 2002).

Woodrow Wilson, *The New Freedom: A Call for the Emancipation of the Generous Energies of a People* (New York Doubleday, Page and Co. 1913).

World Health Organization, *Public Health Impact of Pesticides Used in Agriculture.* (Geneva, World Health Organization, 1990).

Cases

American Civil Liberties Union, et al. v. Department of Defense, et al., Civil Action No. 04-4151 (S.D.N.Y. 2005).

Burka v. HHS, 87 F.3d 508, 151 (D.C. Cir. 1996).

Department of the Air Force v. Rose, 425 U.S. 361 (1976).

Devine v. Marsh, 2 Gov't Disclosure Serv. (P-H) 82,022, at 82,186 (E.D. Va. Aug. 27, 1981).

H.C. 1601-4/90 Shalit et al. v. Peres el at 44(3) P.D. 353.

Houchins v. KQED, Inc., 438 U.S. 1 (1978).

Jones v. F.B.I., 41 F.3d 238, 240 (6th Cir.,1994).

Judicial Watch, Inc. v. Nat'l Energy Policy Dev. Group, 219 F. Supp. 2d 20, 55 (D.D.C. 2002), *aff'd on other grounds*, 334 F.3d 1096 (D.C. Cir.), *cert. granted*, 124 S. Ct. 958 (2003).

Kaneko et. al v. Japan, Keishū ll at 1490 (Sup. Ct. Nov. 26, 1969).

Kissinger v. Reporters Comm. for Freedom of the Press, 445 U.S. 136 (1980).

NARA v. Favish, 541 U.S. 157 (2004).

National Security Archive v. Department of Defense, 880 F.2d 1381 (D.C. Cir. 1989).

Nat'l Sec. Archive v. Archivist of the United States, 909 F.2d 541, 544 (D.C. Cir. 1990).

S.P. Gupta v. President of India [1982] AIR (SC) 149.

Sharif v. Pakistan, PLD 1993 S.C. 471

Tax Analysts v. United States Dep't of Justice, 845 F.2d 1060, 1069 (D.C. Cir. 1988).

United States Dep't of Justice v. Tax Analysts, 492 U.S. 136, 144-45 (1989).

Weinberger v. Catholic Action of Hawaii/Peace Education Project, 454 U.S. 139 (1981).

Reports, Press Releases, and Other Internet Resources

American Society for the Prevention of Cruelty to Animals, "USDA Documents Provide Proof of Circus Abuse of Elephants," March 12, 2002, available at http://www.charitywire.com/charity17/02845.html (last visited September 7, 2008).

The Association of Health Care Journalists, "FOIA survey: FDA's slow response means stories go unpublished," April 10, 2008, available at http://www.healthjournalism.org/about-news-detail.php?id=50 (last visited November 6, 2008).

John C. Baker, et al., "Rand Nat'l Defense Research Institute, Mapping The Risks: Assessing The Homeland Security Implications Of Publicly Available Geospatial Information" 71 (2004), available at http://www.rand.org/pubs/monographs/2004/RAND_MG142.pdf

David Banisar, "Freedom of Information Around the World 2006: A Global Survey of Access to Government Records Laws," available at: http://www.freedominfo.org/documents/global_survey2006.doc (lasted visited August 5, 2008).

BarackObama.com, "Blueprint for Change: Obama and Biden's Plan for America," available at http://www.barackobama.com/pdf/ObamaBlueprintForChange.pdf.

BarackObama.com, "Prepared Remarks for October 2, 2007 Speech," October 2, 2007. Available at http://www.barackobama.com/2007/10/02/on_fifth _anniversary_of_speech.php (last visited November 2, 2008).

BarackObama.com, "Science, Technology and Innovation for a New Generation," http://www.barackobama.com/issues/technology/#transparent-democracy (last visited November 2, 2008).

Bureau of Land Management, "Fact Sheet on Wild Horse and Burro Management Challenges," October 2008, available at http://www.blm.gov/wo/st/en/prog/ wild_horse_and_burro/new_factsheet.html (last visited October 31. 2008).

California Office of Environmental Health Hazard Assessment, "Methylmercury in Sport Fish," available at: http://oehha.ca.gov/fish/hg/index.html (last visited November 5, 2008).

Center for Biological Diversity, Natural Resources Defense Council, and Earth Justice Joint Press Release, "Conservation Groups File Suit for Suppressed Polar Bear Documents," January 28, 2008, available at: http://www.commondreams.org/ news2008/0128-16.htm (last visited October 29, 2008).

Center for Democracy and Technology, "Ten Most Wanted Government Documents," available at http://www.cdt.org/righttoknow/10mostwanted/ (last visited November 4, 2008).

The Center on Law and Security, "Terrorist Trial Report Cards," February 2005-September 2008, available at http://www.lawandsecurity.org/pub_newsletter .cfm?id=3 (last visited November 24, 2008).

Department of Energy, "Final Environmental Impact Statement for a Geologic Repository for the Disposal of Spent Nuclear Fuel and High-Level Radioactive Waste at Yucca Mountain, Nye County, Nevada," DOE/EIS-0250, February 2002, available at: http://www.ocrwm.doe.gov/documents/feis_2/vol_1/ indexv1.htm (last visited November 8, 2008).

Department of Health and Human Services, "Updated Status Report on Executive Order 13392 Review Plan, 2007," available at: http://www.hhs.gov/foia/refer-ence/updatedstatus.html (last visited November 6, 2008).

Department of Health and Human Services, "HHS Fiscal Year 2006 Freedom of Information Annual Report, 2007," available at http://www.hhs.gov/foia/ reports/06anlrpt.html (last visited November 6, 2008).

Department of Health and Human Services, "HHS Fiscal Year 2007 Freedom of Information Annual Report, 2008," available at http://www.hhs.gov/foia/ reports/07anlrpt.html (last visited November 6, 2008).

Edwin H. Clark II, "Water Prices Rising Worldwide," Earth Policy Institute, March 7, 2007, available at http://www.earth-policy.org/Updates/2007/Update64. htm (last visited November 12, 2008).

Environment and Human Health, Inc., "Plastics That May be Harmful to Children and Reproductive Health," June 12, 2008, available at http://www.ehhi.org/ reports/plastics/ehhi_plastics_report_2008.pdf (last visited November 22, 2008).

Environmental Protection Agency, "Accidental Release Prevention Requirements," April 9, 2004, available at http://www.epa.gov/EPA-AIR/2004/April/Day-09/ a7777.htm (last visited November 8, 2008).

Environmental Protection Agency, "Amendment to the Rodenticide Cluster and Zinc Phosphide Reregistration Eligibility Decision (RED) Documents,"

November 28, 2001, available at http://www.epa.gov/EPA-PEST/2001/November/Day-28/p29557.htm (last visited November 22, 2008).

Environmental Protection Agency, "EPA Takes Action to Reduce Accidental Exposures to Rat Poisons," October 16, 1998, available at http://yosemite.epa.gov/opa/admpress.nsf/b1ab9f485b098972852562e7004dc686/81eac9505e72832a8525669f0074f188?OpenDocument (last visited November 22, 2008).

Environmental Protection Agency and Food and Drug Administration, "What You Need To Know About Mercury In Fish And Shellfish," March 19, 2004, available at http://www.cfsan.fda.gov/~dms/admehg3.html (last visited November 5, 2008).

Federal Energy Regulatory Commission, "File a CEII Request," available at http://www.ferc.gov/help/filing-guide/ceii-request.asp (last visited November 8, 2008).

Food and Drug Administration, "FDA Announces Advisory on Methyl Mercury in Fish," January 12, 2001, available at http://www.cfsan.fda.gov/~acrobat/hgadv5.pdf (last visited November 5, 2008).

General Accounting Office, "Update on Implementation of the 1996 Electronic Freedom of Information Act Amendments, CAL-02-493," August, 2002, available at: http://www.gao.gov/new.items/d02493.pdf (last visited October 1, 2008).

Hawaii Department of Health, "A Local Guide to Eating Fish Safely," available at: http://www.hawaii.gov/health/about/family-child-health/wic/pdf/fishsafety.pdf (last visited November 5, 2008).

House Select Committee on Energy Independence and Global Warming, "Letter to President George W. Bush," June 24, 2008, available at http://globalwarming.house.gov/tools/2q08materials/files/0064.pdf (last visited November 10, 2008).

House Committee on Oversight and Government Reform, "Letter to EPA Administrator Stephen L. Johnson," March 12, 2008, available at http://oversight.house.gov/documents/20080312110250.pdf (last visited November 10, 2008).

Human Rights Watch, "The Detainee Abuse and Accountability Project, By the Numbers," Human Rights Watch, April 25, 2006, available at http://www.hrw.org/en/reports/2006/04/25/numbers (last visited November 22, 2008).

Humane Society of the United States, "HSUS Files Suit Against USDA Over FOIA Delays," January 27, 2005, available at http://www.hsus.org/animals_in_research/animals_in_research_news/hsus_files_suit_against_usda_over_foia_delays.html (last visited September 23, 2008).

Humane Society of the United States, "USDA Agrees to Provide Online Animal Research Reports in Wake of HSUS Suit," May 6, 2005, available at http://www.hsus.org/animals_in_research/animals_in_research_news/usda_agrees_to_provide_online_reports.html (last visited September 23, 2008).

Information Security Oversight Office, "2007 Report to the President," May 30, 2008, available at: http://archives.gov/isoo/reports/2007-annual-report.pdf (last visited November 1, 2008).

Intergovernmental Panel on Climate Change, "Summary for Policymakers, 2007," available at http://ipcc-wg1.ucar.edu/wg1/Report/AR4WG1_Print_SPM.pdf (last visited November 11, 2008).

The International Union for Conservation of Nature and Natural Resources, "2008 Red List: Ursus maritimus, 2008," available at http://www.iucnredlist.org/details/22823 (last visited November 11, 2008).

Investigative Reporters and Editors, "Freedom of Information in the USA: Part 1," *The IRE Journal*, March-April 2002. Available at http://www.ire.org/foi/bga/ (last visited November 2, 2008).

ISOO, "Audit of the Withdrawal of Records from Public Access at the National Archives and Records Administration for Classification Purposes," April 2006, available at: http://www.archives.gov/isoo/reports/2006-audit-report.html

Maine Center for Disease Control and Prevention, "The Maine Family Fish Guide," available at: http://www.maine.gov/dhhs/eohp/fish/documents/MeFFGuide .pdf (last visited November 5, 2008).

Massachusetts Department of Environmental Protection, "Fish Consumption Advisories," available at: http://www.mass.gov/dep/toxics/stypes/hgres.htm#fish (last visited November 5, 2008).

Elizabeth Mygatt, "World's Water Resources Face Mounting Pressure," Earth Policy Institute, July 26, 2006, available at http://www.earth-policy.org/Indicators/Water/2006.htm (last visited November 12, 2008).

National Citizens Cement Kiln Coalition, "Downwinders At Risk," available at http://www.cementkiln.com/DARNCCKCHotSpots.htm#TEXAS (last visited on September 24, 2008); see also the website of Toxic Texas, available at http://www.txpeer.org/toxictour/txi.html (last visited on September 24, 2008).

National Security Archive, "A FOIA Request Celebrates Its 17th Birthday: A Report on Federal Agency Backlog," March 2006, available at http://www.gwu.edu/~nsarchiv/NSAEBB/NSAEBB182/index.htm (last visited November 2, 2008).

National Security Archive, "The Ashcroft Memo, ibid.; General Accounting Office, Freedom of Information Act: Agency Views on Changes Resulting from New Administration Policy," GAO-03-981, September 3, 2003, available at http://www.gao.gov/cgi-bin/getrpt?GAO-03-981

National Security Archive, "The Ashcroft Memo: "Drastic" Change or "More Thunder than Lightning?" March 14, 2003, available at: http://www.gwu.edu/~nsarchiv/NSAEBB/NSAEBB84/index.html (last visited November 2, 2008).

Susan Nevelow Mart, "Let the People Know the Facts: Can Government Information Removed from the Internet Be Reclaimed?" LLRX.com, available at: http://www.llrx.com/features/reclaimed.htm (last visited November 11, 2008).

New Hampshire Department of Environmental Services, "Statewide Mercury Fish Consumption Advisory Update," available at: http://des.nh.gov/organization/commissioner/pip/factsheets/ard/documents/ard-ehp-25.pdf (last visited November 5, 2008).

New York University School of Law and the Migration Policy Institute, "Blurring the Lines: A Profile of State and Local Police Enforcement of Immigration Law Using the National Crime Information Center Database, 2002–2004," December 2005, available at http://www.migrationpolicy.org/pubs/MPI_report_Blurring_the_-Lines_120805.pdf (last visited November 15, 2008).

OMB Watch, "Access to Government Information Post September 11th," April 25, 2005, available at http://www.ombwatch.org/article/articleview/213/1/1/ (last visited November 2, 2008).

OMB Watch, "Access to Government Information Post September 11th: Federal Energy Regulatory Commission," April 25, 2005, available at http://www.ombwatch.org/article/articleview/213/1/104/#FERC (last visited November 8, 2008).

OMB Watch, "Benefits of Chemical Information Should Not Be Forgotten," January 16, 2002, available at http://www.ombwatch.org/article/articleview/394/1/39 (last visited November 8, 2008).

OMB Watch, "EPA Proposes Rollback on Toxic Pollution Reporting," October 4, 2005. Available at http://www.ombwatch.org/article/articleview/3117/1/241?TopicID=1 (last visited November 2, 2008).

OMB Watch, "States Sue EPA for Reduced Reporting on Toxics," December 4, 2007. Available at http://www.ombwatch.org/article/articleview/4105/1/241?TopicID=1 (last visited November 2, 2008).

OpenTheGovernment.org, "Secrecy Report Card 2008: Indicators of Secrecy in the Federal Government," a Report by OpenTheGovernment.org, available at: http://www.openthegovernment.org/otg/SecrecyReportCard08.pdf (last visited Sept. 20, 2008).

Rhode Island Department of Health, "Fish Is Good, Mercury is Bad!," available at: http://www.health.state.ri.us/environment/risk/Fishisgood-english.pdf (last visited November 5, 2008).

Jennifer Sass, "NRDC Sues Consumer Product Safety Commission for Withholding Industry Correspondence," NRDC Switchboard, July 30, 2008, available at http://switchboard.nrdc.org/blogs/jsass/nrdc_sues_consumer_product_saf.html (last visited November 22, 2008).

Sunshine Week, "What the Candidates Are Saying About Open Government and FOI," June 10, 2008. Available at http://www.sunshineweek.org/sunshine-week/candidates (last visited November 2, 2008).

SwellNet Dispatch, "Words from Clean Ocean," June 16, 2006, available at: http://www.swellnet.com.au/dispatch.php?dispatch=Clean_Ocean_160606.php (last visited November 5, 2008).

Taxpayers for Common Sense, "Road Woes at the Forest Service," March 29, 2002, available at http://www.taxpayer.net/search_by_tag.php?action=view&proj_id=323&tag=Forest%20Service&type=Project (last visited November 17, 2008).

Mary Thorn, "National Counsel for Research on Women, Missing: Information About Women's Lives (2004)," available at: http://www.ncrw.org/misinfo/report.pdf

The Transactional Records Access Clearinghouse at Syracuse University, "Civil Rights Enforcement by Bush Administration Lags," November 11, 2004, available at http://trac.syr.edu/tracreports/civright/106/ (last visited November 24, 2008).

The United Nations Environment Programme, "Childhood Pesticide Poisoning," May 2004, available at http://www.who.int/entity/ceh/publications/pestpoisoning.pdf (last visited November 11, 2008).

U.S. Department of Justice, "New Attorney General FOIA Memorandum Issued, FOIA Post," October 15, 2001, available at: http://www.usdoj.gov/oip/foia-post/2001foiapost19.htm (last visited November 2, 2008).

The U.S. Public Interest Research Group Education Fund, "Permit to Pollute: How the Government's Lax Enforcement of the Clean Water Act Is Poisoning Our

Waters," August 2002, available at http://www.pennenvironment.org/uploads/Nd/7s/Nd7sho0FW_ZmWKPNJrqOeg/PermittoPolute.pdf (last visited November 3, 2008).

Voice of America, "U.S. Army Officer Expected to Be Charged in Connection with Prisoner Abuse," April 26, 2006, available at http://www.voanews.com/english/archive/2006-04/US-Army-Officer-Expected-to-Be-Charged-in-Connection-with-Prisoner-Abuse.cfm?CFID=67785843&CFTOKEN=52043938 (last visited November 22, 2008).

Washington State Department of Health, "Fish Facts for Healthy Nutrition," available at http://www.doh.wa.gov/ehp/oehas/fish/fishadvmerc.htm (last visited October 10, 2008).

Wisconsin Department of Natural Resources, "Mercury in Wisconsin Fish," available at: http://dnr.wi.gov/org/caer/cea/mercury/fish.htm (last visited November 5, 2008).

World Health Organization, "The World Health Report 2002: Reducing Risks, Promoting Healthy Life, 2002," available at http://www.who.int/entity/whr/2002/en/whr02_en.pdf (last visited November 11, 2008).

World Health Organization, "The World Health Report 2003: Shaping the Future, 2003," available at http://www.who.int/entity/whr/2003/en/whr03_en.pdf (last visited November 11, 2008).

World Nuclear News, "Yucca Mountain Application Docketed," September 9, 2008, available at http://89.151.116.69/WR-Yucca_Mountain_application_docketed-0909087.html (last visited November 8, 2008).

Leticia Yáñez, et al., "Overview of Human Health and Chemical Mixtures: Problems Facing Developing Countries," *Environmental Health Perspectives*, December 2002, available at http://www.ehponline.org/members/2002/suppl-6/901-909yanez/ehp110s6p901.pdf (last visited November 11, 2008)

Laws, Regulations, Treaties, and Conventions

Access to Information Act (Canada).

Access to Public Information Act, 2000 (Bulgaria).

Act No. LXIII of 1992 on the Protection of Personal Data and the Publicity of Data of Public Interest (Hungary).

Act on Disclosure of Information by Public Agencies, 1998 (South Korea).

Act on Free Access to Information and Amendments of Certain Acts (The Freedom of Information Act) (Slovakia).

Administrative Procedures Act, U.S. Code at 5 U.S.C. §501 et seq.

Animal Welfare Act, 7 U.S.C. 2131, et seq

Clean Water Act, 33 U.S.C. § 1251 (1972).

Code on Access to Information, March 1995 (Hong Kong).

Code of Conduct and Ethical Standards for Public Officials and Employees, Republic Act 6713, 1987 (the Philippines).

Constitution of the Republic of Bulgaria.

Constitution of the Republic of Estonia.

Constitution of the Republic of Hungary.

Constitution of the Republic of Lithuania.

Constitution of the Republic of Malawi.

Constitution of the Republic of Moldova.

Constitution of the Philippine Republic.

Constitution of the Republic of Poland.

Constitution of Romania.

Constitution of the Russian Federation.

Constitution of the Republic of South Africa.

Constitution of the Kingdom of Thailand.

Constitution of the Argentine Nation.

Consumer Product Safety Improvement Act of 2008, Public Law No: 110-314.

Council of Europe, Convention for the Protection of Human Rights and Fundamental Freedoms, E.T.S. No. 5, (Nov. 4, 1950).

Electronic Freedom of Information Act Amendments of 1996, Pub. L. No. 104-231, 110 Stat 3048 (1986).

EPA, Advance Notice of Proposed Rulemaking: Regulating Greenhouse Gas Emissions under EPA-HQ-OAR-2008-0318, July 11, 2008, available at http://www.epa.gov/climatechange/anpr.html.

Emergency Planning and Community Right-to-Know Act, 42 USC 11011-11050 (1986).

The Faster FOIA Act of 2007, H.R. 541.

Federal Advisory Committee Act, 1972, 5 U.S.C. App. II.

Federal Funding Accountability and Transparency Act of 2006, Pub. L. No. 109-282.

Freedom of Access to Information Act, October 2000 (Bosnia and Herzegovina).

Freedom of Information Act, 1982 (Australia).

Freedom of Information Act, 1994 (Belize).

Freedom of Information Law, 1999 (Czech Republic).

Freedom of Information Act, 1999 (Trinidad and Tobago).

Freedom of Information Act, 2000 (United Kingdom).

Freedom of Information Act, 5 U.S.C. 552, 1966.

Freedom of Information Act Amendments of 1974, Pub. L. No. 93-502, 4, 88 Stat 1564.

Freedom of Information Reform Act of 1986, Publ. L. No. 99-570, tit. I Subtit. N. 1801, 100 Stat 3207-48,

Freedom of Information Law, Law 5758-1998, May 1998 (Israel).

The Freedom of Press Act, December 2, 1766 (Sweden).

Government in the Sunshine Act, 5 U.S.C. 552b.

Homeland Security Act of 2002, 116 Stat 2135 (2002).

Illinois Open Meetings Act Amendment, P.A. No. 93-0523, § 5 ILCS 120/2.06

Inter-American Court of Human Rights, Compulsory Membership in an Association Prescribed by Law for the Practice of Journalism, 30, Advisory Opinion OC-5/85 (Nov. 13, 1985).

Law No. 26301, 2 May 1994, implementing the constitutional right to habeas data (Peru).

Law No. 104, 1998 (the City of Buenos Aires).

Law No. 8503 on the right to information about official documents, 1999 (Albania).

Law on the Right to Receive Information from the State and Municipal Institutions, 2000 (Lithuania).

Law on Access to Information, 2000 (Moldova).
Law on Freedom of Information, 1998 (Latvia).
Law of Georgia on Freedom of Information, 1998 (Georgia).
Law on Information, 2 October 1992, Law No. 2657-XII (Ukraine).
Law on Information, Disclosure and Protection of Information, 25 January 1995, Act No. 24-FZ (Russia).
National Environmental Policy Act, 42 U.S.C. 4321 (1970).
No Child Left Behind Act of 2002, U.S. Public Law 107-110 (2002).
Official Information Act, 1982 (New Zealand).
Official Information Act, December 1997 (Thailand).
The Open FOIA Act of 2008, S. 2746.
OPEN Government Act of 2007, Pub. L. No. 110-175.
Open Meetings Law, Fla. Stat. sec. 286.011 et seq.
Open Records Law, Fla. Stat. sec. 119.01 et. seq.
Organization of American States, American Convention on Human Rights, adopted at San José, Costa Rica (Nov. 22, 1969), entered into force, July 18, 1978.
Privacy Act of 1974, 5. U.S.C. 552a.
Promotion of Access to Information Act, Act No. 2, 2000 (South Africa).
Public Information Act, 2000 (Estonia).
The Public Information Act, Texas Government Code, Chapter 552 (1993).
Public Records Act, Calif. Stat. §§ 6250 - 6276.48 (1968).
Universal Declaration of Human Rights, G.A. Res. 217A (III), at 71, U.N. Doc A/ 810 (Dec. 10, 1948).
Wis. Stat. § 19.31-19.39 (2003).

Miscellaneous Resources

Attorney General's Manual on the Administrative Procedure Act, 1947, available at: http://www.law.fsu.edu/library/admin/1947cover.html
E-mail from Ray George, EPA West Virginia/Western Pennsylvania State Liaison Officer, to Kathy Hodgkiss, EPA Region 3 Acting Director, Environmental Services Division (December 29, 2002, at 1:37 pm), available at http://www.tlpj.org/ briefs/wvhc-ovec.exhibits44-75.pdf (page 31).
George Kennedy, How Americans Got Their Rights to Know: Getting Congress to Guarantee Access to Federal Information through FOIA 30 Years Ago Was a Press Triumph," available at: http://www.johnemossfoundation.org/foi/kennedy.htm (last visited Sept. 24, 2008).
Statement by the President Upon Signing the Freedom of Information Act, 2 Pub. Papers 316 (July 4, 1966). Available at The American Presidency Project: http:// www.presidency.ucsb.edu/ws/index.php?pid=27700&st=&st1= (last visited Oct 30, 2008).

Index

About the Author

JACQUELINE KLOSEK is Senior Counsel in Business Law for Goodwin Procter LLP, where she practices in intellectual property, data privacy, and technology security. A certified information privacy professional, she serves on the advisory board of the International Association of Privacy Professionals and as vice chair of the Information Services, Technology and Data Protection Committee of the American Bar Association. As adjunct professor at New York University, she taught international intellectual property law and the law of e-commerce. After taking her LLM in European and international law from the Vrije Universiteit, Brussels, she served as consultant on U.S. information law to the directorate general of the European Commission. Klosek is the author of *War on Privacy* (Praeger, 2006), *The Legal Guide to e-Business* (Greenwood, 2003), and *Data Privacy in the Information Age* (Greenwood, 2000).